# Traveling India in the Age of Gandhi

Jeffrey N. Dupée

UNIVERSITY PRESS OF AMERICA,® INC.
*Lanham • Boulder • New York • Toronto • Plymouth, UK*

**Copyright © 2008 by**
**University Press of America,® Inc.**
4501 Forbes Boulevard
Suite 200
Lanham, Maryland 20706
UPA Acquisitions Department (301) 459-3366

Estover Road
Plymouth PL6 7PY
United Kingdom

All rights reserved
Printed in the United States of America
British Library Cataloging in Publication Information Available

Library of Congress Control Number: 2007940300
ISBN-13: 978-0-7618-3949-1 (paperback : alk. paper)

∞™ The paper used in this publication meets the minimum requirements of AmericanNational Standard for Information Sciences—Permanence of Paper for Printed Library Materials, ANSI/NISO Z39.48-1992.

To my aunt, Lois Boyer,

For teaching and modeling compassion

KASHMIR
Srinagar
AFGHANISTAN
Lahore
Amritsar
PUNJAB
TIBET
Indus
Meerut
Delhi
NEPAL
BHUTAN
RAJPUTANA
Jaipur
Agra
Lucknow
Darjeeling
Cawnpore
Patna
UDAIPUR
Allahabad
Benares
Ganges
GUJERAT
Kathiawar
CENTRAL
PROVINCES
Calcutta
BURMA
Arabian
Sea
ORISSA
Bombay
Poona
HYDERABAD
Bay of
Bengal
Hyderabad
Goa
Bangalore
Madras
Mysore
Pondicherry
Calicut
Travancore
CEYLON

# Table of Contents

# *Acknowledgments*

I wish to express my gratitude to a number of individuals who assisted me in this project. First, to my son Justin, who edits online news for a living but then was found captive during off-duty hours staring at my manuscript long into the night replicating the meticulous tasks of his day job. His time hunched over a computer carefully editing this manuscript marked a distinctly different sort of father-son interaction from former times of Little League, backpacking expeditions, and nights out at the movies. Having traveled much and written a few travel pieces of his own, the world of travel and travel writing are familiar terrain to him. Next, to Felisa Meier, a former student of mine currently doing graduate studies at La Sierra University. Felisa checked on footnote, bibliographic and related research items, tirelessly and painstakingly assisting me in many tedious tasks. She also worked on the index, formatting and similar responsibilities with great cheerfulness, enthusiasm and professionalism. A word about Paul Davies, the marvelous artist who created the book cover and map insert. Paul, a resident of Maine, has had many successful art shows, demonstrating both a distinctive yet diverse style and a unique visual sensibility on the world. It was a privilege to have him consider and then take on the task of creating what turned out to be a most haunting and beautiful image of Britain's imperial legacy. The image is of an architectural creation designed by Sir Edwin Lutyens, a sandstone structure intended to canopy a seventy-two foot high statue of King George V, installed in 1936 but later withdrawn to Delhi's Coronation Park, today a graveyard of sorts for old imperial statues, symbolic of Britain's vanished imperial realm. Next, many thanks to several of my students and student workers at La Sierra University: Katie Parsons, Hillary Sparks, and Diana Krueger in particular for hunting down sources, biographical material, and similar items during the past several years. As always, a big thanks to my wonderful wife Elizabeth, born and reared in England, who is an ever-crucial guide through the sometimes strange world of British colloquialisms and mentalities – a most useful resource in interpreting the Raj and the many British travel writers who visited India during the Gandhian Age. As has been said before, Americans and the British may share the same language, but they often befuddle each other in the complex world of thought and language. I would also like to thank Ralph Christie, a close friend since high school, who has traveled and read more than any person I know. We have spent many long hours discussing travel sites, stories and issues, not to mention works of history and literature that span the globe. Those sessions have contributed richly to my understanding of the traveler's universe. Additionally, a nod to Don Haas, another old friend from school days who in my young adulthood reshaped my mental map of India. In his journey to the East many years ago he sent me a postcard, penned somewhere near the Khyber Pass, as he made his way to India in search of a culture *in extremis* to test his intellectual and spiritual mettle as he embarked on life's journey – not unlike many of the travel writers featured in this study. Meeting him months later trekking across Europe, he filled my mind with extraordinary images of the subcontinent. Finally, a thanks to La Sierra University where I teach, to Kitty Simmons and her library staff for their constant and energetic support, and particularly to Jim Beach, Dean of the College of Arts and Sciences, who never forgets amidst the myriad duties and competing budget demands of an Academic Dean, that scholarly research remains an ever important obligation of a university's mission.

# *Introduction*

To travel writers the Age of Gandhi was a magical time. Not only did it offer the ultimate travel experience, what one writer described as "the best show on earth," it was also heralded as the world's premier political drama. The Age of Gandhi lasted approximately three decades. It began in 1919 as Gandhi's persona accelerated in public acclaim and independence aspirations became dominant in Indian politics. It ended with Gandhi's assassination in 1948. Yet, despite its celebratory aura, today it is of another era, far distant from our present world of the twenty-first century. William Dalrymple, an astute observer of things Indian, has noted that in his native Britain memories of Empire's Indian heritage retain a unique hold on British consciousness, but in India "the British Empire was referred to in much the same way as I referred to the Roman Empire." Britain's residual influence on Indian politics and ways may have been pervasive, but in contemporary India the British Raj is ancient history, a faint memory of a bygone era.[1] Nonetheless, reading travel accounts from the time resurrects memories of its earlier primacy on the world's stage, an imperial society vying with indigenous independence aspirations that commanded international attention. Moreover, India's political drama played out in an environment that was arguably the globe's most exotic human and cultural landscape—a site of extraordinary diversity that fascinated writers even as it bewildered them. For India is unlike any other place in the world. It is an astonishing locale of nearly impossible complexity and contradictions, a point that travel writers who have journeyed there typically acknowledge in the opening pages of their books. Take for example the *India* segment of the popular *Travelers' Tales Guides* edited by James O'Reilly and Larry Habegger. Their introduction to the volume opens with the line, "We confess to a bias towards India," going on to assert that travelers who brave its formidable challenges will be treated to the "best bazaar of human experiences that can be visited in a lifetime"—a place that will "dissolve your ideas about what it is to be a human being, what it is to be compassionate, what it is to be spiritual or conscious."[2] Lowell Thomas, an equally popular travel tales raconteur from the first half of the twentieth century expressed similar sentiments, remarking that he found India to be a "spectacle" like none other.[3]

Writing about India, it seems, typically unleashes a torrent of verbal description. Travel writers have characteristically gushed about its exotic variety on one page only to shrink in horror on another in describing scenes of wrenching poverty or hygienic repulsion. The term *kaleidoscope* was frequently invoked to somehow capture India's mystifying complexity. One writer, in attempting to summarize his fourteen-month stay in India, complained that the "whole thing kept breaking up into a series of pictures and patterns, like a *kaleidoscope*. I could not stick to one opinion." In fact, he lamented, "I was never going to make a statement without qualifying it."[4] Another bemoaned similarly that although his travel writing on India had bestowed upon him a "practical doctorate" he questioned its utility because he knew India "intimately" yet couldn't explain it.[5] And yet another writer, asking a Canadian traveler what he thought of India after extensive travel there, exclaimed: "he looked at me rather wild-eyed (the way I felt), and said: 'I scarcely know. I feel breathless, as if I had been hit by some sort of staggering blow and left gasping. I'm still at loose ends.'"[6] Some writers deflected their bewilderment by resorting to a syrupy romanticism, attempting to convey India's essence with lines like "India has gifts for you—she offers her marvels and mysteries to all who seek—in return she demands only intensity of purpose... life then streams like a fabulous dream, a picture pageantry of shadow shapes."[7] Whomever the scrivener, those who write about India invariably struggle to adequately articulate its uniqueness.

In reading a multitude of travel accounts about India—both past and present—I readily acknowledge both the difficulty in grasping India's essence and in interpreting, fairly, travel writer perceptions about the subcontinent. People who write about India are continuously conflicted about how to represent what is in front of them. And, they carry with them a host of preconceptions, even though most state to their readers that they enter India's domain as an "open book." One writer claimed that his was not a travel book, but rather "a book that has written itself. India is the speaker, and I am merely the scribe."[8] If one were not intuitively suspect of such a claim, post-modern theory has surely disabused us of the notion that we function as independent observers existing outside of the reality we seek to interpret. Yet, early twentieth century writers still believed that such neutral objectivity was possible. A survey of their writings suggests otherwise. Nevertheless, many writers clearly *aspired* to openness and objectivity, some desperately so.

The travel writers I have chosen to survey went to India in a particular period of its history, what has sometimes been termed the "Age of Gandhi," placed, as stated earlier, between 1919 and 1948. Clearly, Gandhi had been a well-known figure in India for several years prior to the Great War's ending, but 1919 ushered in a host of events that marked it as a kind of launch-date for the big push towards Indian independence. As British Raj historian Lawrence James has suggested, "nineteen nineteen was a decisive year in Indian history." The Amritsar Massacre occurred in April, irrevocably altering British-Indian relations. Deeply affected, India's Congress Party was reborn with new resolve. And, according to James, Gandhi "stamped his personality and principles on Congress,"[9] ultimately leading to an independence movement that integrated diverse elements of Indian society. 1948 as a concluding date is more obvious; it is the year of Gandhi's assassination. I have utilized travel accounts prior to and subsequent to the 1919 and 1948 dates, but most of this work focuses on the many writers who understood this era to be a unique time in world history—in India and elsewhere on the globe. The lingering trauma of World War I, the rise of radical state ideologies in Russia, Italy, Germany, and Japan, world-wide depression in the 1930s along with a host of other unsettling and transforming social, cultural, and technological realities presented a world of great complexity and uncertainty. For many of the travel writers surveyed here, India was the main drama in this shifting global landscape.

Of the writers who traveled to India in the first half of the twentieth century, quite a number were famous. Aldous Huxley, Carl Jung, Herman Hesse, Annie Besant, E.M. Forster, to name only a few, journeyed there and most penned their reflections. Studies in travel literature typically focus on such figures and understandably so. Their work lives on and thus academic studies in particular value such travel accounts as important material for interpreting literary and other distinguished careers. I have acquired a particular affection for a breed of largely forgotten travel writers—people who penned travel books for either a living or for a certain passion for a particular place in the world. Their books can often be found in larger libraries, whereupon a brief glance inside their dusty covers reveals that they have not been exposed to human eyes for many-a-decade. Some authors had marginal, if not temporary fame as travel writers; others, like journalists, had connections with publishers or with social or political establishments sufficient to get their travel memoirs into print. Taken together, they form a collage of such diverse personalities and writers that summarizing them into a coherent whole is extremely difficult. The post-colonial critique of such travel writers suggests that they were little more than rhetorical clones of their age, spewing out travel musings saturated with Western sensibilities and "essentialistic" representations of the global sites they encountered. To characterize them in that manner simply inverts the rhetorical form, where Western travel writers are all lumped together as an undifferentiated mass of "Western natives"—chronicling their way through India in myopic bliss. As a group, they are hardly as diverse as the India they sought to reveal, but they are surely *kaleidoscopic* in their own way, carrying Western cultural baggage, but still seeing India in varied and complex ways.

How does one write about such a diverse range of characters? In attempting to do so I face the same dilemma they constantly confronted in their own writings; namely, that India was a site of such great complexity that it was nearly impossible to describe it without becoming entangled in one's description. Thus, like the travel writer quoted earlier, I am haunted by the lingering fear that I can never "make a statement without qualifying it." Consequently, borrowing advice from their pages, I have yielded to the notion that "openness" to that complexity, embracing it as an inescapable literary hazard, is the only way in which to engage it. That said there are identifiable trends and patterns among the authors. When apparent I attempt to identify and present them. Where contradictions and confusion reigns, I hold that it is indigenous to the genre and attempt to sort it out in some sensible way. For travel writing is notoriously autobiographical, impressionistic, rambling, and quirky. That is a part of its great charm. So to be overly deductive with these writings would, in my opinion, cast them unnecessarily into a rigorous mold. On the other hand, they are era-oriented writings and thus the great events of the 1920s through the 1940s do impact the material in many ways. Hopefully, that will be evident in my analysis.

Something else should be said about these authors. Even if their opinions and sensibilities sometimes differ from those we embrace in the twenty-first century, to understand and appreciate them we need to respect their peculiar mentalities and enter into the sense of wonder at what they were seeing—whether enchanting or problematical in their representations. And we need to appreciate the great difficulties, stresses, and irritants that are inevitably inherent in any extended travel experience—particularly in a locale like India. Revealingly, late twentieth and current travel accounts on India, as will be shown later, express many of the frustrations and difficulties of their earlier twentieth century counterparts. India is frequently cited as one of the most forbidding travel sites in the world. As in much travel writing, a certain peevishness frequently surfaces in their accounts. Nonetheless, traveling with these writers, albeit vicariously, is a wonderful journey in itself. Their books were mainly targeted for "armchair travelers," so this study is an effort to capture some of the wonder and enchantment that so thoroughly inhabit their works, a traveler's sense of awe and delight they were determined to pass onto their readers. For purposes of clarification, I should elaborate on my use of the word "armchair." It is utilized here in a dual sense. First, to designate the authors ("armchair authors" as it were, practitioners of a genre often referred to as armchair travel books)—writers targeting a particular type of audience, namely "armchair readers"; and secondly to denote the readers themselves, a specifically envisioned audience of compatriots who vicariously journeyed with the author as he or she traveled about the far reaches of the globe, but within this work the explicit site of India. As Benedict Anderson has suggested, a nation is "an imagined community" constituted of fellow members where "in the minds of each lives the image of their communion."[10] Travel writers from the Gandhian Age typically appropriated that image, serving as communal guides to a presumed group of armchair readers who they bonded with in imagined solidarity yet most likely would never encounter personally. Although most writers wrote to a specific national audience, some clearly were targeting multiple ones, particularly American and British authors whose books were marketed on both sides of the Atlantic. With those works, the national emphasis was de-emphasized; nevertheless, a sense of intimacy invariably pervaded the writings, a type of trans-spatial bonding where separation by geography and time was bridged by surrogate travel and conversational narrative.

Represented among the authors are numerous journalists and adventurers—often one and the same; several old India hands, a few soldiers, several minor novelists, a healthy contingency of self-proclaimed travel writers, and an assortment of other types that will be apparent later in the book. Many of them were women. Almost all of them had established "contacts" in India at various levels of the Raj's political and social scale prior to arrival. A large segment of them interviewed Ganhdi personally—for Gandhi was famous for his openness to all types of visitors—particularly journalists who could serve as surrogate spokespersons articulating India's aspirations for independence. The works surveyed in this book hardly exhaust the number of travel accounts written about India from the 1920s through the end of the 1940s. In fact, no magazine or journal articles are represented—another rich source for mining travel accounts. Instead, the focus is on a cadre of "armchair" travel writers who crafted book titles beckoning readers to journey with them to the subcontinent—titles such as *See India with Me, Foot-Loose in India,* and *My Road to India*, to name only a few. Such titles were personalized invitations recruiting readers to buy their books and join them on their journeys.

Apart from briefing readers on India's urban itineraries—Bombay, Calcutta, Delhi, Benares and Agra (the Taj Mahal)—which were almost universally covered—most writers exerted considerable effort towards "understanding" the political and social currents that were buzzing around independence and Indian religious and cultural practices. To a lesser extent, the Princely States, British Hill Stations, India's villages, and other locations were travel destinations as well. Since this book focuses on "armchair" narrators, it is their impressionistic musings that will receive the most attention, even if some observations, at times, risk appearing as recycled touristic pulp. For whether these authors were tourists or travelers could ignite an interminable debate concerning travel nomenclature. Tourist and traveler are highly contested linguistic categories rife with class-ridden assumptions, often privileging or decrying the motives behind and the nature of an author's journey. That aside, for the purposes of this work, they will be referred to here as travelers. Almost all journeyed for months, some for years in India. A few accounts are from expatriate writers, chronicling their travels across India while engaged in imperial service. As stated, most of the focus will be upon armchair writers who set off to India to discover what India was about, and more particularly to penetrate its exotic complexity and dynamic political climate. In doing so most of them understood themselves to be a type of travel savant, individuals who were wise to the ways of travel and were skilled at extracting new ways of seeing India, stripped of colonialist patter or Western preconceptions.

Before entering the rich fauna of Gandhian Age travel accounts perhaps a cursory historical sketch of Britain's imperial India would be in order. For many readers, covering that ground would be entirely unnecessary. Moreover, there are other works that engage the task most effectively. Clearly, this book is not a history of India—it is a study of how travel writers selectively mined from their travel experiences various interpretations of what they saw and encountered during the Gandhian Age. Nevertheless, for those less familiar with India in this era, a brief historical presentation may provide helpful context in which to situate the travel writings surveyed here. For those better informed or simply not interested in such matters, I am reminded of George Orwell's remarks in *Homage to Catalonia*—the chapter explicating the dizzy complexity of leftist politics in Barcelona during the Spanish Civil War: "if you are not interested in the horrors of party politics, please skip."[11] Similarly, if you want to sidestep a brief, generic history of British India, "please skip."

Britain's initial foray into India sprung from the formation of the British East India Company under the reign of Elizabeth I in the early seventeenth century. Among other formational purposes, the Company had its eye on the lucrative Indian spice and cotton trade. In 1619 a British mission to India persuaded India's then Mughal Emperor Jahangir to grant the Company the first of what eventually became several dozen forts along India's coastline. From these and other bribery-induced or manipulative dealings, Britain gained a foothold on the subcontinent and such trading centers as Bombay, Madras and Calcutta became key commercial players in Britain's global empire. By 1700 trade with the East became increasingly profitable, a trend accelerated by the burgeoning trade with China during the course of the eighteenth century. The British East India Company's policy was singular in design and action—to make money. Company employees were to stay out of local Indian politics and avoid reform and missionary endeavors. But over the course of the eighteenth century the Mughal Empire progressively weakened and India became increasingly chaotic and politically unstable. The Mughal government and local princely administrations were incapable of providing adequate security, forcing the Company to impose political authority over the territories in which they operated.[12] That eventually led to increased British interference if not aggression in Indian affairs. Traditional imperial historiography has characterized Britain's rise to empire as something of an accident, a response in part to the chaos about it requiring military security and proficient administrative control in order to protect legitimate national interests. That interpretation has been severely tested in recent decades. Today it is suggested that the chaos in India and its consequent political vacuum "were in part of the Company's own making, in part an invention of apologists, and in part the result of a misreading of India's history."[13]

It was also a response to Britain's intense rivalry with France in the mid-eighteenth century, a rivalry quickened by the appointment of Joseph Dupleix as governor general of the French East India Company's operations at Pondicherry. Dupleix aggressively promoted his company's influence, establishing alliances with local princes, creating an army of native troops (hence the name *sepoys*), and expanding territorial possessions. Beginning in the 1740s Britain and France vied for control of India, culminating in the Seven Year's War (1757-1763) when British commander Robert Clive triumphed over the French in a series of political and military maneuvers that left India to the British. The Treaty of Paris of 1763 formalized the reality, launching what many scholars believed to be the inception of the British Empire in India. The British East India Company continued its operations in India but its independence and power were increasingly diminished and regulated by parliamentary authority in London from the 1770's until its political demise in 1857. Warren Hastings was the first among many governor-generals who through diplomacy, war, and various forms of skullduggery increased Britain's territorial possessions, economic domination and authority in India. As one historian has noted, "the company had become a sort of Frankenstein's monster, out of control and capable of wreaking havoc both in India and Britain." Thus, it became necessary to curb financial and other abuses and gradually assert more direct control over India's administration. By the mid-nineteenth century, Britain had "acquired a monopoly of power in India."[14] The system was maintained by three pillars: puppet princes, seduced or coerced by carrot or stick policies that bestowed the pomp of power, absent any significant voice outside of their fairy tale realms; a predominantly sepoy army of precarious loyalty, later revealed by the dramatic events of the 1857 Rebellion; and an efficient civil service comprised of British expatriates assisted by lower level minions from indigenous groups.[15] However, Britain's territorial domain in India peaked at approximately 60%; 40% remained as part of India's 540 Princely States, from large principalities such as Hyderabad that approximated the size of Ireland to smaller ones reminiscent of miniature European states such as Monaco.

1857 was a dramatic marker in British-India and more specifically British-Indian relations. In addition to numerous underlying Indian economic, religious and political grievances, the British military began the use of the Enfield rifle in India, igniting a disputed belief that its cartridges were lubricated with a mixture of pig and cow fat. Since sepoy troops thought that they were expected to bite off the ends of the cartridges in order to expedite loading and firing procedures, in the minds of Hindu or Muslim soldiers doing so confronted them with a most horrendous defilement of their faith. Added to the mix was a pervasive suspicion that the cartridge ritual was only one more insidious effort to impose Christianity on India. When a number of sepoy troops were court-martialed at Meerut for refusing to load their rifles at a regimental parade (even though loading was to be done by hand, not by mouth), a rebellion ensued that spread across many parts of northern India. The Rebellion's most notorious event occurred at Cawnpore several hundred miles southeast of Delhi. There an infamous rebel leader named Nana Sahib ordered the slaughter of the settlement's surviving European women and children, a task carried out by a local butcher before the bodies were cast ignominiously into a nearby well. As one historian noted, when the British arrived later, "the sight of the place of slaughter, blood-stained and littered with ladies' dresses, children's clothing and locks of hair, provoked an explosion of anguished rage among the soldiers." Thereafter the massacre at Cawnpore became an inflammatory symbol that unleashed a torrent of British atrocities—atrocities perpetuated by both sides until the British finally restored control of their realm nearly eighteen months later.[16] Studies of post-Rebellion literature reveal that more than fifty novels were written about the crisis prior to 1900; another thirty prior to World War II. Moreover, innumerable eyewitness accounts, journal articles, poems, and plays were generated in the Rebellion's aftermath. The nature of this production was largely sensationalist or maudlin, with Nana Sahib infamously memorialized as "the Demon of Cawnpore."[17] Cawnpore was commemorated by a grand marble memorial, designed by an Italian sculptor, with the site thereafter permanently placed on the 'mutiny tour' that became so popular with British travelers over the next century[18], including a few covered in this study. The root causes of the Rebellion were subsumed by melodramatic accounts of oriental treachery and savagery, and of course, British suffering and victimization. The West's grand civilizing mission, to bring the East into conformity with Western aspirations for it, deflated before increasingly dominant attitudes that India was a site of recalcitrant ignorance and superstition, peopled by a race prone to variant forms of debauchery and stubborn resistance to change.

In 1858 Britain's Parliament passed the Government of India Act, formally ending the East India Company's authority in India, replacing it with that of the British Crown. With it came a host of policy changes. Among others, they included a feudal-like strategy that privileged the role of India's aristocratic elites as a reliably conservative ally for the Raj; a recasting of the British army, transforming its sepoy ranks from Rajput, Brahmin, well-born Muslims and Bengali troops to those of the more politically reliable "martial races"—such as selected Sikh, Pathan, Punjabi Jats and Rajputs, and Nepali Gurkhas recruits; and an extensive financial reorganization that expanded revenues from traditional sources such as the land tax to income tax and tariff revenues, laying the foundation for future income-producing resources into the twentieth century.[19] There were other changes as well. Except for carefully ritualized ceremonies and social events, fraternization between the British and their Indian subjects decreased significantly after the Rebellion. One casualty was relations between British males and indigenous women. Prior to the eighteenth century, intermarriage or cohabitation between the two was more easily accepted, in part due to official British attitudes that sexual relations between British residents and indigenous women fostered heterosexuality and other "manly" qualities crucial to maintaining imperial control. However, by the 1860s. a near-half century of Western missionary efforts, the consolidation of increasingly restrictive imperial social codes, and the arrival in large numbers of British women all contributed to policies and attitudes that severely disapproved of such unions. In fact, to many Victorian and Edwardian observers, the influx of British women to India from the mid-nineteenth century on with their presumed airs of overwrought domesticity and social insularity, contributed significantly to imperial woes if not its eventual decline.[20]

Such was the growing conservatism among Britain's imperial ranks in the Rebellion's aftermath. India, to their minds, was changeless. An impressive rail network, extensive irrigation works, and other infrastructure improvements might modernize India's landscape, but its soul was deeply entrenched in the past. The idea that India should be prepared for self-government surfaced intermittently among British officialdom but the dominant attitude was of an India projected to be under imperial control long into the foreseeable future. The period from the Rebellion into the early twentieth century has been characterized as Britain's "imperial heyday."[21] Lord Curzon, who presided over India as its viceroy from 1898-1905, perhaps more than any other British official of the era best symbolized Britain's pre-occupation with India's place as the "crown jewel" of Empire, the loss of which to his mind—however unlikely in his or any successive generation—would ensure Britain's descent from imperial greatness.[22] What Curzon failed to realize was that at the point of his departure in 1905 Britain's imperial grip on India was already slipping. As Lawrence James has commented, "henceforward the Raj he had tried so hard to strengthen was thrown on the defensive against the mounting pressure from a growing number of its own subjects and left-wing politicians in London, whose natural sympathies lay with underdogs of all kinds and for whom empires, however benevolent their intentions, were essentially despotic."[23] Most importantly, it should be added, demands for change came from indigenous elements groomed on the principles of Western democracy, political and social reform, and equality before the law. As Percival Spear has noted, long before the surge of independence activity in the twentieth century, "beneath the burnished cover of the British administration the mind of India was actually in ferment."[24] Eventually such sentiments crystallized in organized form, most prominently in the formation of the Indian National Congress in 1885, an institution in its inception that was primarily loyal to the Raj but nonetheless insistent that Britain hold true to its promises. "Congress" then and later billed itself as the voice of India and would be the institutional vehicle through which Indians would eventually achieve independence.[25]

In many ways, World War I provided the opportunity for significant gains towards indigenous rule even if form prevailed over substance. India united behind the British during the conflict; even Gandhi urged his countrymen to support the British cause with the general hope that sharing the burdens of the hour would ultimately reap the benefit of shared rule as well. For Indians, dominion status (as in Canada or Australia) was the objective. The reality turned out to be the Montagu-Chelmsford reforms, proposed in 1918 and adopted as law a year later. In essence it was a two-tier system of government housing two levels of elected governments. Known as "diarchy," the system provided for eight provincial assemblies in which Indian ministers presided over various "lesser" ministries (education, health, agriculture) but where British provincial governors retained control over the more crucial domains of taxation and security. The reforms were controversial. Imperialists viewed them as concessionary weakness; anti-imperialists and Indian nationalists saw them as political sops yielding symbolic but not real power to India's electorate.[26]

The event that fully opened the era of Indian independence aspirations was the Amritsar Massacre of 1919. The riots that provoked the event arose from the passage of the Rowlatt Acts at the end of 1918, a legislative response to what the British believed to be an ever-increasing terrorist threat in India, particularly in the post-war climate of global unrest and the fact that large numbers of British troops were departing for home. Lawrence James has suggested that if the Rowlatt Acts had failed to materialize "Gandhi might have stayed an eccentric philosopher on the fringes of Congress, well-loved but with little influence." Instead, in the aftermath of the massacre, Gandhi emerged as the voice and soul of the nationalist movement. What precipitated these developments was the arrest of Amritsar's two leading nationalists, resulting in general rioting throughout the city, the ensuing murder of three Europeans, and the general sense of terror felt by 100 other traumatized Europeans holed up in a local fortress, thereby by inviting the British military to solve the crisis and rescue them from harm's way. A crusty old British general named Rex Dyer was sent to the city to confront the emergency. Dyer was determined to stop the rioting dead in its tracks and by doing so set an example throughout all of India that such behaviors would be unmercifully squelched and punished by the authorities. He issued a proclamation forbidding all public processions or gatherings. In defiance of the order, an estimated fifteen to twenty thousand Indians congregated in an enclosed area about the size of Trafalgar Square known as the Jallianwala Bagh. General Dyer and his troops marched to the site and without warning fired 1,650 rounds, killing 379 and wounding approximately 1,500.[27] For anyone who has seen the film *Gandhi*, the sight of the Mahatma peering over the horrifying remains of the slaughter can easily visualize why the Massacre was such a catalytic event for the independence movement. One historian perhaps sums it up quite effectively for most of the event's historiography: "the Amritsar Massacre united Indians behind Gandhi's campaigns of civil disobedience, and destroyed any claims the British might try to advance that they were bringing values to the Indians which were more 'civilized' than what they could evolve for themselves."[28]

After Amritsar organized campaigns of civil disobedience, what Gandhi referred to as *Satyagraha*, or non-violent resistance, persisted throughout the 1920s. They were marked by endless cycles of civil obedience, arrest, trial, incarceration, release and subsequent perpetuation of the same rituals as Gandhi and his charges sought to wear down the British. There were also incidents of violence, most notably in Bengal where communist and trade union elements shot or threw bombs at British officials and generally attempted to disrupt governmental operations. By 1930, Gandhi, shaken by the decade's legacy of violence and losing faith in the Raj's dithering efforts at compromise, became convinced that only outright independence, not a dominion-like arrangement or other interim status, could secure India's aspirations for self-government. In 1930 he led the famous 240 mile Salt March to the sea to not only break the state's monopoly on the commodity but to also to exact a toll on British patience and policies. Approximately 100,000 of his Congress supporters were jailed. However, the March produced its desired effect. Lord Irwin, Britain's Viceroy in India, invited Gandhi to Delhi to discuss India's status, yielding on the salt issue and agreeing to a plan whereby Congress would join with Britain to formulate a strategy concerning India's political future. In turn, Gandhi called off the civil disobedience campaign. Shortly thereafter, Gandhi was invited to London to participate in the Round Table Conference's effort to draft a federal constitution for India. The event was more of a propaganda coup for Gandhi than it was a substantive step towards independence. Nonetheless, by 1935 various negotiations resulted in the Government Act of India, a statute that pointed towards eventual self-government and which liberalized various aspects of British-Indian relations.[29]

In the interim, civil obedience continued, Gandhi being jailed once again soon after his return from London. By 1939, on the eve of World War II, "Congress had established itself as an alternative raj." It propagated a martyr's image where aspiring Indian politicians sought imprisonment by British authorities in order to enhance their electoral chances. Meanwhile, as one historian has observed, "the declaration of war against Germany brought the constitutional experiment to an end, but, in truth, by then Britain had lost her imperial touch in India."[30] Moreover, the declaration exacerbated relations with Congress by its wholly unilateral nature, proving once again that the imperial mind presumed to know what was best for it subjects, pulling India into the conflict as if it chiefly concerned Indians as well. Nehru and other Congress leaders were sympathetic to Britain's struggle against fascism but they were not about to be blithely absorbed into another imperial conflict without exacting some significant concessions for their efforts. At the outset of the war such concessions were not forthcoming.[31] Nevertheless, several years into the conflict, apart from numerous resignations by Indian government officials, the imperial machinery continued without significant challenge from Congress even if the time appeared ripe for open rebellion. Gandhi's tempering influence was crucial, contributing, among other matters, to the marginalization of the one Indian figure who appeared most likely to lead a revolution in India—the radical Bengali leader Subhas Chandra Bose. Bose, normally of leftist sympathies, managed among other escapades to visit Nazi Germany to seek assistance for his revolutionary objectives. He eventually ended up in Japan to spearhead the enlistment of Indian troops to fight with the Japanese against the British in Burma.[32] Bose, who served there as well, fled Rangoon as the British retook the city in April of 1945, dying from injuries sustained in an airplane crash en route to Tokyo. Despised by the

British, Bose nonetheless was and remains a "national hero in India." Lawrence James has suggested that "in Indian mythology Bose had become a King Arthur figure who had gone into some secret retreat from which he might emerge to save his people," a notion that survived into the 1980s.[33] Yet, however threatening his movement may have appeared during the war, the real threat to British control of India came from Gandhi and Congress. After the Japanese entered the conflict, Gandhi and Congress initiated the "Quit India" campaign in the wake of Britain's failed Cripps Mission to broker post-war plans for independence. Congress wanted an immediate turnover of power and used the campaign to force action on the independence issue in what appeared to be a shift away from traditional tactics of non-violent resistance. British authorities responded by jailing Gandhi and other Congress leaders for the duration of the war.[34]

The "Quit India" campaign engendered random forms of disobedience in various parts of India. There were significant attacks against or destruction of rail stations, track lines, telegraph poles, police stations, post offices and other infrastructure sites. Fear of the 1857 Rebellion reborn rippled throughout the British community. However, the acts of sabotage and violence were quickly contained, aided in large part by the unorganized nature of the uprising and the fact that India housed large numbers of troops due to the War. Meanwhile, Muhammad Jinnah and other leaders of the Muslim League became increasingly uneasy about what shape the inevitable new India would take, fearing that a Muslim minority would find itself marginalized once independence was granted. Although Muslims had worked closely with Congress in Gandhi's non-cooperation movement, by the 1940s visions, however vague, of a Muslim "Pakistan" became increasingly prominent. In July of 1945 Labour's Clement Attlee defeated Winston Churchill in British elections, removing perhaps the nation's most ardent imperialist for retaining the Raj in some form. Attlee, as well as many others in Britain, realized it was time for the Raj to end. Britain had neither the means nor the will to further sustain the demands of Empire. In February of 1947, Clement appointed Lord Mountbatten as India's last viceroy. By August of that year Mountbatten had expedited the reality of Indian independence and that of a controversial Pakistani state. However, there was a price. In the midst of independence tens of thousands of Hindus and Muslims were slain in large-scale rioting and carnage as citizens scrambled to re-locate into the newly formed India and Pakistan or simply survive the sectarian violence within their own districts. In January of 1948 a disaffected Hindu nationalist assassinated Gandhi. The British were gone, a new India and a new Pakistan were formed, yet Britain's stamp upon the subcontinent had been significant, leaving historians and others with the task of sorting out Britain's imperial legacy in India.[35]

Suffice it to say that such a task is beyond the reach of this study. Opinions about the Raj range variously from an imperial realm that was intrinsically evil and largely fraught with catastrophic results to that of a benevolent one bringing peace, security, prosperity and democratic values to a fractured and impoverished land. In an article written for the *Cambridge Illustrated History of British Empire,* titled "British Rule in India: An Assessment," Tapan Raychaudhuri argues, "historical writing about India under the Raj has been hag-ridden by the strong emotions that often inform ostensibly rational debates. The preoccupation with giving good or bad marks to British rule has overshadowed exercises in serious analysis." Raychaudhuri states further that few serious thinkers or historians in post-independence India see any significant benefits from the Raj (Raychaudhuri clearly being among that majority). One writer even characterized British India as "the Nazis of their time."[36] Among the British writers I surveyed, there is a more balanced perspective—one that readily concedes the problematic nature of imperial realms generally and the significant failures of the British in India specifically. Yet, they tend to view today's democratic India, among other contributions, as a most important legacy of the Raj. As will be seen in this study, most travel writers from the Gandhian Age characterized the Raj similarly, even if their perceptions were largely impressionistic and based upon anecdotal evidence or personal encounters. Thus, most reflected a range of opinions generally less severe than current historiography, even if the analysis lacked the depth and perspective of late twentieth or early twenty-first century hindsight and scholarship. Imperial governments are by their nature oppressive and exploitive in some form, however well-intentioned. Nation-states in the post-imperial age have generally proved to be no less so. But they are sovereign entities, whatever their faults—unlike subjects living under an imperial order. That was what the Gandhian Age was about—seeking national self-determination. And that aspiration, cast as it was in perhaps the world's most exotic human environment, was a lure travel writers of the times could hardly resist.

As a final note, the reader will observe that I have retained the era-utilized names for Bombay (Mumbai), Calcutta (Kolkatta), and other Indian geographical sites. Since the old European names were the ones used by the travel writers surveyed and remain in common usage to today—irrespective of official changes—I thought it best to continue the practice.

## NOTES

1. William Dalrymple, *City of Djinns; A Year in Delhi* (London: Penguin Books, 1993), 71.

2. James O'Reilly and Larry Habegger, ed,. introduction to *Travelers' Tales Guides India: True Stories of Life on the Road* (San Francisco: Travelers' Tales, 1998), xix.
3. Lowell Thomas, *India: Land of the Black Pagoda* (New York: P. F. Collier & Sons, 1930), 6–7.
4. Louis Hagan, *Indian Route March* (New York: Pilot Press, 1946), 187, 191.
5. John Frederick Muehl, *American Sahib* (New York: John Day Co., 1946), v-1.
6. Agnes Rush Burr, *India: The Land that Lures* (Boston: L.C. Page & Co., 1929), 5–6.
7. Patricia Kendall, *Come With Me To India* (New York: Charles Scribner's Sons, 1935), 3.
8. Ranjee G. Shahani, *Indian Pilgrimage* (London: Michael Joseph, 1939), 14.
9. Lawrence James, *Raj: The Making and Unmaking of British India* (New York: St. Martin's Griffin, 1997), 464–465.
10. Benedict Anderson, *Imagined Communities: Reflections on the Origin and Spread of Nationalism* (London: Verso, 1983).
11. George Orwell, *Homage to Catalonia* (London: Harvest/HBJ Books, 1952), 46
12. John P. McKay, Bennett D. Hill, and John Buckler, ed., *A History of World Societies*, vol. B, 3rd ed. (Boston: Houghton Mifflin Company, 1992), 759–761.
13. John Keay, *India, A History* (New York: Grove Press, 2000), 384.
14. Lawrence James, *Raj: The Making and Unmaking of British India* (New York: St. Martin's Griffin, 1997), 49, 63.
15. McKay, Hill, and Buckler, 760–762.
16. James, 233–254.
17. Patrick Brantlinger, *Rule of Darkness: British Literature and Imperialism, 1830–1914* (Ithaca: Cornell University Press, 1988), 199–206.
18. Barbara D. Metcalf and Thomas R. Metcalf, *A Concise History of Modern India*, 2nd ed. (Cambridge: Cambridge University Press, 2006), 107.
19. Percival Spear, *A History of India, Volume Two* (London: Penguin Books, 1965), 145–150.
20. Margaret Strobel, *European Women and the Second British Empire* (Bloomington: Indiana University, 1991), 1–3, 7, 9.
21. Spear, 146–153.
22. Keay, 460–462.
23. James, 417.
24. Spear, 158.
25. James, 352.
26. Ibid, 439, 458–461.
27. Ibid, 468, 472–474.
28. A.N. Andrews, *After the Victorians, The Decline of Britain in the World* (New York: Picador, 2005), 209.
29. Trevor Royle, *The Last Days of the Raj* (London: John Murray, 1989), 52–56.
30. Ibid, 70–71.
31. Metcalf, 203–204.
32. Royle, 78–80.

33. James, 575.
34. Royle, 82–87.
35. Metcalf, 205–223.
36. Tapan Raychaudhuri, "British Rule in India: An Assessment," in *The Cambridge Illustrated History of the British Empire,* ed. P.J. Marshall (Cambridge: Cambridge University Press, 1996), 357.

## *Chapter One*

# India's Lure: Traveler Motivations and Aspirations

Edward Holton James related how one day in the drawing room of a Geneva hotel he overheard a discussion among British subjects chatting about India's independence movement and Gandhi's role as spokesman for its objectives. Fascinated, he formulated a plan to travel there, telling his readers "the best way after all to get the facts is to go to India, to get them on the spot." As an American, James contended that he and his fellow countrymen had a particular fascination and empathy with the Indian independence movement. However, he exclaimed, they were "short of trustworthy and impartial information." Moreover, he contended, "no country in the world furnishes such dramatic and thrilling newspaper material as India . . . [a place where] the greatest human drama of the world is being enacted."[1] These sentiments, in varying ways, surfaced in many travel accounts on India during the Gandhian period. Robert Bernays, on a world tour, intended to stay in India for only a few weeks, pen a few articles, and then move on. Instead, he stayed for five months, writing *Naked Faquir*, a "diary of my reactions to the Indian scene and the chief characters upon its stage." Was Gandhi, Bernays queried, no more than "the half-naked faquir" of Winston Churchill's imagination, or would he, as Bernays suggested, go down as "one of the great men of the world in the class of Mahomet or St. Paul?" Some like Louis Hagen were initially skeptical about traveling to India. His travel memoir opened with the sentiment: "Drafted to India, I hated the idea . . . India was about the only country in the world that I had no desire to visit." But he was quickly captivated by its sweeping social and political landscape, going on to write a reflective work wrestling with his nation's legacy of colonialism there.[2]

The independence question was clearly front and center in many travel accounts. Albert Farwell Bemis, traveling through India in 1921 and 1922, wrote a representative sample of the genre, telling his readers that as he embarked on his voyage to India and other parts of the globe that "everything seems unsettled: society, politics, industry, religion, and even climate and weather." He referred to Sovietism as the "great *political* experiment"—a part of a larger world upheaval in which the people of India are also participating, but where such "hazy, elusive demands for the democratization of everything is leading us, we know not where."[3] The Indian independence drama transpired principally within the inter-war period, an era in which the foundations of traditional Western liberalism were being challenged by a host of more radical political ideologies and carping socio-cultural critiques of Western capitalism, colonialism, and Judaic-Christian morality. Closer scrutiny of the British imperial project only reinforced such challenges as peoples in and outside of India increasingly viewed the Raj as a dying institution, surviving tenaciously on Britain's reluctance to give up its so-called "jewel in the crown" of Empire. The question "to quit or not to quit," or some variation of the phrase, fascinated almost every travel writer who visited India. Was India prepared for independence? Would India go communist like Russia if it did? These and many related political issues provided compelling reasons to travel to India.

However, the political drama was often matched by intense socio-cultural debates concerning India's religious traditions, particularly Hinduism. The catalyst for the debates was a self-appointed American muckraker named Katherine Mayo, whose incendiary work *Mother India* ignited a furor in and outside of India regarding Hindu traditions and practices. It spawned as well a barrage of responses from Gandhi and other Indian leaders, innumerable editorials, and several books reacting to or supporting Mayo's claim. Nearly every travel writer who journeyed to India after its 1927 publication date commented on *Mother India*—some supporting and others refuting its claims. By February of 1928, a year after its publication, it had entered into its seventeenth printing. For travel writers, it provided a structured analysis in which to pit their own observational and critical faculties as they journeyed across India, however they perceived Mayo's work. For Mayo, like many other writers on India during this period, her research on and travels in India afforded Americans with much-needed insight into this huge domain beyond the usual clichés—such as beguiling snake charmers, the adventures of *Kim* or the dreamy imagery of the Taj Mahal. And also like her travel-writer contemporaries she laid claim to a rigid objectivity that would be ferociously challenged in the years to follow. She contended, for example, that Gandhi's "hazy notions" were unthinkingly absorbed by "professional propagandists out of one camp or another," from travel books to novels to mystical sources, all "having India as their scene." Katherine Mayo, however, was determined to set the record straight about the *real* India. Her research and travels, she claimed, would uncover what "the Indian does not confront in its entirety . . . and what the traveler in India misses."[4]

Yet, for all of the political and cultural debates about India, its exotic kaleidoscopic allure was usually central to the travel writer's motives for venturing there. For some, it subsumed all other motives. One could choose from an intriguing set of travel-writer characters to make the point, but perhaps three will suffice. The first, Nilla Cram Cook, was an extraordinarily interesting and flamboyant personality. Her *My Road to India* is a roller-coaster ride of romantic adventures and quirky characters—chronicled not only by her but also by 1930s paparazzi equivalents—bent on getting stories on her even if it required devising "orgiastic rumors" and other fictional creations. She was the daughter of George Cram Cook, a prominent American poet. Her book is scattered with references to prominent personalities of her era: her grandmother had been a friend of Rudyard Kipling, her mother was once bailed out of jail through the efforts of Upton Sinclair, and another family member helped Eugene O'Neill produce his plays. On her own merits, she claimed to have had Clifford Odets ("a curly-haired boy who wanted to write plays") write poems to her "in purple ink." And as a young teen, she carried on a lengthy correspondence with H.L. Mencken, challenging him over remarks he made in the *American Mercury* about Margaret Sanger and birth control in addition to related issues—pleased with herself that he finally recognized that she was no ordinary "Massachusetts matron."[5]

Nilla Cook's adventure to India commenced at the age of 14 and ended eight years later with a celebrated return to New York, where from a casual challenge over issues of social class, she became engaged to a ship hand in a fury of Cook's version of political correctness. Cook visited the "boy" after he had had a pleasant encounter with her young son, inquiring about his health, when the "boy" remarked "it was nice of you to come and see me . . . I've heard you are quite a social worker—quite a friend of the lowly." Cook was indignant at his class-based remark, nevertheless the "boy" persisted with phrases such as "it could not exactly be called a visit to a social *equal*" and "you were a grand lady, magnificently visiting the lowly. You did the same in India, stooped to be nice to your inferiors." Cook became increasingly irritated at his remarks when the "boy," in an effort to call her bluff on the issue blurted out "I mean you'd never marry me." Cook accepted on the spot. From there the story turned increasingly bizarre as Cook was intent upon honoring her pledge. She recognized the irony that she was marrying him to break down social barriers while "he looked upon the Jews, the Italians, the Greeks, the French, as dirt under his feet." When they arrived in New York, Cook and her fiancé scuttled about town from taxi to taxi trying to avoid the "pack of hyenas" bent on covering her ceremony. They then married at City Hall. Cook's friends were appalled, but their efforts to persuade her otherwise had been futile, Cook assuring herself that "not to care what they said about you was the key to the *Bhagavad Gita.*" Shortly after the ceremony, Cook, by her own account, became very ill. While recovering, she notified the "boy" that it had all been a mistake—that she was profusely sorry but she was going to annul the union. However, in a tongue-in-cheek gesture to the media hounds Cook and the "boy" posed for some honeymoon pictures to add a final touch to the strange affair.[6]

The nuptial drama in New York was representative of Cook's eight-year odyssey that began in Greece and eventually led to a lengthy series of event-filled travels in India. For Cook, India had been a place of dreams, where even in the California of her childhood "I danced in the ocean foam and saw the temples of India in the clouds of the Pacific sunset." As a bi-coastal commuter between divorced parents, she reminisced about a childhood love named Vernon from Vermont (whose mother was a relative of Walt Whitman's) who "had a dream of India that dated as far back as mine." India was an early fixation that never waned. While in Greece, she determined to sail on to India, even though she had married in her mid-teens, borne a son, and her family sought to dissuade her from the adventure. Finally, Cook's mother relented and then persuaded the trustees of the Cook estate to disburse trust funds for Nilla's education at the University of Athens—concealing the real purpose—because an Indian venture would presumably never be approved. For Cook, "going to India was going to paradise."[7]

Once in India Cook met a wide assortment of Indians including a stay at Gandhi's ashram. However, prior to even meeting him, while on a visit to Kashmir, she received "infuriated letters from American Protestants, enclosing newspaper clippings announcing that I had been dipped in the Ganges by Mahatma Gandhi and baptized a Hindu." Complete with pictures taken from her earlier days adorned in ancient Greek robes, she is represented as dancing before Gandhi, whose picture had been conveniently inserted in place of Prometheus. Thus began a journey through India plagued by the journalistic excesses of the American press—an element that not only constantly irritated Cook but also complicated her travels. One report, which later generated a libel suit against a New York newspaper, inferred that she and Gandhi had traveled from Bombay to Wardah in a "romantic escapade, in which the two of us eloped for a joy ride." She had indeed been on the train, but only as part of a very large entourage. In spite of these frustrations, she immersed herself in India, its peoples, its customs, and its rich heritage—adopting Indian dress and ways and spending extensive time with Indian personages—studiously avoiding British compounds and social events. Upon her eventual departure to the

States from Calcutta, she reflects, "I could under no circumstances *see* myself leaving the shore of India, or hear myself saying good-bye. And so I took a vow of silence and closed my eyes."[8]

A character of an entirely different sort was Gordon Sinclair, a swashbuckling Canadian journalist of such myopic depths that one "Indian" reader of his work could not refrain from handwriting, in bold penciled letters, indignant remarks about the book's contents in select sections of the volume. One entry, sprawled across an entire page, reads as follows: "if you really want to know about India do not waste your time reading this biased book written by a stupid author who should have never been allowed to enter India." Such sentiments were understandable, particularly if the "Indian" scribe were a Hindu, because Sinclair frequently demeaned them, whom he variously described in condescending or denigrating terms. In one remark Sinclair characterized Hindu troops as "puny chaps who die young." In a commentary on reincarnation, Sinclair tells his readers "no Hindu will kill any animal, bird or reptile under any condition, anywhere. That's because they believe you and I and the iceman come back to this world as some other being after we die, and by killing a mouse or a monkey they may be killing Aunt Susie's little Willie who died young." Sinclair's work is filled with flippant remarks about nearly everything he encounters in India. Even Gandhi was harpooned by his supercilious wit. Sinclair arranged a meeting with Gandhi while he was incarcerated in a Poona jail. The Mahatma was described as an "emaciated and embittered holy humbug." Sinclair questioned him in a pretentious and rude manner, designed more for an anticipated audience back home than for any desire for insight. In one exchange, concerning East-West habits of hygiene, he queried of Gandhi, "but surely, Mr. Gandhi, you, who have traveled, agree that India is undoubtedly the filthiest, smelliest, unhealthiest country in the known world. I know that it is not polite for me to say all this but I'm almost in hygienic terror." To which Gandhi responded: "my son these things are too deep for you. Why don't you run along to play golf and drink beer and bathe in your many, many bathtubs?" Later in his account, while making snide remarks about mill workers in Poona who refused to move into public housing, Sinclair informed his readers "they quote Gandhi as their patron saint of filth." Gandhi, according to Sinclair, "would break up every hospital as 'a place of quackery and creator of vice'—and he would prohibit the importation or manufacture of bathtubs."[9]

Sinclair entered India by way of the Khyber Pass in what he refers to as "this he-man land of adventure . . . without companions, plans, worries, prejudices, guidebooks, a message to the heathen or something to sell." His objective was "to explore this fantastic land of India as the mood suited me, going when, where and how I pleased; if possible off the beaten path." He referred to India as part of a "terrible trio of front page babies," namely, India, Russia and China. He frequently disparaged tourists, privileging his own exploits as an exemplary form of travel outside the usual circuitry of tourist itineraries. Much of his work is tinged with the flavor of sensational journalism. Chapter headings are filled with catchy titles such as The Pass of Death, Pagan Frenzy, Brides and Boobs, Hello Sucker, and Buckets of Blood, to name only a few. Of all the armchair travel narrators, his India account is the most extreme example of Western arrogance. Sinclair blithely struts across the subcontinent more in search of a sensational subject or catchy phrase than for any real insight into the drama unfolding there. But like his travel writer contemporaries, he contended that his journey through India was conducted "without prejudice." However, as the previously mentioned scribbler on his volume noted, "he (Sinclair) has never taken any trouble to see the real India."[10]

Louis Hagan, a naturalized British citizen who fled Nazi Germany with his parents in the early 1930s, represented a studied contrast from Gordon Sinclair. Hagen, after fighting in the European theatre for several years, served out the rest of his tour of duty in India, grudgingly at first, but then engaged India with intense interest and commitment. He arrived on the subcontinent quite cynical about Britain's imperial legacy, loaded with questions such as "if ninety-five per cent of the population was illiterate, why the hell hadn't we taught them to read and write?" He admired Gandhi and Jinnah and believed that the Indian independence movement was natural and inevitable. In short, he didn't want to fight "for something rotten," commenting, "I felt I should have to be ashamed of being British." Although he never retreated from some of those sentiments, he admitted to his readers that during his fourteen months in India that "I noticed myself—in common with almost everyone I met who came out there and kept his eyes open—becoming less and less didactic as my knowledge increased." Hagan constantly ran up against situations and people that challenged any simplistic interpretation of the Indian scene. He warned his readers that they will "find this book contradictory, full of theories that lead nowhere in particular and quite devoid of solutions." In final reflection he states, "the only thing that was constant now was my reluctance to criticize . . . the Indians or the British Raj."[11]

Like many travelers in India, Hagen was overwhelmed by the poverty and suffering he encountered. "The first time you see this sort of thing, it leaves you stunned . . . overcome with an inarticulate pity." And like others, what was first a surge of heart-felt sympathy turned to irritation and then anger as gangs of clinging children and chattering beggars flooded him with demands for *backsheesh*. Later in his account he described a sexual encounter with a young Indian prostitute, realizing how far he was from his homeland, but then forcing himself "to forget about England." He had an affair with a British memsahib where he learned about the quirks and refined snobbery of British society in India. He never tired of visiting local villages, continuously fascinated by what he saw, and eager to absorb and understand the India he was encountering. What separates Hagen from other armchair travel writers is his more intense self-scrutiny, a constant battle with pre-conceptions or accumulated ones as he travels through India. At times, he is as contradictory as he admits—sometimes championing Indian independence and at others conceding that the whole question is too big for him. Nonetheless, his honesty and determined effort to understand what he beholds negates his frequent turns towards ambiguity. To expect much more of him would perhaps be its own failing.[12]

Most of the works surveyed in this study were written by travelers passing through India over a period of months—sometimes up to a year or more. A few were penned as colonial memoirs, recalling travels across the subcontinent while carrying out imperial duties. Not infrequently the question arose as to whether the traveler's or the expatriate's views on India was of more value to readers. Did it take, as some suggested, twenty years in India to cultivate the requisite expertise to really *know* India and its peoples? Some claimed it did. Travelers, in their view, were merely superficial observers who experienced India as wide-eyed ingénues. Or, as some contended, did extended time in India only serve to dissolve one's curiosity, to blunt one's sense of wonder and openness where slowly but surely, as so many expatriates demonstrated, one retreated back to the sheltered insularity and pervasive racism of colonial life? As will be discussed more later in this study, Indians were often astonished, sometimes amused at the refreshing openness and politeness of first-time visitors or newly-arrived expatriates. There is a conversation between Indians in Forster's *Passage to India* that effectively illustrates the point. They debate whether, unlike *in* England, it was possible to be friends with an Englishman *in* India. They cite specific experiences noting that initial encounters are quite promising only to disintegrate in the wake of social sabotage by calcified British expatriates. In short, real friendship in India between Indians and the English was highly unlikely, if not impossible. And as one of the conversationalists noted, the women were the worst: "granted the exceptions . . . all Englishwomen are haughty and venal."[13]

Some travel writers were apologetic about doing a book on India based on only a few months of travel there. It was as if they were anticipating the disdain of old India hands or the sniping of potential literary reviewers. And they expressed concern that their readers might be wary of their India credentials. By raising the issue and being suitably modest in their claims they sought to ward off such criticisms. A case could be made that their short-term travel accounts were more insightful than those written by expatriate authors. There is something about seeing sights for the first time. An exhilarating sense of wonder and fascination with detail can both enrich and define the experience. Imagine, for a moment, coming around the bend and seeing a valley stretched before you—a visual panorama composed of a town with architectural features, topographical surroundings, and other distinguishing characteristics that make the sight, and moment, unique in one's experience. Imagine the eyes surveying those sights with intense concentration, studying (as an observant traveler would) the distinctive forms and traits before one, enhanced even more once the viewer enters the town, roams the squares and markets about him, and interacts with locals. Imagine living in the same town for twenty years. Everything would be familiar and would most likely blend and blur into an amorphous mass of commonality. Something is lost over time even as on some level much is accumulated. Perhaps the foregoing is little more than an insipid analogy hardly serving to creditably validate the short-term travel writer over the expatriate chronicler. Yet, it is important to bear in mind that almost every short-term travel writer surveyed in this study journeyed through India for months and had the advantage of a shared language. Obviously, not all Indians spoke English (few villagers did) but sufficient numbers of them were fluent enough to permit extended interactions and conversations with indigenous residents. Of the three travel writers profiled in this chapter—Nilla Cram Cook, Gordon Sinclair and Louis Hagan—Cook and Hagan truly engaged the India before them. Sinclair surely experienced extraordinary adventures (if all are to be believed) but he never opened his eyes to India and Indians beyond clever, demeaning clichés. The same travel writing varieties can be found in expatriate authors. Some smugly dispensed the imperial line; others were more thoughtful and insightful in their observations. Having done travel writing studies on both China and India, I would tilt towards the short-term travel writer as the more vibrant and interesting practitioners of the genre—and on balance the more insightful. There are many exceptions. But of course, there always are. Ultimately each author has to be evaluated individually on his or her own terms because block or "essentialistic" assessments, much like ethnic stereotyping or racial profiling, is simply one more variation of the human tendency to over-generalize observations and beliefs. Such is the travel writer's dilemma but if poised in thoughtful equilibrium between the need to synthesize impressions and the duty to honor vital distinctions, the travel narrative can inform us much about peoples and places—in this case India and Indians.

## NOTES

1. Edward Holton James, *I Tell Everything: The Brown Man's Burden (A Book on India)* (Geneva: Imprimerie Kundig, 1931), 9–11, 94.

2. Louis Hagan, forward to *Indian Route March* (New York: Pilot Press, 1946).
3. Albert Farwell Bemis, preface to *A Journey to India, 1921–22* (Boston: Privately Printed, 1923).
4. Katherine Mayo, *Mother India* (New York: Harcourt, Brace & Co., 1927) 11–12, 16–17.
5. Nilla Cram Cook, *My Road to India* (New York: Lee Furman, 1939), 8, 14, 47, 51.
6. Ibid, 438–449.
7. Ibid, 3, 52–54.
8. Ibid, 189, 399, 435.
9. Gordon Sinclair, *Foot-Loose in India* (New York: Farrar & Rinehart, 1933), 6, 32, 81, 87, 197.
10. Ibid, 1, 2, 23, 125, 196, 197.
11. Hagan, forward to *India Route March*, 187, 191, 192.
12. Louis Hagan, *Indian Route March* (New York: Pilot Press, 1946), 13, 25, 27, 28.
13. E.M. Forster, *A Passage to India* (London: Harvest/HBJ Books, 1924), 11–13.

## *Chapter Two*

# Katherine Mayo and the Great 'Mother India' Debate

India's diverse religious, cultural and political climate provided India-observers with a formidable range of issues to absorb. Gandhi himself embodied such a perplexing mixture of the old and the new that the travel writers surveyed in this study found it nearly impossible to untangle the political idealist from the ashram reactionary. If aspirations for democracy and eradication of the caste system signaled a progressive embrace of Western-styled politics and social reform, a return to homespun textile production represented a regressive retreat from modernity. Gandhi, like the India he symbolized, confronted observers with such a crazy quilt pattern of desirable and undesirable traits that it stretched one's capabilities to interpret either the individual parts or the Indian monolith in any type of coherent analysis. Some writers, like Katherine Mayo, focused on the perceived evils of child-marriage, prostitution and related Hindu cultural traditions. Others, like Clive Branson, a member of Britain's communist party, railed at imperial rule in India as a "howling disgrace."[1] To embrace a reformist vision as Mayo and Branson did provided a singular interpretational structure in which to conduct one's analysis, but it did not necessarily yield more enlightenment as to the *real* India they sought to portray. In what ways do the parts, or at least the parts selected, unlock the mysteries of the whole? In a place like India, understanding traditions such as child-marriage or British imperial policy, if pursued with openness to different points of view, would reveal so many perspectives that it would look like the shifting sets of a kaleidoscope so often referenced by travel writers. Yet to dismiss certain realities such as poverty and racism as subject to the vagaries of different perspectives, and thus beyond any assertive effort to cast them for what most people knew them to be—evils deserving elimination from society—seemed a dereliction of one's duty.

Most travel writers narrating their experiences in India did tackle such issues, no less so than we do today when we condemn the Taliban's treatment of women in Afghanistan or ethnic cleansing in Sudan. But the line between Western political and cultural imperialism, thrusting itself into the internal affairs of other nations and the proper condemnation of global evils in need of eradication was and continues to be a problematical divide—dependent in great part upon the perspective of the observer. Some writers waffled on the tough issues of the day; others attacked them furiously in an effort to make right historic wrongs. Post-colonial critics, often justifiably, have assailed Western travel writers as Eurocentric and frequently racist interpreters of the non-Western cultures they portrayed. But writing about foreign cultures, if one is honest, inevitably involves critical judgments; otherwise one's descriptions and analysis is little more than a sterile, one-dimensional production yielding little of interest let alone significant discourse on a topic. Of course, figures such as Katherine Mayo represent the opposite extreme—sensationalist interpreters of a culture's more problematic traditions. Wrestling with the variable spins of the "India debate" that sprung from her *Mother India* tome seems an appropriate place to explore the diverse forms of representational quandaries that surfaced during the Gandhian Age.

Katherine Mayo's *Mother India* has been described by one contemporary scholar as the "single most brazenly 'orientalist' work on India that I know."[2] C.S. Ranga, in his 1928 publication responding to Mayo's claims, described the work as "a tirade against India, written in the style of a Cassandra-like propagandist."[3] Nearly all major Indian figures of the era, including Mahatma Gandhi, Rabindranath Tagore, Lala Lajpath, Sarojini Naidu, to name only a few, responded vigorously to *Mother India* in some fashion. Gandhi, for example, suggested that it resembled "the report of a drain inspector sent out with the one purpose of opening and examining the drains of the country to be reported upon, or to give a graphic description of the stench exuded by the open drains . . . [and] the drains are India."[4] Some have contended that Britain's colonial government drafted her to write the book in order to subvert the aims of the Indian independence movement, and thus it was little more than a polemic imperial rag.

By her own account she was an American innocent, "commissioned by no one," who dropped by London's India Office in early October of 1925 to "state her plans"; namely, write a book on India, "leaving untouched the realms of religion, of politics, and of the arts" but instead focusing on issues of public health and related matters. When asked what the Office could do for her, she blithely answered "nothing"—except to recognize that she was neither a busybody nor a political agent, but "merely an ordinary American citizen" investigating public health issues that affected not only Indians but

"John Smith of 23 Main Street" as well. The British, in her words, responded by stating "but whatever you do, be careful not to generalize." Mayo told her readers otherwise; that indeed "there are perhaps certain points on which . . . you *can* generalize about India." And generalize she did—armed with collected statistics and lurid examples from her India travels. What was purportedly a "public health" inquiry devoid of religious, political or artistic concerns, quickly turned into a diatribe against Hindu marriage and sexual practices, the waffling indolence of British and Congress Party political figures, and what she and others interpreted as the lurid imagery of Hindu art. Mayo informed her readers that the ordinary traveler who visits India would fail to see the horrors she uncovered and that British officialdom assiduously ignored it. But she, "shouldering this task," had fully engaged it and was "fully aware of the resentments" that she would incur; "of muck-raking; of injustice; of material-mindedness; of lack of sympathy; of falsehood perhaps; perhaps of prurience."[5]

Before discussing how the armchair travel writer of the era understood Mayo's work, perhaps a few specifics concerning her claims should be presented. Much of the storm revolved around Hindu marriage customs. Mayo emphasized that Hindu tradition, concerned about early mortality rates, mandated that a young male produce a legitimate son as soon as procreation was physically possible in order to ensure proper administration of the father's burial rites. Such early sexual activity, she contended, sapped the energies of young manhood with the result that "seven to eight of every ten males between the ages of twenty-five and thirty are impotent." Although she provided no source for the statistics, she contended that they were "not random."[6] Moreover, she quoted statements from Indian figures supporting her claims. She cited an article by Gandhi in his weekly paper *Young India* titled the "Curse of Child Marriage" in which Gandhi, among other points, stated that the practice "is a very important cause of the gradual and steady decline of Hindu society in point of (1) numbers, (2) physical strength, courage, and (3) morality."[7] Mayo also referenced other indigenous Indian and British reform efforts to curtail the practice, ultimately dismissing them as halting and irresolute in the face of fierce traditionalist Hindu resistance. Mayo's supporters also frequently referenced reformist statements by Indian national leaders to defend *Mother India's* claims. But what angered so many of Mayo's opponents was the broad indictment of Hinduism in general and the racist undercurrents that permeated her work. The following excerpt is but one example of her many broadsides against Hindu culture:

> Once more, then, one is driven to the original conclusion: Given men who enter the world physical bankrupts out of bankrupt stock, rear them through childhood

in influences and practices that devour their vitality; launch them at the dawn of maturity on an unrestrained outpouring or their whole provision of creative energy in one single direction; find them, at the age when the Anglo-Saxon is just coming into full glory of manhood, broken-nerved, low-spirited, petulant ancients; and need you, while this remains unchanged, seek for other reasons why they are poor and sick and dying and why their hands are too weak, too fluttering, to seize or to hold the reins of Government?[8]

Mayo's Hindus, like Gordon Sinclair's "puny chaps who die young," were so ostensibly feeble that they were ill-equipped to assume independence and self-rule. And of course, Hindu sexual practices were to blame; one need look no further, certainly not to poverty, malnutrition, nor disease for health problems, alleged impotency or premature death. It was, according to Mayo, an intractable Hinduism, steeped in such ignorance and reactionary menace, that to resist its will "has ever meant the eclipse of Indian reason in madness, riot and blood." *Mother India* labors on in an onslaught against Indian religious and cultural practices, particularly those of Hindu origin with a notable preoccupation with sexual themes. If Mayo's coverage of early male sexuality was deemed provocative, her extensive treatment of female childhood marriage, prostitution, or widowhood was even more explosive material.[9] As critic C.S. Ranga Iyer argued in a book-length rebuttal of Mayo's claims,

A book to be popular must be sensational. A sensational book must deal with the sex-side. Shocking things must be expressed either with cool courage or holy horror. A woman is best qualified for the job; if she can "fire off" in the yellow press style, she can command a good sale. Give the lady her due; Miss Mayo does the job thoroughly well; good, on the whole, from the sensuous and the sensational standpoint. The tourist authoress deserves all the limelight of the world."[10]

Iyer's work directly challenged many of Mayo's findings. For example, he claimed "early marriage is not part of India culture. In the Vedas, one finds no sanction for it," but admitted that the fourteen year-old Hindu mother existed, albeit as an exception to the norm. Moreover, he claimed that pre-puberty betrothals, mistakenly characterized as "marriages" also existed, but they were no more than ceremonial pledges with the young boy and girl returning to their respective homes to await marriage at a date when they reached maturity. Such traditions, Iyer argued, prevailed principally among the Brahmins and certain regions of India—representing a "very small fraction" of India's population. He was also irked by Mayo's failure to utilize even one quote from the Vedas, what he termed the Hindu Bible, contending that Mayo studiously avoided it as a source for interpreting Hindu practices.[11] In reading competing reactions to *Mother India*, one is immediately struck by not only the intensity of the debate but what at first impression appears to be irreconcilable statistics, claims and counter-claims, and ultimate conclusions concerning Mayo's claims. To tackle the range and complexity of the debate is beyond the scope of this work. Nonetheless, it is important to address Mayo's book because of its impact upon the armchair narrators who chronicled their journeys to India during the Gandhian Age. Was India a hell-hole—a "world menace" of vile religious practices and a cesspool of horrific diseases—or was it a wondrous kaleidoscope of colorful cultures with warm and gentle people maturing inevitably towards independence and political maturity? These are only several of the many competing images of the era.

Before departing Iyer's *Father India,* a few observations should be addressed towards not only the substance of his work, but also several underlying strategies designed to discredit Mayo's personally. Iyer's sardonic sexist remark that "a woman is best qualified for the job" (to muckrake India) surfaced in comparable variation in other rebuttals as well. Women travel writers from the late nineteenth century on had increasingly cornered a significant share of the travel narrative market. Invariably, they were seen as global busybodies, poking their heads into imperial realms and foreign cultures bent on creating at best innocent fluff, at worst, sensational works distorting social and political realities. They tended to deal more with the social and the cultural and less with the political aspects of the sites they visited. Hence, in the eyes of many commentators, a woman's travel account was soft, mushy material, often discounted as feminine patter. Iyer, by condescendingly referring to Mayo as "the tourist authoress," invoked a familiar tactic to challenge her findings. Had a male written the same work, no doubt the attack would have been strenuous given the nature and tone of the work, but a woman writing such an account invariably triggered stronger and more cynical responses.

It should also be noted that Iyer launched his work by establishing two prototypical visitors to India: Mayo with her sex-laden yellow journalism bent on slandering "a great and simple-hearted nation," and Aldous Huxley's record of his India travels, *Jesting Pilate,* where an observer of intellectual acumen "has said very unpleasant things [about India] in a pleasant way, for he had no desire to hurt; he wished to help." In short, Huxley's "style is literary, because he is a scholar . . . an Englishman of culture."[12] This juxtaposition of high and low literary styles—the scholar versus the yellow journalist—further buttressed Iyer's efforts to denigrate Mayo's book. No doubt *how* one writes about unpleasant aspects of foreign cultures is a critical dimension in how we understand the subject matter. In Mayo, we find the single-minded reformist, seeking to root out what she refers to in hyperbolic terms—a "world menace." In Huxley's *Jesting Pilate*, we find a more reflective and melancholic quality, particularly in his conclusions. Upon parting India he tells his readers "it is because I do not desire to grieve that I am glad to be going. For India is depressing as no other country I have ever known. One breathes in it, not air, but dust and hopelessness."[13] On several occasions, Huxley criticized Indian religious traditions no less so than Mayo, but his remarks read less like an all-out assault and more like a thoughtful reflection on India's troubles—an atheist's distaste for religious influences, wherever found:

> Admirers of India are unanimous in praising Hindu 'spirituality.' I cannot agree with them. To my mind 'spirituality' (ultimately, I suppose, the product of the climate) is the primal curse of India and the cause of her misfortunes. It is this preoccupation with 'spiritual' realities, different from the actual historical realities of common life, that has kept millions upon millions of men and women content, through centuries, with a lot unworthy of human beings. A little less spirituality, and the Indians would now be free—free from foreign dominion and from the tyranny of their own prejudices and traditions. There would be less dirt and more food. There would be fewer Maharajahs with Rolls Royces and more schools. The women would be out of their prisons, and there would be some kind of polite and conventional social life—one of those despised appearances of civilization which are yet the very stuff and essence of civilized existence.[14]

Most travel writers, unlike C.S. Ranga Iyer, did not journey to India for the express purpose of challenging *Mother India*. However, most were aware of the book and the cross-cultural storm it had aroused. Nilla Cook, having married at sixteen herself, was openly disdainful of Mayo's interpretation of child brides, stating that she "never personally saw or heard of one anywhere but in the books of foreign pornographists." It was, she claimed, an elementary matter to photograph engaged children and then characterize them as married when in fact "no marriage is celebrated until years after the engagement." Cook's 'pornographists,' in her words, look for the "sick exception . . . seeking ghoulish material from which to draw conclusions about three hundred million Hindus."[15] Gertrude Williams, in her *Understanding India*, informed readers that *Mother India* brought "away such different impressions of the same country. I think the difference in what Miss Mayo and I saw was due in part to the way we saw it." Williams traveled through India for a five-month period the year after Mayo was there. She traveled alone across the subcontinent for more than 6,000 miles. She journeyed, by her own account, by first, second, and third class travel, spending time in Indian villages, markets, and homes—unaccompanied by white males. She contended that "without being sentimental or blind to India's failures," what Mayo attacked were evils that were universally existent elsewhere in the world, and not unlike Western cultures until very recent times. As for child marriage, she noted how surprised she was to discover that twelve was the legally marriageable age in fourteen

American states, whereas in India it was thirteen. For Williams, "some of the indignation lavished on India might well be turned to reforming our own marriage laws."[16]

Mayo certainly had her ardent supporters. Harry Field, in his *After Mother India,* suggested that Mayo's work would go down in history as one of those seminal literary "social forces," like *The Origin of Species* or *Uncle Tom's Cabin*. According to Field, "all who know anything of India are aware, of course, of the prime evils of Hinduism, of the horrors of the child marriage system, of the universality of sexual vice in its most extravagant forms." In short, *Mother India* thoroughly documented and discussed what English officials and missionaries feared to debate openly because of the serious repercussions it would have in India's Hindu community. Only one in a thousand of her critics, according to Field, had actually read the work—ignorantly tabbing Mayo as little more than a lackey drain inspector, bought and paid for by British political and commercial interests. Field proclaimed that the evidence he had surveyed from Indian sources clearly "substantiated the paramount thesis of *Mother India.*"[17]

By contrast, Edward Holton James contended that *Mother India* gave him a false sense of what India was like, leading to him to believe that it was a filthy place where the locals lived like animals. He titled a chapter of his travel narrative on India "The Gospel According to Saint Katherine," telling readers that "it is very easy to get things wrong on India," and Mayo had particularly been wrong on the issue of cleanliness—that Indians "are as clean as or cleaner than any other people I know anything about." James claimed that except for a five-year old boy relieving himself on the edges of a remote road, he had traveled more than 10,000 miles across the subcontinent "poking into every conceivable place" but had never once seen human excrement along India's roads and pathways. Other travel writers, including current ones, have found their experiences to be otherwise, but frequently put their own spin on public displays of bodily functions. Two English Buddhists, journeying as pilgrims to India over the winter of 1990-91, put it this way:

> A ragged man came shuffling along in the half light, paused about a dozen paces in front of me, turned and squatted, pulled up his dhoti, and proceeded to empty his bowels. A dawn attack on the bastions of propriety! This area of life is the one above all that the West cannot accept into consciousness, and which *Mother India* therefore thrusts before our cringing gaze. Despite our "openness" on sexual matters—and our yielding recognition of death—the daily business of the body is still socially unacceptable. In India, back at Mother's bosom, we learn toilet training anew. Every morning in the country, people make their way out into the treeless fields with their little cans of water to defecate and then wash the anus with water and the left hand. Food goes in by means of the right hand

> and out to the ministrations of the left: there's symmetry in that. One can grow to like the cool matter-of-factness of something that is, actually, matter of fact.[18]

Did James not see what was obvious to many other travel writers? Perhaps for him it was simply a "matter-of-fact" activity of the day, not entering his consciousness or worthy of reference in his travel notes. The left hand/right hand antithesis cited above is symbolic of the split perceptions that emerge about India, oppositional characterizations where one side sees the left hand's function as repugnant habit and the other side sees its singular function as part of a larger symmetry of hygienic requirements.

James, besides taking issue with Mayo over "latrine" matters, also pointed out that most of what she focused on, namely child marriage and untouchability, was "not particularly original." Gandhi and other reformers had been advocating change for some time. As for Indian sexuality, Mayo, according to James, "sees sex everywhere." But where and when, he questioned, did Mayo have the opportunity to discover such allegedly lascivious practices? For one—in the symbols of Hindu temples—but James contended that he had not seen any of the promised sexual contact in temple sculptures, frescoes, or paintings. In fact, James queried, "would Miss Mayo, for the help of earnest investigators like myself, furnish information as to where she found her sex-contact materials? India is a big place to investigate in and time is valuable." When in India James carried *Mother India* with him, "conveniently condensed," as he put it "for the use of travelers." Moreover, he informed his readers, if one is out of harm's way from angry picketers or the occasional bomb but still craving some cheap thrills, an "abundant supply may be found in Miss Katherine Mayo's sensational book."[19]

These are only a few samplings of the great *Mother India* debate. As stated earlier, the combatants on both sides marshaled innumerable statistics, observations, and examples to bolster their contentions. Often, they do not seem to be writing about the same India. In fact, at times authors seemed reluctant to concede any facts or points to the other side, suggesting a deep-seated fear that any such concession would invariably be used as ammunition by opposing forces, or be seen by compatriots in the struggle as yielding to the dark side of the debate. To evade being situated so extremely on one or the other side of such controversial debates, most travel writers frequently invoked cross-cultural comparisons as a way of handling critiques of foreign cultures and peoples—much like Gertrude Williams' statistic that twelve is the legal age for marriage in fourteen American states—whereas in India it starts at thirteen. Does Calcutta have slums? Yes, but so does London or New York. Does India have troubling child-marriage practices? Simply travel to rural Utah. Or, there is the historic variation of the strategy. Does India suffer from severe poverty, disease, and public sanitation problems? One need only revisit the urban reform movements of nineteenth and early twentieth century New York or London. Is untouchability a hideous social tradition? Then note the Jim Crow Laws of the American South. One more equalizing strategy should be mentioned: India is simply too large and complex to possibly generalize upon. As French novelist Maurice Dekobra wrote in 1930 following a six-month tour of India,

> Having digested both these books [Mayo's *Mother India* and Iyer's *Father India*] with considerable care, I have come to the conclusion that it is superlatively difficult to judge of the customs of so composite a country. I have said: country. Continent would have been better. And the Hindus? One must take into account the Bengalese, the Punjabis, the Dravidians, the Parsees, the Mahrattis, the Sikhs, the Malabars, and so on indefinitely. There are 500,000 cities or towns in India. There are 2,000 distinct and separate castes. There are 50 religious sects. How is any one man or woman to really know and understand them all? The lifetime of a centenarian would not suffice.[20]

Dekobra dryly remarked, "far be it from me to hurt Mr. Iyer's feelings by asserting that India's cooks are dirty. He would doubtless respond that he had seen equally dirty ones in Europe, sweating over hot ovens." Dekobra commented upon the relativity of concepts like cleanliness, referencing how offensive it is to Orientals that Westerners use handkerchiefs. He then told a story of an English woman who was visiting Bombay. Having been previously informed of the beauty of the Parsee faith, she found herself having tea one day nearby the Towers of Silence (Parsee funeral rites involve placement of their dead on the Towers for vultures to consume) when a vulture "thoughtlessly dropped" the eyeball of a deceased Parsee beside her. As Dekobra mused, "you can well imagine the opinion which the poor old lady formed of Zoroaster's religion." Were other more beautiful and touching funeral ceremonies the real Parsee faith, the real India? Or did the Towers and its gruesome image of the falling eyeball more accurately define Parsee traditions? For those of Mayo's persuasion, no doubt the Tower and its plunging eyeball; for those of Iyer and his India, no doubt the more beatific act of the youngest girl of the house placing crystal bowls of pink and white flowers, at dawn each morning, in a specially designated prayer room to honor the dead. According to Dekobra, "India is probably the country where the European experiences the most varied sensations—sensations which go all the way from profound admiration to intense disgust—sensations which oscillate between the sublime and the ridiculous."[21] If so, travel writers in India could surely choose to see and elaborate upon whatever engaged their fascination or reflections.

Many who traveled there after 1926 had read and commented upon *Mother India*; not as many had read or referenced *Father India*. It should be said that travel writers typically chose to keep their distance from so-called authoritative or acclaimed works in writing about the sites they visited. They were occasionally referenced, but the aspiration to discover sights and peoples on their own terms, presumptively "without pre-conceptions," was the travel writer's mantra. Otherwise, what would compel the armchair reader to buy their books? What fresh insights or adventures could they narrate if the "definitive" work had already been penned? The travel writer's persona was bound up in a self-projected image of the unbiased, free-spirited independent, dispensing original observations and insights fresh from India's shores. Of course, most works betrayed evidence of bias and few portrayed India in novel terms. Nevertheless, the best travel writers transported their readers to India as if it were the reader's own journey. Even Katherine Mayo, as problematic as her travels turned out to be, represented herself as unbiased, independent, and free-spirited—and surely she transported readers to India—though many questioned whether it was the real India or one constructed from carefully selected fragments to represent what was really a more elusive whole.

## NOTES

1. Clive Branson, *British Soldier in India: The Letters of Clive Branson* (London: Communist Party Press, 1944), 13.
2. Veena T. Oldenburg, a review essay of Elisabeth Bumiller's *May You Be the Mother of a Hundred Sons: A Journey Among the Women of India,* in *Manushi A Journal About Women and Society*, 39–43.
3. C.S. Ranga Iyer, *Father India: A Reply to Mother India* (New York: Louis Carrier & Co., 1928), 10.
4. V. Sundaram, "Let Not the West Mislead India," in *News Today*. <http://newstoday.net.com/04jun/ss1.htm>
5. Katherine Mayo, *Mother India* (New York: Harcourt, Brace & Co., 1927), 11–18.
6. Ibid, 26–29.
7. Mahatma Gandhi, "Young India," August 26, 1926, 302, as quoted in Mayo, 59.
8. Mayo, 32.
9. Ibid.
10. Iyer, 10–11.
11. Ibid, 21, 24–25.
12. Ibid, 9–11.
13. Aldous Huxley, *Jesting Pilate: The Diary of a Journey* (London: Chatto & Windus, 1948), 159. Huxley traveled to India in the 1920's. This work, along with *Beyond the Mexique Bay*, represent two of his contributions to travel literature.

14. Ibid, 109.

15. Nilla Cram Cook, *My Road to India* (New York, L. Furman, Inc., 1939), 231.

16. Gertrude Marvin Williams, *Understanding India* (New York: Coward-McCann, 1928), xi, xii, 251. Williams had previously collaborated with Bishop Frederick B. Fisher on a work entitled *India's Silent Revolution.* Since most of her efforts on that project were confined to the Congressional Library, she decided to strike out on her own, without her husband, to see India for herself.

17. Harry H. Field, *After Mother India* (New York: Harcourt, Brace and Co., 1929), ix, 4, 9, 244. Field's entire work is a defense of Mayo. Since, in his words, nine books had been written to attack *Mother India*, his book is an effort to set the record straight by demonstrating the truth of her findings and the hypocrisy of her critics.

18. Ajahn Sucitto and Nick Scott, *Rude Awakenings: Two Englishmen on Foot in Buddhism's Holy Land* (Boston: Wisdom Publications, 2006), 42. This quotation derives from Ajahn Sucitto's observations; Sucitto and Scott write separate and distinctive yet generally parallel accounts of their experiences, alternating entries every few pages.

19. Edward Holton James, *I Tell Everything: The Brown Man's Burden (A Book on India)* (Geneva: Imprimerie Kundig, 1931), 43, 139–143.

20. Maurice Dekobra, *The Perfumed Tigers: Adventures in the Land of the Maharajahs* (Oxford: Brewer and Warren, 1930), 4.

21. Ibid, 4–6.

## *Chapter Three*

# The British Colonialist Debate: 'A Pigmentary Aristocracy?'

In chronicling their journeys through India travel writers seldom failed to dispense observations concerning Britain's colonial system, particularly the British expatriate "character" in interaction with Indian subjects. Americans in particular exhibited a tendency to be critical of what they perceived to be British aloofness and snobbery, hearing distant echoes of their own colonial experience from the eighteenth century. The colonialist debate revolved around whether the British were indeed benevolent rulers bestowing justice, prosperity and progress upon an otherwise unruly, ungovernable continent, or were they simply imperialist intruders imposing their will on India principally for commercial gain? One writer, subscribing to the latter sentiment, stated sardonically, "there is an unpleasantly commercial odor, even today, about our whole system in India."[1] Frederick Muehl, an American who traveled and wrote extensively about India, was aghast at how impervious many Britishers could be to the "Indian question." In one argument with a British Colonel over the issue, Muehl nearly lost his temper. The officer, armed with a quiver of supercilious barbs, contemptuously remarked to Muehl: "don't tell me that you're concerned with the welfare of the wogs hereabouts. Well, no matter, you'll get over that in a hurry—that is, if you know what's best for yourself." Peeved, Muehl remarked in turn: "I was brought to India under false pretenses Colonel, under a pretense that Britain is interested in these people." Moreover, "we are told that the rule is kind and humane, designed to prepare these people for self-government." The Colonel, irked at Muehl's idealism, cynically characterized such notions as hogwash, advising Muehl "to forget these imperial apologetics."[2]

The encounter with the Colonel was not a singular event. Muehl noted that the British habitually thought in nationalized terms. To in any way question the imperial system was to indict every British subject in India; "a disagreement with anything British amounts to a large-scale assault against England. When I argue with them it is like the circling of two planets in the farthest reaches of outer space." Muehl thought that the British operated in a self-enclosed sphere, holding to a belief that peoples from other nations could never understand their position in the East, typically expressed by the retort: "well, you're American and I am British, so it's quite natural that we cannot agree." That cliché exasperated Muehl. He pondered whether the big questions of morality and national behavior were so relative, and if they were, then what basis would there be to object to Nazi doctrine? It was Muehl's view that the longer a Britisher remained in India the less he seemed to know about the place and its peoples. Prejudice gripped them, followed by ignorance, leaving most of them "thoroughly blind" in the end.[3]

Muehl's remarks echo themes found in E.M. Forster's classic *A Passage to India*. Set in India shortly after the Great War, Forster launches his novel with the arrival of two India novices, Miss Quested and her projected mother-in-law to be, Mrs. Moore. They traveled to India in anticipation of a potential union between Miss Quested and Mrs. Moore's civil servant son, Ronny Heaslop—the quintessential British-India sahib. However, once there, they are soon bored by the snobbish insularity of British club life and society. They have come, in the familiar traveler's mantra, to see "the real India." When Ronny mockingly asks Fielding, the local headmaster of Government College "how's one to see the real India?"—Fielding responds—"try seeing Indians." Thus, Mrs. Moore and Ms. Quested embark on a series of pre-arranged encounters to meet and interact with local Indian society. Much of it is officious, forced and awkward. Fielding, however, invites them to tea at the college with a small gathering of local Indians. Forster conveys to his readers that "as a rule no Englishwoman entered the College except for official functions, and if he [Fielding] invited Mrs. Moore and Miss Quested to tea, it was because they were newcomers who would view everything with an equal if superficial eye, and would not turn on a special voice when speaking to his guests."[4]

Forster's remarks do little to recommend the traveler's insight. At best his 'travelers' eschew the patronizing voice, but if they encounter local Indians with a refreshing openness, they do so with a "superficial eye." And once the novelty of India and Indians wore off, could they retain the openness and engage local conditions and peoples on a deeper level? According to several of Forster's India characters, probably not. One remarks: "I give any Englishman two years . . . and I give any Englishwoman six months"—ultimately they all slide back into arrogant communal insularity, detaching themselves from the real India.[5] In the end Miss Quested sees more of the real India than she bargained for. Dr. Aziz, one of the visitors at Fielding's informal social, decides in a surge of hospitable emotion to invite Miss Quested and Mrs. Moore to an excursion to the mysterious Malabar Caves. There, in a bizarre episode of spelunking confusion, Miss Quested becomes disoriented, panics, and in an effort to extricate herself from a tangle of potential exits, mistakes Dr. Aziz's efforts to help as sexual assault. In a subsequent trial against Dr. Aziz, he is found innocent—but not before Indians and British colonials line-up in respective righteous indignation and ethnic unity against the alleged wrongs each side had presumably inflicted upon the other. In the end, the perky, curious seeker for the real India is overwhelmed by India's kaleidoscopic images, leading to an expedited passage back to England.

Forster's characters re-appear in different guises among travel writers of the same period. Walter Lawrence, in writing his resident and travel memoirs of several journeys to India, related an experience shortly after his arrival in Bombay where a native host took him about the city to an Indian social event. When they later passed a British club, Lawrence invited the Indian in, who in turn warned Lawrence of its impossibility. When Lawrence inquired why not, his friend stated simply, "you seem to know very little about India. In two years' time you will know why we cannot go into your clubs, and I doubt whether you will even remember my name. [And] you will certainly not dine with me and talk to my friends as we talked yesterday." Reminiscent of Forster's Indian characters in *A Passage to India*, Lawrence's native companion reasserted the common perception that an extended stay in India inevitably led to British insularity and indifference to the real India one inhabited. Lawrence, disturbed by the remark, assured his readers that four years later he returned to Bombay to visit and socialize with his friend, unaffected by the colonial curse so many others had succumbed to.[6]

Clive Branson represents another type of traveler—the communist ideologue who saw India through the prism of class struggle. Branson was stationed in India during World War II, adding a visiting soldier's perspective to his Marxist one. Born in India, but reared and educated in England, Branson was an artist by profession who converted to Marxism in his early twenties. He later joined the Republican cause in Spain's civil war, ending up in a Franco concentration camp before his eventual release back to England. In India, Branson traveled extensively, seeking to discover what the place was about and to crusade against what he perceived to be Britain's active neglect of India's peoples. When Churchill gave a speech in 1942 claiming that India's Congress Party had deliberately fomented riots to assist the Japanese, Branson opined that "Churchill's speech on India was just filth." He complained that he and his fellow soldiers were "never allowed to learn anything about India or the Indians." He was excited by the discovery, so often discouraged by others, "that Indians are human beings." Branson also complained about the fact that he and other common soldiers could clearly see the lovely homes and manicured gardens of British officers, but their lodgings, when not tents, were crude with few of the most basic amenities. In short, Branson believed that India was run for the benefit of a capitalist elite that showed little regard for not only indigenous Indians, but also the ordinary British sent to serve there. Branson was killed in action in 1944 but his notes on India were preserved and then published by Britain's communist party that same year.[7]

Branson's anti-imperial rhetoric was predictable; Gordon Sinclair's, the Canadian journalist whose sophomoric remarks could seem so condescendingly racist at times, was not. In Bombay Sinclair was victimized by an angry female beggar, who miffed at his refusal to respond to her pleas, grabbed a glass jar in a bazaar stall and smacked him over the head with it. Bleeding, he tried to get to a hospital but over the subsequent hours found himself in the midst of "100,000 howling Hindus in diapers looking like a prize fool in a dress suit." British riot control was swift and brutal. In spite of his demeaning remarks about Hindus, he was aghast at British policy. He learned that two Indian lawyers he became acquainted with were jailed for extensive periods for simply failing to report to a police station on time for alleged political offenses against the Raj, Under the British emergency they could he hanged for their failure to report. "Imagine that," Sinclair pondered, "hanged for not reporting."[8]

A corollary to the larger colonial question was the perception that the expatriate Englishman personified a peculiar kind of colonialist "character," usually assumed shortly after exposure to not only Indians, but perhaps more telling, extended contact with British nationals residing abroad. Aldous Huxley observed that British subjects who loved life in the East invariably did so because "in the East, they say, a man is somebody; he has authority and is looked up to . . . at home, he is lost in the crowd, he does not count, he is nobody."[9] One Indian expatriate explained it this way: "it's the bastard sons that ship off to the colonies. If you're the black sheep of some prominent and wealthy family, or illegitimate son of an earl and a chambermaid, or if you simply can't make it at home, then you drink yourself to death in British Siberia."[10] In short, the colonialist "character" was a defective one, if not originating from questionable circumstances at home, then surely formed shortly after arrival on the subcontinent.

Gertrude Williams noted how in the homeland English manners were impeccable whether exhibited at bus stops, shops or relations between employers and employees. However, once in India, a "curious change" occurred; expatriate Britishers rarely engaged in the common verbal courtesies towards Indians so familiar at home, instead barking instructions in sharp tones and yelling out the abusive 'B-h-o-y" when seeking assistance from Indian servants. Moreover, Williams observed, "an Englishman of any pretensions does not carry so much as a book," leaving that modest task to his Indian servant. In short, Huxley's British expatriate in the East—once there "a man is somebody"—even if insufferably so to Indians. Like others, Williams also commented upon an extraordinary British insularity in India, a trait that commenced once they boarded ship in Britain for the East. Every winter the P. & O. boats were filled with British officials heading to India, some to return and others, many young subalterns, embarking on the venture for the first time.[11] She recounted this odd experience at the outset of her journey:

> The first morning out, as I took my place at table, I said good-morning to my English neighbors. The men looked embarrassed and the women looked blank. No one replied. It is a three weeks' trip from London to Bombay. We had our permanent places at table. I never spoke to any of them again, and they never spoke to me. Nor did they usually speak to each other unless they had been introduced before sailing.[12]

Silence, at table, on deck, or in the saloon sipping coffee after dinner, was the operative behavioral code. Promenading along the decks also entailed well-defined rituals: people walked with prescribed hand placements and body movements in rhythmic, silent pacing. The males always wore blazers with their school crest prominently displayed, for without it, it was clear to others that one had not attended the right school. When lining up for her morning wash each day, Williams once again observed an extraordinary reserve, as silence ruled the line-up of the five to ten women that were invariably in front of her. Williams remarked that in one way this silent parade was the one time when the women broke from their usual reserve, wearing "the most ravishing negligees, passionate pinks and languorous lavenders; the homeliest old dowagers were rather the most fastidious." As they crossed the Red Sea, the tropics seemed to melt the behavioral chill some; suddenly several women spoke to Williams and she dabbled in casual conversation for the first time. If this stuffy band of travelers seemed to represent the ultimate in British diffidence, a British army Captain, surprised at Williams' perceptions of British formality, remarked, "you don't call this crowd reserved, do you? This is a rummy crowd of nobodies. That is what makes them so sociable."[13]

Ranjee Shahani, a native Indian who journeyed home on a self-described pilgrimage evoked, in his words, by a "veritable hurricane of longing," sought to discover whether the India of the 1930s, as so many had claimed, was a substantially changed India from the one of his past. Shahani was a self-admitted Europhile, clearly comfortable with his English friends and his life in Britain. He reminded his readers that friendship between an Englishman and an Indian is "not only possible but really exists," but then added, "in India, however, the story is quite different." Shahani contended that except for the rare personality "the Englishman in India becomes acutely aware of his pigmentary aristocracy." He behaved not like a gentleman, but more like a "savage" who treats all Indians with arrogance and disdain. Shahani then provided several examples of this trait, lamenting the fact that such behavior was sponsored and perpetuated by British officialdom. Shahani further contended that Europeans (particularly Anglo-Saxons) committed many a *faux pas* upon arrival in India, so many so that he should be provided with a tract titled "What a Westerner Ought to Know."[14] Generating a mini-tract of his own, below is a sampling of Shahani's recommendations:

1. Indians criticize one another freely, even bitterly, but they hate to be criticized by a stranger;
2. All Indians are not coolies or clerks; so do not speak to everyone in the same lofty manner. Above all avoid the word "native" as you would the black plague. Talk naturally, man to man. The younger generation appreciates that.
3. Indians are very tolerant. You can do what you like among your own kind; but when among Indians refrain from slighting references to their women and their religions.
4. Wherever you go, to a post office or to a theatre, wait your turn, as in any European country. Don't insist on being attended to first.
5. India—note well—has always had great men.
6. The Indian, like the Englishman, is a sentimentalist at heart. Only the Indian cannot hide his feelings.
7. If you wish to know the real India, go into the country, especially among the peasantry.[15]

As Mona Gardner suggested in her travel work on India, *The Menacing Sun*, "I believe hurt pride manages to be the dividing point between a successful and unsuccessful colonization in India."[16] Not all would agree that colonization in any shape or form could possibly sustain a successful Raj; nevertheless, Gardner, Shahani and many other India observers noted that a serious failure in human relations was at the heart of Indian discontent with British rule. Yet, in the view of most British colonials, maintaining distinct lines between themselves and the colonized was essential to Empire's success. The insularity of club life, the social rituals, the *Upstairs, Downstairs* divide between those who serve and the served, and many related behavioral modes preserved those lines even as it dissolved the prestige and authority the British sought to retain. Shahani's mini-tract of travel etiquette, designed for India travelers, was clearly universal in aspiration. Such advice surfaced in proximate variation in many travel accounts but rarely as an itemized list of recommended or proscribed conduct as set forth by Shahani. Some India observers believed that the inter-war period had brought significant change. J.A. Spender traveled in India for three months over the winter of 1925-1926. He undertook the journey as a correspondent for the *Westminster Gazette*. He contended that in the fourteen years since he had been to the subcontinent, "now there is a real desire to understand what Indians want and to meet them more than half-way."[17] Spender's remarks are not atypical of British resolve to portray a Raj of ever-emerging tolerance of Indian sensibilities and aspirations. Like the old adage that one can find whatever one desires to see in India, travel writers frequently characterized British colonial attitudes in contradictory terms. Undoubtedly, the truth existed in many versions, but the dominant one, from American travel writers, and British ones less so, was of a haughty colonialist regime staffed by insensitive and aloof officials. As one writer put it, "one hears again and again about the unchanging East. But what of the unchanging and unchangeable Britisher in India?"[18]

## NOTES

1. John S. Hoyland, *Indian Crisis: The Background* (New York: Macmillan Co., 1943), 129.
2. Frederick Muehl, *American Sahib* (New York: John Day Co.), 87–88.
3. Ibid, 41, 49.
4. E.M. Forster, *Passage to India* (London: Harcourt, Brace, Jovanovich, 1924), 24, 27, 67.
5. Ibid, 11.
6. Walter Lawrence, *The India We Served* (London: Cassell and Co., 1928), 15–16.
7. Clive Branson, introduction to *British Soldier in India: The Letters of Clive Branson* (London: Communist Party, 1944); and Clive Branson, *British Soldier in India: The Letters of Clive Branson* (London: Communist Party, 1944), 17, 29, 34, 49, 84.
8. Gordon Sinclair, *Foot-Loose in India* (New York: Farrar & Rinehart, 1933), 174–195.
9. Aldous Huxley, *Jesting Pilate: The Diary of a Journey* (London: Chatto & Windus, 1948), 4.
10. Muehl, 5.
11. Gertrude Marvin Williams, *Understanding India* (New York: Coward-McCann, 1928), 5, 9, 127.
12. Ibid, 5.
13. Ibid, 6–12.
14. Ranjee G. Shahani, *Indian Pilgrimage* (London: Michael Joseph, 1939), 17, 39–42, 172–175.

15. Ibid, 149–150.

16. Mona Gardner, *The Menacing Sun* (New York: Harcourt, Brace & Co., 1939), 334.

17. J.A. Spender, *The Changing East* (London: Casell & Co., 1926), 108.

18. Shahani, 141.

## *Chapter Four*

# The Independence Debate: Wrestling with the "Peter-Pan Theory"

The independence debate dominated Indian political life and British-Indian relations in the first half of the twentieth century. Some travel writers went to India specifically to investigate the issue, none more earnest than retired British colonials who returned to the subcontinent to witness changes first-hand, burnishing their "expert" credentials before their readers as beacons of seasoned political judgment. Some like noted American historian Will Durant happened upon the issue inadvertently while researching the first volume of his sweeping study of world history, *The Story of Civilization*. Durant traveled to India to "visualize" its peoples and cultures "merely hoping to add a little to my material." Once there he became so infuriated by British policies that he wrote a passionate polemic titled *The Case for India*. Durant lathered the book with scathing accusations against the British, including a contention that their rule in India was "the most sordid and criminal exploitation of one nation by another in all recorded history."[1]

Not all observers were as singularly devoted to India's quest for self-government as Will Durant. The spectrum of opinion on independence matters from the 1920s to the 1940s stretched from Durant-like demands that Britain "quit India" immediately to sentiments that India was not, and would not be ready for independence at any time in the near future. By the 1940s, few clung to the latter notion; the shattering consequences of World War II, the liberation rhetoric from the war's propaganda machine, and Britain's exhaustion at the conflict's end quickly deflated any ideas of a continuing British imperialism, assuring that India's sovereignty was soon to be expedited. Prior to the war's outbreak, the independence debate rarely focused on *if* India would become a sovereign nation but rather *when* the transition should occur. The issues revolved around India's aptitude for self-government—sometimes referred to as the 'Peter Pan' theory of India's political maturation. In other words, could India ever grow up and responsibly separate from the British Empire? And if so, in what form? Would it mature into a British-styled democracy embodying what many believed to be the best that Britain had bestowed, so graciously and benignly, over several centuries of enlightened rule? Or would it turn into a federated conglomerate of Indian states of mixed religious and ethnic identities—perhaps continuously devolving into political and religious factionalism? Or would it regress to an old-style Oriental despotism, ruled from above by hereditary elites? Or worse yet, would the Bolshevik disease spread south to India, turning it into an Asian communist state?

In seeking answers to the independence question, travel writers frequently conveyed to their readers their concerted efforts to seek opinions from diverse elements of British Indian society. Most of them had contacts in British officialdom and eagerly sought out Congress Party members to sound out their views on independence. Additionally, most assured their readers that they had traveled through much of the subcontinent while engaging varied elements of Indian society, some boasting that they had traveled in first, second *and* third class rail compartments, mixing with British colonials and ordinary Indians in their quest for objectivity. Or that they had hung out in British clubs and compounds, roamed the bazaars and back streets of India's major cities, wandered into remote Indian villages, talked with university students, attended political rallies—all designed to gather as much information as possible on the subject. Moreover, they read the papers—British and Indian—monitoring public debates on independence aspirations. Finally, many of them met with Gandhi face-to-face, or at least attempted to, settling in some cases for discussions with Gandhi's followers.

The quest for objectivity was central to their travel writer persona, even if the actual content of their reporting by current standards might at times appear otherwise. Surprisingly, most were not as taken by Gandhi's *Satyagraha* movement of strategic non-violent protests, rallies, marches, and boycotts to achieve independence as one might suppose. For those who have witnessed later twentieth century civil rights movements in the United States, South Africa and other places, Gandhi's peaceful civil obedience campaign was arguably the most prominent legacy of India's independence movement—at least outside of India. For the travel writers surveyed for this work, the focus was more on whether India was ready for independence than upon the strategies employed to achieve it. As one writer argued paternalistically,

> Before the people of England will consider India ready for self-government, India must demonstrate her ability to govern herself under British supervision. The basis of democratic government is the privilege, right, and even obligation of the members of a fairly homogeneous electorate to scrutinize and criticize the acts of the party in power, and eventually to develop an opposition party to oust and

> succeed it . . . How can such a system succeed in a country where the party in power, the British, remains in power regardless of elections? Where in India, in blood or tradition, in habits of thought and action, exists any evidence of probability that replicas of Anglo-Saxon political institutions can successfully function there?[2]

The suggestion that Indians somehow required a period of "British supervision" to demonstrate their ability to self-govern or that a "fairly homogenous electorate" was necessary to conduct a functioning democracy betrayed elements of a continuing racism, attitudes seldom missed by Indian nationals. Yet, the author of this particular colonialist perspective noted that everywhere he traveled in India people were obsessed with politics. That obsession, he argued, demonstrated that Indians were diligently seeking after "Western ideals." In fact, after awhile, the Indian obsession with politics irritated him, crowding out other areas of discussion that he wanted to pursue—such as religion, philosophy and art. Efforts to shift to other domains were inevitably skirted as Indian nationals returned inexhaustibly to the independence question.[3] Frederick Muehl experienced similar preoccupations in his encounters. While riding a train he struck up a conversation with an Indian military officer named Jam, who in spite of being in her majesty's service, assured Muehl that "my soul and my politics are entirely my own." Fascinated by his openness and frankness, Muehl skipped his intended stop and engaged Jam in an afternoon train ride of lively political conversation. When Muehl asked him "is India ready for independence," he answered back: "you Americans think in peculiar terms! What bearing does a country's technical development have on her readiness to rule herself?" Indeed, Jam went on, China was little more than a "mere geographic aggregation" but no one seemed to question its right to self-government. Even though embarrassed by his questions, Muehl pushed the issue into inevitable terrain—nearly always raised in the self-government question—could independence survive India's religious strife? How could the problem be resolved in the new India of the future? Jam's responded: "there are no doubt differences but they are quite manageable." In fact, he argued conflict between religious groups surfaced mainly when the British administered justice between them in an inequitable manner. Moreover, Jam added, even if the Hindus were to attack other minorities upon independence and civil war broke out, how would that be different from the American civil war or similar conflicts in European history? Finally, Jam summed up his position by stating: "you cannot learn self-government from a correspondence school. You've got to try, and you've got to make errors."[4] Obviously, Jam's perspective had little use for the 'Peter Pan' developmental theory—dispensing it as little more than calculated Eurocentric tripe designed to sustain an unwanted colonial government.

Yet, so many writers anguished over "the errors" that threatened the subcontinent if independence was to be granted prematurely. Basil Mathew traveled through India in the mid-1930's, having yearned to discover it for himself for over twenty-five years, and now, at long last having a three-month journey "to interpret her . . . [while] on the verge of the greatest political experiment that the world has ever seen." Mathews claimed to "passionately sympathize with the desire of India for self-rule" but fretted that Indian Nationalists had no concept of the "Himalayan" task before them. According to Mathews, there was no historic or geographic equal to the formidable challenges before India: disease, pestilences, child-marriage, religious strife, nepotism, corruption, to name only a few obstacles, were of near-impossible proportions. Compounding these difficulties was the blind fanaticism of Indian nationalism, so intent on ridding India of the British that it effectively strangled any effort at rational discourse on the complex ramifications of the independence issue. Mathews greatly admired, and in fact, stood in awe of Congress leader Jawaharlal Nehru. He was able to meet with him while in India, noting his ferocious hatred of oppression wherever found, whether an exploitative capitalist, British official, Indian prince, or zemindar landlord. Yet, Mathews, for all of his sympathy with Indian leaders and their aspirations for self-determination, remained pessimistic that India was ready for or could survive the task before it without descent into catastrophic consequences.[5]

Beverley Nichols' *Verdict on India* is a quintessential example of Britain's great discomfort at yielding India to the winds of independence. Nichols' originally traveled to India as a correspondent for Allied Newspapers during World War II. That relationship was interrupted by an extended illness; thereafter he carried on his inquiry into the state of India on his own, or in his words, as an "independent observer" with no ax to grind. However, in his book's preface he fretted that his Hindu hosts, so hospitable and gracious, would upon reading his work "hate it from the first sentence to the last." In fact, he confessed, "in some ways I hate it myself," originally envisioning a different book from the one he eventually wrote. In a chapter titled "To Quit or not to Quit" ("Quit India" was a ubiquitous slogan found everywhere Nichols traveled in India), Nichols set forth three central facets of the question: *should* we quit; *can* we quit; and *will* we quit? Nichols began the first segment by setting up a prototypical British family (the Smiths) and how they might understand the issue. In short, he characterized them as essentially ignorant of India's realities but generally sympathetic to the idea that Indians were entitled to their independence. The Smiths, according to Nichols, were "warm-hearted people; they believe in 'freedom' in the same way that they believe in being kind to animals; they can find India on the map and they know that at any rate it *looks* like a single country, and they have a sneaking affection for Gandhi." As for soldiers serving in India, they were no better. Nichols maintained that their "ignorance was boundless . . . they did not know the difference between a Hindu and a Muslim." Nonetheless, Nichols recognized that the "*should* we quit" India was fundamentally a moral question. On those grounds, he conceded whether to depart must be answered with an emphatic "yes . . . if the Atlantic Charter means anything, if the whole war means anything."[6]

As for "*can* we quit" India, he succinctly responded "of course we can," but then proceeded to totally dismantle the concession as an absurdity because India would neither have an army at independence nor would it have one in less than twenty years. Consequently, it would be vulnerable to outside threats and civil wars. Thus, for the "*can*" component of the issue, Nichols focused entirely on military matters. The counter-response "that India is eager to defend herself only if she is free" Nichols dismissed as muddle-headed nonsense even unworthy of the Mad Hatter. In Nichols' "*can*" analysis, one could surmise that the Atlantic Charter's ideal of self-determination dissolved the 'Peter Pan' political problem, only to be replaced by a "Peter Pan" security problem stemming from the war's preoccupation with military defense. To an Indian, however, it was simply a variation of the imperialist argument that India was in some form incapable of managing its own affairs. If the ardent colonialist had his way, some form of statehood deficiency would invariably surface to defeat self-governance.[7]

In Nichols final element of the equation, *will* we quit, the 'Peter Pan' theory resurfaced once more, albeit in somewhat different guise. According to him, determining whether the British *will* quit depended "on the attitude of Indians themselves," a rather suspect prospect in Nichols' estimation as evidenced by Hindu intransigence during the War. However, Nichols does not really correlate how Indian attitudes would appropriately expedite Britain's exit. In short, he was resigned to Britain's inevitable departure, but whether in haste, which he speculated would be an "unredeemed tragedy," or over an extended period, which he favored as a necessary strategy for adjustment, Britain would quit India physically but would never do so in the "spiritual sense." As far as Indians were concerned, the British were welcome to their "spiritual" attachment; it was the imperial, physical one that needed shedding.[8] Some would argue, perhaps with some justification, that Britain's hasty exit from India several years later (1947) resulted in the very chaos and violence that so many feared. It has been estimated that more than 100,000 were slaughtered when Hindus and Muslims frantically scrambled to re-locate upon the establishment of Indian and Pakistani borders.

However, what Indian independence looked like from a post-1947 perspective was quite different from that of the vortex of political and social rebellion earlier in the century. Robert Bernays traveled in India in 1930-31, observing riots first-hand in Bombay, telling his readers "I was now in the storm-centre of India, face to face with the Congress situation as it really existed." Bernays portrayed Indian resistance as largely peaceful but characterized by occasional violence. The brutality perpetuated by British efforts to control events disturbed him. He traveled across India observing, interviewing, and assessing events from many vantages points, finding in India an environment that "at once fascinates and repels." Bernays in one turn could be found worrying about whether he had enough money to get to his next destination and in the next he was interviewing Lord Irwin and other dignitaries. Bernays admired Irwin, citing one incident where the Viceroy slipped into slum areas one night to inspect squalid conditions, much to the dismay of the local police force. He also admired Irwin for his broad vision, yet Bernays held to a critical stance regarding British policies in India. And, although sympathetic to the Indian cause, he was at times disdainful of certain elements of Indian society, as evidenced by this remark: "I have been studying the university student here. He is one of the lowest things on earth. When he is not making bombs in the laboratory he seems to be stealing examination papers." But it is for his British compatriots that Bernays reserved his harshest criticism. He sensed that for the British "there is a queer atmosphere of impending tragedy . . . that the shrewdest of them are beginning to realize in their hearts that the game is up."[9] In one of several summations on the British view of things, Bernays clearly revealed where his sympathies lay:

> They [Civil Service types] are seldom sincere in any gesture of goodwill they make. They are determined to hold on to power to the last, and so far they have been remarkably successful. Challenged, they 'will speak of liberal things', but their attitude is that of the arrivisite Labour members, who say, 'Socialism by all means—but not in our time.' The Civil Service says, 'self-government is splendid – but not in our time if we can help it.' It is all very natural.[10]

Bernays also perceived the independence issue from a post-colonial perspective. He stated, rather poignantly, "no one finds any music now in the sputter of the machine-gun, and the idea of the white man's burden is distinctly *démodé*. Jingoism that barely survived the Black Week of South Africa perished altogether on the sliding duck-boards of the Passchendaele ridge. It is only in years a generation that separates us from Kipling, but in actual fact it is another century."[11] Bernays found it ironic that Britain's power was ten times what is was during the 1857 Mutiny, but "morally our position is thirty times as weak." He concluded his book by stating, "we are all in at the death of an epoch, and, what is more, we are all conscious of it."[12]

Edward Holton James, visiting India at about the same time, replicated in even harsher terms many of Bernays criticisms of the Raj. He interpreted British colonialism in India as a systemic problem arising from an inevitable imperial hubris. The British, he contended, were no rougher or arrogant than other peoples, in fact, he maintained, "when an Englishman is polite, he *is* polite." Nonetheless, when in India "he often thinks he must treat the Indian like a dog."[13] James' analysis of the independence drama was that it was neither a despotism nor democracy in action, but rather "a disintegrating condition, sometimes bordering on anarchy." Reporting India under such conditions was not only disturbingly problematic, it also revealed the British at their worst:

> The censorship of telegraphic news is such that the outside world knows nothing about the real conditions. No country in the world furnishes such dramatic and thrilling newspaper material as India, but the great newspapers of the west will not throw away their money to send correspondents here who will promptly be gagged when they arrive. The greatest human drama of the world is being enacted here. Boys and girls all over the country are seeing before their eyes jailings, beatings, shootings, destruction and confiscations of property. Secret and invisible forces are daily gathering volume under this surface of apparent Indian inertia and helplessness. While men are being bayoneted and beaten to death in Bombay, the English patrons of the Taj Mahal hotel dance, drink, and eat. Make merry today, for tomorrow we die.[14]

For James, Britain's behavior towards its Indian subjects was comparable to that of ancient Rome's persecution of the Christians. He noted the brutality of British sergeants versus the more restrained tactics of Indian sepoys. The latter urged protesters to run away, risking immediate dismissal from government employment. However, when the British either participated directly or had more immediate control over specific police actions, the violence frequently escalated. On Gandhi Day, December 5, 1930, James witnessed a "lathi charge,"[15] which resulted in dozens of Indian protesters being beaten and then carted off to hospitals or jails, "their cloaks soaked and splattered with blood."[16]

Such critiques of British policy in India were hardly new to the post-World War I era. Keir Hardie, the British Labor Leader, Socialist and Member of Parliament skewered imperial policy in India in a series of writings he penned while traveling there in 1907. Hardie reiterated the familiar argument that Britain's central objective in India was not to improve conditions there but rather to extract revenues to maximum effect. Moreover, Hardie was shocked at his countrymen's behavior, noting from his travel recollections that he could "fill a decent-sized volume" with examples of racist incidents. In one such case, Hardie related the humiliating experience of an Indian who had once been knighted by Queen Victoria. To further accentuate the Indian's

British credentials, Hardie informed his readers that the man was also a Christian, known for his active missionary work in India, and to cap off his claim to respectability, was married to a proper English lady. Certifiably British, the Indian was nevertheless thoroughly disrespected when he attempted to enter a rail car with his "darker" son. A British official quickly lit upon them, informing the father, "look here, we tolerated you because you don't look so bad, but I'll be damned if we allow that black dog in beside us." Such stories abound in travel narratives of India, and Hardie no less than others was profoundly disturbed by what he witnessed or by stories related to him in his travels. He reminded his readers that Indians, like the British, are from Aryan stock, and that if one exchanged their picturesque costumes and dressed them in Western garb, one would have difficulty determining whether they were from Manchester or Madras. That recognition, he argued, had a "very important bearing upon the question of how far the Indian people can be trusted with the right of self-government."[17] An odd argument for sure, but it does illustrate Hardie's sympathy for the nationalist cause Hardie concluded with these thoughts on Indian independence:

> I went to India to see the people, and to learn of their grievances; during the two months I was there I mixed with the people, companioned with them, and found them sociable, trustworthy, and lovable. Their ability is not open to question. A great intellectual awakening is shaking this ancient empire to its foundation. A sympathetic interpretation of the facts will bind the people more closely to us and lead to their becoming a loyal self-governing part of the Empire. Repression will only intensify their determination to secure self-government, and may lead finally to the loss of what has been described as the brightest jewel in the British Crown. It is for statesmen to choose which path they will follow.[18]

To be sure, some travel writers were more sympathetic to the British perspective. One complained that England "had for years poured into India her noblest sons and daughters to give unwearying service to the peoples she had sworn to uplift and protect" . . . but is ill repaid by intimidation and boycotting, to say nothing of dastardly deeds of murder and violence."[19] Others, less fawning of the imperial legacy, nevertheless expressed the belief that the Raj had been an enlightened and benevolent rule. It had developed India's rail and irrigation systems, it had contributed the rule of law and maintained peace between diverse religious and ethnic groups, and it had mentored India on the progressive traditions of the West—all of which would greatly contribute to the success of India's future. Thus, nationalist protests, boycotts, and from extreme quarters, terrorist acts, were seen as either evidence of ungratefulness or further evidence of India's political immaturity. Some writers, attempting to sort out what at first impression seemed to be interminable antagonisms, "harped on by quantities of travelers," in the end concluded that the gulf between the differing sides was ultimately irreconcilable, reverting to an East-West or Orient-Occident paradigm of 'neither the twain shall meet.'[20] Several writers expressed a sentiment not unlike this one: "it seemed so easy before I came out here to solve the Indian problem in a sweeping statement about the rights of nations."[21] The "bright chaos" of India was beguiling, but it could also have the effect of disorienting one's pre-conceptions of how to solve the Indian dilemma. One thing was for sure: the world *had* changed. Imperial authority was disintegrating on many fronts. Even American films had their effects. As one writer put it, "if we lose the Indian Empire, the fault will lie neither in New Delhi nor in Whitehall, but in Los Angeles. The white man's superiority myth disappeared forever in the studios of Metro-Goldwyn."[22]

## NOTES

1. Will Durant, *The Case for India* (New York: Simon & Schuster, 1930), ix, 2.
2. Richard Maurice Elliot, *The Sunny Side of Asia* (New York: Century Co., 1928), 135–136.
3. Ibid, 131–133.
4. John Frederick Muehl, *American Sahib* (New York: John Day Co., 1946), 64–68.
5. Basil Mathews, preface to *India Reveals Herself* (London: Oxford University Press, 1937); and Basil Mathews, *India Reveals Herself* (London: Oxford University Press, 1937), 38–41, 46–47.
6. Beverley Nichols, *Verdict on India* (London: Jonathan Cape, 1944), 7–8, 249–251.
7. Ibid, 249–254.
8. Ibid, 255–256.
9. Robert Bernays, *"Naked Faquir"* (New York: Henry Holt & Co., 1932), 27, 44, 45, 52, 53, 136.
10. Ibid, 136.
11. Ibid, 56–57.
12. Ibid, 150, 335.
13. Edward Bolton James, *I Tell Everything: The Brown Man's Burden (A Book on India)* (Geneva: Imprimerie Kundig, 1931), 90.
14. Ibid, 94
15. http://dictionary.reference.com/. A "lathi" was a club consisting of a heavy stick (often bamboo) often bound with iron; used by police in India. The charge itself was a coordinated assault, in this case against protesters, designed to disperse and break the collective will of crowds. It succeeded, with people stampeding in different directions to escape the heavy blows, although approximately fifty were wounded in the charge.

16. James, 94–95.

17. Keir J. Hardie, *India: Impressions and Suggestions* (New York: B. W. Huebsch, 1919), 90, 98–99, 102. Hardie spent two months in India contributing a series of letters to the *Labour Leader*. He complained that while in India he was accused of urging sedition and "libeling Anglo-Indian officials. One journalist, sending a wire off to London through Reuters, claimed that Hardie had compared British actions to atrocities committed by Turks against Armenians. The release ended up in the *London Times*. Miffed, Hardie assured his readers that five of his "brother journalists" accosted him on the veracity of his claims, which the man was unable to provide (112,113).

18. Ibid, 126.

19. John W. Mitchell, *The Wheels of India* (London: Thornton Butterworth, 1934), 47.

20. Maurice Dekobra, *The Perfumed Tigers: Adventures in the Land of the Maharajahs* (Oxford: Brewer & Warren, 1930), 293–297.

21. Bernays, 106.

22. Ibid, 260.

## *Chapter Five*

# The Gandhi Debate: Indian 'Fakir' or Heroic Independence Leader?

Gandhi was the great soul and driving force of the Indian independence movement. Nearly every travel writer devoted parts of their narrative to the man, many having interviewed him personally in the course of their travels. Gandhi was such a tangle of paradoxes that capturing his personality and value to the nationalist cause inevitably generated mixed reviews. Some writers expressed admiration, others profound skepticism. Often the two perceptions emerged from the same author. Almost all were amazed that someone of his personal appearance and philosophy could generate so much devotion and worldwide attention. Many writers surveyed for this work did not know what to do with him. In an era filled with demagogic leaders orchestrating mass political movements, images of a stooped, loin-clothed holy man directing his people rapidly towards nationhood contrasted sharply with the political methods of Mussolini, Lenin, Hitler and other twentieth century figures. Writers were sometimes tempted to find Gandhi medieval, daft, or comic but this was no marketplace sideshow—some Indian fakir performing rope tricks or laying on a bed of nails to the befuddlement of a few Western tourists. Gandhi was someone to be reckoned with. Millions followed him and he articulated a vision that although Eastern in part was equally composed of familiar Western political and legal concepts.

For those who met him, what initially struck them were his physical features. As one writer put it, at first blush he is nothing less than "the ugliest man I have ever seen." Yet, he went on, "the moment you see Gandhi you catch the atmosphere of royalty." Later in the same volume he reiterated his first impression—that "in appearance he is almost ridiculous." Yet, even though "ugly to the point of repulsion," he projected a spiritual majesty borne of quietness and dignity. And even though "when he walks he looks almost like a dwarf on the music-hall stage," he could command the most earnest devotion from every corner of India's great expanse. If Gandhi befuddled travel writers who met him personally, Winston Churchill was mystified as well, who only saw him from photographs, eliciting the oft-quoted remark that Gandhi was little more than a "half-naked faquir." Some wondered whether Churchill would have chanced the same remark if he were to have met him personally.[1]

> My own experience is that all thought of Gandhi's repulsive appearance vanishes the moment he begins to talk. In a flash one realizes that one is in the presence of one of the great men of the world. Though he speaks very quietly and without a trace of passion or bitterness, his power is almost hypnotic. His words so grip and absorb the mind that half an hour's conversation with him produces real physical exhaustion. For he speaks not as other men do, but with the power of a prophet.[2]

American travel writer Patricia Kendall obtained an audience with Gandhi as he was about to embark upon his legendary Salt March in 1930. She noted the suspicious glares of his entourage, particularly the women. Gandhi, by contrast, was all smiles, greeting her graciously and beckoning Kendall to sit down for a chat. Awed by her surroundings, Kendall gushed, "we study the face of the most publicized man on earth." Then like many observers, she immediately commented upon his toothless grin, large ears, outsized nose and bald pate. Thereafter, Kendall ventured into more delicate terrain. Sympathetic to Katherine Mayo's campaign to attack India's custom of child-marriages, she inquired of Gandhi as to whether or not he was gratified that the proposed enactment of the Sarda Bill, reforming the custom, was about to become law. Gandhi, according to Kendall, recoiled at the notion, stating, "we need no such laws . . . our law of love is the true answer." Kendall, expressing surprise, reminded Gandhi that he had spoken publicly against child-marriages. Gandhi simply rejoined that such laws were government-inspired and that "nothing good can come from government," later in the conversation referring to government acts as "satanic." Kendall then proceeded to matters of rape, another issue about to be addressed by government reform measures. Gandhi responded that no such measures were needed, that for a woman "perfect purity" was its own defense, and that she should not turn to violent resistance for to do so would constitute a "sin"—that *Satyagraha*, Gandhi's philosophy of non-violence—demanded that women not respond to sexual assaults by violent means. Understandably, this was a bit much for Kendall. Thereafter, the conversation halted and Gandhi excused himself to attend to his impending Salt March.[3]

Although not stated in the text, the chill which Kendall felt upon entering Gandhi's compound was no doubt precipitated by the general knowledge by all present that she would hammer on women's issues during the course of her interview. Others had commented upon the reserve and occasional hostility of Gandhi's entourage, but not all chronicled frosty receptions. Kendall saw Gandhi as a "political opportunist." He was at once a "gentle apostle" and "militant politician."[4] Her reaction to him mirrors that of almost every Gandhi-observer whether they adored or despised the man. He was a man of Himalayan contradictions. As one writer quipped, "to make an entertaining catalogue of Gandhi's inconsistencies of word and deed is as easy as rolling off a log."[5] In that sense it could be said that Gandhi was the quintessential representation of India itself—an image of kaleidoscopic diversity and contradictions. It was impossible to get a firm grip on the man because for all his saintliness and nobility of cause, including his courageous and determined campaign to rid India of the evils of caste, here was a leader that advocated non-resistance to rape, spewed vitriolic tirades against technological innovations, and issued many other highly problematical statements.

Albert Bemis, who traveled to India in 1921–22, early on in the Gandhian crusade, characterized him as "an educated socialist or communist, and probably believes in 'social revolution' as the means for bringing about the communistic conditions he favors." He contended that Gandhi was working closely with international socialists and had reportedly received ten million rupees from Lenin to aid "the socialist campaign in India." Gandhi's movement, according to Bemis, was poisoning young Indian minds and seeding India with seditious policies of passive resistance.[6] Bemis never met Gandhi. His odd remarks tying the Mahatma to international communism reflect his preoccupation with events in Russia or were perhaps derived from nervous business contacts in India, Bemis' reason for traveling there. By contrast Clive Branson, a young communist stationed in India during World War II, failed to detect anything faintly communist about Gandhi's actions, arguing that his actions were generally ludicrous: "how stupid Gandhi's fast looks compared to the grandeur of a handful of Indian peasants and workers uniting to demand their human rights! No wonder the Viceroy corresponds with Gandhi and then sends the police after his people."[7] Beverley Nichols, a reactionary imperialist, likewise disparaged Gandhi, albeit from a different perspective, devoting a chapter to him titled "Heil Hindu!" Nichols cynically remarked: "I have no incense to spare for Mr.Gandhi, except the small pinch which one grudgingly tosses at the ugly feet of any other dictator, as a reluctant tribute to his theatrical abilities." In another diatribe, Nichols asserted: "it is not with Gandhi the man that we are here concerned, but Gandhi the dictator, and the Fascist organization which he has created, called Congress, which obeys the slightest crack of his whip." On and on the comparisons go with Mussolini, Hitler, Laval and others—Nichols quoting crackpot sources and drawing absurd inferences between Nazi ideology and tactics with those of India's Congress Party officials, and of course, Gandhi himself.[8]

Given the complex and tense political environment of the Gandhian era—both within India and abroad—it should come as no surprise that Gandhi and his movement was interpreted through the tenets of communism, fascism and other era-dominant ideological filters. Yet, clearly Gandhi's movement was of a different order and most observers recognized the difference. J.A. Spender, a more reflective British writer than Nichols, interviewed Gandhi in 1926 while in India for three months. Recalling an old political cartoon that caricatured William Gladstone as "politically dead," Spender paid a visit to Gandhi at a time when Gandhi had deemed himself "politically dead," announcing that he was heading into a year's seclusion to renounce politics in favor of an interim turn to asceticism and reflection. Gandhi appeared disheartened by events in India and had gone into retreat mode. Spender's conversation with him, at least that which was focused upon in Spender's account, reflected that shift as Gandhi spoke at length concerning the evils modernity had inflicted upon India. Gandhi contended that Western industrialism had ravaged Indian village life. Gandhi's love of spinning cloth and his desire that Indians should return to the practice in order to arrest the damage that machines had wrought in India, led Gandhi to the conclusion that British westernization had done more than just damage India's economy and the life of its villages, it had as well devastated India's soul. Spender took issue with the point, maintaining, "if we may believe eighteenth and early nineteenth century travelers, the old self-dependent life of which Gandhi is thinking had already been irretrievably spoilt by the incursions of traders before we came on the scene." Spender speculated that if Gandhi were to become Emperor of India that he would most likely restrict European immigration to India not unlike South Africans had imposed regulations upon Indian immigrants to that state. And argued Spender, Gandhi's "retreat to Medievalism" would no longer find sympathy among most Indians who had experienced and were committed to modern ways. Yet, Spender clearly demonstrated respect for Gandhi, recognizing that however foreign to Western ways of thinking, in India Gandhi was a saint and the independence movement was indissolubly wedded to his timetables and decisions.[9]

D. Clouston, who had traveled in India extensively, met Gandhi in 1926 in Bangalore while Gandhi was a guest of the ruler of the princely state of Mysore. Clouston claimed to have caught him at a time when politics, propaganda and the art of spinning were given a brief medical sabbatical. In their place Gandhi was momentarily enthralled with a government cattle-breeding farm, making daily visits to the establishment and eventually bonding with Clouston and the farm's workers. Although the operation was mechanized,

Gandhi dispensed with his usual Luddite sentiments in order to admire the farm's efficient methods. Clouston painted a picture of bovine bliss, where "clean and comfortable cow-sheds . . . fields of luscious fodder-crops were tokens of the humane manner in which the sacred cow was being treated." The cows all enjoyed pet names, their milk yields were carefully recorded, and they existed pleasantly in a regimented yet animal-friendly environment. Gandhi, according to Clouston, was impressed. He was particularly taken with a cow named Jill, the senior citizen of the herd of alleged mixed British and Indian ancestry. But Jill's true claim to fame was that of being "the best cow in Asia." Supposedly she had produced 14,000 gallons of milk and sixteen healthy calves during her tenure. Although not the cow she once was, Clouston informed his readers that she enjoyed the life of a "privileged pensioner," lollygagging about the farm at her pleasure. As for Gandhi, he had his picture taken with her and continued to visit the farm on a daily basis with Miss Slade, one of Gandhi's well-publicized British disciples. Everyone on the farm found Gandhi a most charming and gracious guest.[10]

The dairy farm episode was typical of Gandhi's penchant for wandering off to what appeared to others to be tangential diversions from the main business at hand, namely, the march to independence. It tended to disarm Westerners even as they wrestled with what they deemed to be willful, unlawful acts against the British Raj. Clouston, like others, found Gandhi extremely likeable on a personal basis. He was humble, cheerful, selfless, and engagingly chatty with friends and foes alike. To Clouston, Gandhi's interest in the dairy farm demonstrated his more constructive side, dedicated to the economic improvement of the Indian people. That said, Gandhi's "satanic government" diatribes were, in Clouston's view, hypocritical, celebrating a government dairy farm in one moment and condemning government institutions as evil the next. Furthermore, Clouston asserted, Gandhi's civil disobedience campaign was destructive and showed "contempt [for] the sanctity of law."[11] These apparent inconsistencies made Gandhi an easy target for criticism. Katherine Mayo, who once met Gandhi, could not resist throwing in a disparaging Gandhi story in her *Mother India*. She quoted Gandhi's reported statements that "hospitals are institutions for propagating sin" and that "European doctors are the worst of all." One day, Mayo related, Gandhi fell ill with appendicitis while in a British prison. The attending British physician, aware of Gandhi's views on Western medicine, recommended that he seek out an Aurvedic physician. When Gandhi pushed the surgeon to proceed with an operation, the surgeon balked, fearing that if not successful he would be blamed for Gandhi's death. Ultimately, Gandhi provided the necessary assurances; the operation took place and was entirely successful.[12] If a smirk were visible on a printed page, Mayo's countenance would surely have beamed one. Even though such barbs against Gandhi's obvious inconsistencies never ceased, they were wobbly arrows that never seemed to inflict any real damage to Gandhi's reputation nor to the independence movement. Gandhi's contradictions played more like personality quirks then serious character flaws. Ultimately, the moral force of his character and the rightness of the independence cause trumped all other considerations.

Thus, attacks on Gandhi's supposed hypocrisy along with flurries of derisive name-calling such as "naked faquir" or "holy humbug," only added to his strange allure. Moreover he seemed impervious to such attacks, forever concentrating on the task or diversion at hand. Edward Holton James, an American writer referenced earlier in this work, had his own cow story to relate—one that further illustrated the undeniable charm and disarming tactics of Gandhi's personality. James met Gandhi in 1931 through James Mills, a reporter with the Associated Press. Gandhi, seeing that James was a stranger, asked him if he would like to ask a question, to which a flummoxed James had no response. Regaining his composure, James remarked that Indian cows were more beautiful than American cows, to which Gandhi replied: "but American cows give more butter than Indian cows." James, in full stride now, countered that American cows were more productive only because they dwelled within a republic. The conversation was typical of Gandhi's delight in playful banter. Eventually, James was granted an interview with Gandhi that ranged from jokes about his camera (an instrument of torture) to references to Thoreau and Emerson.[13] But as always, Gandhi controlled the conversational agenda. Although on the brink of bringing the world's greatest empire to its knees, Gandhi always possessed that harmless-as-a-fly demeanor. To many it seemed incredulous that a man of such playful innocence could pose a serious threat to the Raj. Moreover, some queried, why indeed would Congress Party yield, even if reluctantly, to the seeming whims of Gandhi's methodology and personal schedule?

The answer lay in the fact that Gandhi brought the masses of India with him, an observation that surfaced repeatedly in contemporary accounts and has been reiterated by historians in succeeding years. Maarten Matisse, a rather quirky Dutchman who wandered India in search of spiritual meaning, related an experience that amply illustrates Gandhi's grip on India's masses. Matisse spent a period of time in a Hindu center and school near Delhi when an announcement came that Gandhi would be traveling through to enlist support for the *Swaraj* movement (Indian self-rule). Everyone at the school was ecstatic at the news. For weeks they had organized teachers and students in a wide range of endeavors to spruce up the compound and raise money for the cause. One member of the group exclaimed: "our uncrowned king is coming to visit us"; another stated, "he is the savior of the fatherland, the greatest man alive." Before Gandhi had arrived, the school had a new park, new pathways, flags were posted along the route, and nine hundred rupees had been raised for the *Swaraj* cause. Students even enlisted Matisse to assist them in organizing an exhibition—"a gallery of all the great heroes of freedom."[14] At last the great day came, a cavalcade of cars, dust, and frenzy:

> From a magnificent luxury car, badly dressed in a loincloth of milk-white khaddar, alighted a thin, slender little figure with a frail body, a large shaven head, prominent ears and a toothless mouth around which played a wonderfully happy smile: Gandhi. The director of the school bowed and touched the feet of the Mahatma devoutly. The crowd pressed forward. Many figures in snow-white dhotis surrounded the leader. Next to him stood Mirabhai, his secretary, the daughter of Slade the British general; she looked adoringly at her master. But upon me it made an unpleasant impression to see this man so honored. 'He rides in a luxury car and is looked after like a small child, I thought.'[15]

By the time Gandhi had whizzed off to three other appointments that day, those at the compound had lost some of their enthusiasm for him. To some he turned out to be a bit of 'holy humbug' after all as some critics had alleged. He chastised the director when he saw an abandoned spinning wheel set off in a corner; he expressed displeasure at seeing a garland draped over the image of Baghat Singh in the freedom hall exhibition (Singh had engaged in terrorist activities); he sternly rebuked everyone for allowing a garland of flowers to be placed upon his neck and broken petals thrown at his feet, lamenting the fact that such beautiful emblems of nature had been cruelly "maimed" in frivolous display; he reprimanded everyone for holding his lecture indoors when outdoors "in free nature" would have more rightly honored their forefathers; and, he lectured them on the fact that few students had taken up spinning—a far more significant task than raising nine hundred rupees. He concluded by urging all present to improve Indian agriculture, stockbreeding and religion. "For every Indian the motto should be: either in prison or busy with social work."[16]

As Gandhi rushed off to his next *Swaraj* event, teachers and students at the compound were unhappy that they had not received even the slightest bit of praise for their efforts. Most likely this episode, or some variation of it, occurred repeatedly across India. Dissatisfaction and displeasure with Gandhi and his methods repeatedly surfaced, but his identity, gestures, and acts were so closely woven with Indian aspirations for a new and free India, that Gandhi's perceived failings were dwarfed by grander hopes and dreams. And it is often forgotten in the lush sentimentality that surrounds Gandhi's legacy (of which Richard Attenborough's 1982 Academy Award winning film *Gandhi* so fittingly illustrates) that Gandhi was by many standards an odd sort filled with eccentric beliefs and habits. V.S. Naipaul has suggested that Gandhi's retreats into defensive postures and self-made vows left him "seemingly headed for lunacy . . . [but] was constantly rescued and redefined by external events and the goadings of other civilizations." In other words, being confronted with "the terror and strangeness of England . . . the racial pressures of South Africa . . . and British authoritarianism in India" forced him out of an otherwise personal tendency towards self-absorbed insularity.[17]

Naipaul observes the irony of Gandhi's Gujarati merchant class origins, which he characterizes as "one-time great travelers"—yet as Gandhi embarked for his legal education in England, that same caste had banished notions of foreign travel as potentially pollutant to its members. Thus, the journey was an agonizing decision for both Gandhi and his family, tainted by prospective defilement of caste rules. Once in Britain, Naipaul observes further that Gandhi's memoir of events was devoid of landscape descriptions, talk of climate or seasons, observations of the British character, or any other travel-like reflections on his environment. Except for a few references to odd religious or social movements, it was as if Gandhi had never been to England. He arrived, he studied, he graduated, and then departed its shores. Naipaul's rather heavy-handed critique of India (and Gandhi) in his work *India: A Wounded Civilization*, casts its peoples and Gandhi as tied to a civilization burdened by profound yet insular attachments to faith, family, and caste, where rationality wanders off into legends and magic, individuality is subsumed by an overbearing collective, and where the self drifts through this world ultimately turning inward, away from reality's grounding. Naipaul, ever the Westerner, concludes of Gandhi and Indians in general: "when men cannot observe, they don't have ideas; they have obsessions."[18] Yet, in Gandhi's case, even if faintly chronicled in his memoir of three years in England, close observation clearly manifested itself in many ways. His encounters with travel writers, for example, evidenced astute observational qualities used to advance the idea of Indian independence, moments, as it were, when "ideas" and "obsessions" met in mutual purpose—where the self was subsumed by a cause-collective in rational and epic march towards personal and collective freedom. The fact that Gandhi was a litany of part saint, politician, revolutionary, reactionary, crank, charmer, lawyer, peasant—to list just a few characterizations—should not come as a surprise. If the travel accounts are to be believed, and they do roughly correspond to like sources on Gandhi, Gandhi was a man who lived squarely in the public square yet frequently ventured off into eccentric private pursuits. One could never fully wrap around his essence. For travel writers and many others, that was a part of his fascination. He was India. Yet he was not. Much like India's relationship with Britain. It might absorb selective features of British civilization, but India was never of Britain, preferring instead to march to the drummer of its own civilizational past. Gandhi, as well, adhered to his own calling, mixing and matching the traditions of different civilizations at his choosing.

Chester Bowles served as United States Ambassador to India for eighteen months in the early 1950s. His memoir of the experience included a chapter's homage to Gandhi—an effort to place the Mahatma in historical perspective both as to India's newly achieved independence and earlier twentieth century developments. Bowles journeyed to Rajghat, a memorial park on the Jumma River where Gandhi was cremated, shortly after he arrived in India. The trip was part pilgrimage, part diplomatic gesture. An Indian friend had told Bowles: "to understand India today you will need to know the India of the Gandhian Age." Bowles, having already seen an India saturated with photographs of Gandhi's image and other objects of devotion to his memory, was struck as to how massive his life and legacy were to the nation's identity, to its hope and aspirations for the future. Like so many of the era who had witnessed decades of violent revolutionary turmoil and global conflict, Bowles found in Gandhi an alterative revolutionary ethic, one that sought change through non-violent means. Bowles compared Gandhi with Lenin, Mussolini, Hitler, Stalin and Mao—noting the obvious distinctions between the violent upheavals they had wrought versus Gandhi's legacy of political change through peaceful protest, diplomacy and patience.[19] Clearly, there was nothing original about Bowles analysis. He was simply reiterating stock reflections of the age. Nonetheless, it demonstrates the pervasiveness and power of Gandhi's imprint upon India—indeed the larger world as well—evidenced by Martin Luther King, Jr.'s American version of *Satyagraha* only several years after the Mahatma's death. Pitted against that vision of Gandhi's grandeur, the fact that many Gandhian Age travel writers often focused on his personal idiosyncrasies seems petty in retrospect. Yet, such traits were surely a part of Gandhi's character. Today, as one contemporary observer has remarked, Gandhi "continues both to divide Indians and to haunt their dreams." His condemnation of Western-styled materialism arguably retarded economic development in India for nearly a half century after independence. Many of his views now seem strangely out of place in twenty-first century India as it hurtles towards enthusiastic embrace of global capitalism. His devotion to village ways continues to resonate among India's elite but at the expense of sorely needed strategies to foster better urban planning.[20] Travel writers of the Gandhian Age, nearly all adherents to the virtues of modernity, saw in Gandhi's anti-materialist stance a philosophy that would not only impede India's march towards independence but would also cripple its development long after the British had departed. Although it is important to see Gandhi in personal and historical context, it is also important to understand where travel writers were coming from. Material progress of the techno-industrialized kind pointed towards a world that could become increasingly shorn of poverty, ignorance, and disease. Whatever Gandhi's virtues, and they were legion, some of his views on life and society would, in their eyes, obstruct efforts to build a better life for the very Indians he championed. To travel writers, modernizing India made perfect sense. Indeed, it was inevitable. Thus, when Gandhi lashed out at technological and governmental efforts to better India, he was exhibiting reactionary traits no less regressive and harmful than the antiquated imperialism he sought to eradicate.

As a final sampling of travel writer perceptions of Gandhi, we turn to the travel memoir of Agnes Burr, who was granted a one-hour session with him in the late 1920s. Like others, Gandhi's smile, his eyes, and his gracious hospitality both fascinated and charmed her. Burr perceived him through the filter of Christianity, commenting that she saw striking similarities between Gandhi and Christ, particularly Gandhi's penchant for bearing the guilt of his people's violent transgressions and his commitment to non-violent change. Burr asked him how he defined religion. Gandhi response was vague and ponderous, expressing eclectic views that frequently surfaced in other travel writing accounts. But on the issue of Indian independence Gandhi's response was typically more pointed. Burr asked him: "will you give a message to America?" To which he responded: "tell America to study carefully, if possible, reverently, what is going on in India, and in this study not to rely on what the newspapers say."[21] This was, in essence, what Gandhi and travel writers sought to accomplish in their interviews—a means by which fresh and open dialogue could be used to communicate to the rest of the world what Gandhi and India were all about. That the Mahatma and his followers were on a noble mission to fulfill India's sovereign destiny, an aspiration that all peoples of world, no less than Americans, could surely appreciate and embrace.

## NOTES

1. Robert Bernays, *"Naked Faquir"* (New York: Henry Holt & Co., 1932), 83, 125.
2. Ibid, 125.
3. Patricia Kendall, *Come With Me to India* (New York: Charles Scribner's Sons, 1935), 328–329.
4. Ibid, 352.
5. Basil Mathews, *India Reveals Herself* (London: Oxford University Press, 1937), 136.
6. Albert Farwell Bemis, *A Journey to India, 1921–1922* (Boston: Privately Printed, 1923), 58–59.

7. Clive Branson, *British Soldier in India: The Letters of Clive Branson* (London: Communist Party, 1944), 54.

8. Beverley Nichols, *Verdict on India* (London: Jonathan Cape, 1944), 157–163.

9. J.A. Spender, *The Changing East* (London: Casell & Co., 1926), 20–21, 208–209, 214–215.

10. D. Clouston, *From the Orcades to India* (London: Oliver and Boyd, 1936), 142–146.

11. Ibid, 147.

12. Katherine Mayo, *Mother India* (New York: Harcourt, Brace & Co., 1927), 387–388.

13. Edward Bolton James, *I Tell Everything: The Brown Man's Burden (A Book on India)* (Geneva: Imprimerie Kundig, 1931), 178–180.

14. Maarten Matisse, *Wanderer from Sea to Sea* (New York: Harcourt, Brace and Co., 1936), 296–297.

15. Ibid, 299–300.

16. Ibid, 300–301.

17. V.S. Naipaul, *India: A Wounded Civilization* (New York: Vintage Books, 1976), 98.

18. Ibid, 85–98.

19. Chester Bowles, *Ambassador's Report* (New York: Harper & Row, n.d.), 60–61.

20. Edward Luce, *In Spite of the Gods: The Strange Rise of Modern India* (New York: Doubleday, 2007), 8–10.

21. Agnes Rush Burr, *India: The Land That Lures* (Boston: L.C. Page & Co., 1929), 428–434.

## *Chapter Six*

# 'An Observation of No Value': India's Poverty, Disease and Suffering

V.S. Naipaul contended that Indian poverty was of a special kind. He characterized India as a culture enchanted, strangely, by poverty's allure, its function as a path to spiritual enlightenment; what Naipaul termed "an exercise of the purest sensibility." Thus, efforts to eradicate poverty through reform and remedial action were perpetually diverted by a perverse romanticism, a belief that poverty could transform its victims, or more precisely—the victims' observers—despite its troubling effects. For Naipaul, poverty was so endemic to India that to view it "is to make an observation of no value."[1] One hears echoes of Somerset Maugham's comment on Chinese poverty—to encounter it is to experience "a useless compassion." The very titles of Naipaul's two travel accounts to India—India as *An Area of Darkness* and India as *A Wounded Civilization* reify standard notions that India was and remains a site of poverty and despair—a fact often noted by his critics. Naipaul was overwhelmed by what he encountered in his first visit, disembarking in Bombay and then suddenly realizing that unlike other ports of call (Alexandria, Port Sudan), "there was no ship to run back to." In describing his initial impressions of India, it is interesting to note the language he employed to characterize the sights before him: words and phrases like "wasted body, swollen-bellied, chaos, decaying, odours of mingled filth, rubbish dump, stinking corridors, stench of gutters and latrines, revulsion, prostitutes, degradation" to reference only a representative sampling. Describing India invariably conjures up disturbing images of poverty, disease, deformity, and variant forms of human suffering. Arguably, writing about India leads one into a linguistic trap from which few can escape because, as some would contend, how else does one describe what one sees?

John Hutnyk, in his work *The Rumour of Calcutta: Tourism, Charity and the Poverty of Representation*, examines how Calcutta, a localized version of a larger India, is likewise imaged as a site of incalculable poverty and despair, wherefrom, as he puts its, "the rumour of Calcutta travels all over the world." He quotes from Frommer's 1984 guide to India, stating, "everything you ever heard about Calcutta is true" as a representative trope of the city's continuous standing as a type of "urban monster, a city of hell." Arguably, the same application has been assigned to India today as larger geographic entity, however unique Calcutta may be in its specific expression of the Indian whole. Hutnyk's study examines, among other sources, representations of Calcutta by Western backpackers, charity workers, and Roland Joffe's cinematic *City of Joy*, debunking what he perceives to be a pernicious cultural imperialism in how Calcutta is portrayed, yet suggests as well that "a rumour is also a gift of truth lying under cover of deceit—a surplus representation, a doubled sign."[2] India's multiple representations, surplus if you will, renders many truths about its diverse landscape and complex civilization, so that for every so-called 'truth,' such as poverty and despair, there are many corresponding 'counter-truths' that tell a different story.

Such multiple images of India abound in travel literature. For example, Sarah MacDonald's recent popular travel memoir of India, *Holy Cow*, captures the ubiquitous poverty exemplar from its outset, introducing India as a menacing site heavy with heat, stench, and unwelcome beggars:

> For three days my friend Nic and I have been sitting on plastic airport chairs waiting for the stifling, stinky smog to lift. For three days I've lain on a bed in an airport hotel listening to Nic bounce the sounds of violent double-ender projectile vomits and diarrhea explosions off the bathroom walls. [Now a beggar] hovers around us patient and persistent as a vulture waiting for death. He can smell our exhaustion and weakness, and we can smell him—his blue overalls are stained with urine and the stink of mothballs; his breath reeks of *paan*, the red chewing tobacco that smells of overripe fruit and fluoride . . . With her final energy, Nic digs in her pocket and gives the man our last few filthy notes, saved for an emergency toilet supply . . . Good-bye and good riddance, India, I hate you and I'm never, never, ever coming back.[3]

Of course, she does return—with her boyfriend several years later when he is assigned to cover the region as a journalist for the Australian Broadcasting Company. The above quotation was from MacDonald's earlier and briefer trip in 1988. In her next journey, the one upon which she bases her travel memoir, India remains a site of foul air, grasping beggars, and never-ending exasperation, but MacDonald in time settles in and finds India to be a wonderland of delightful memories, fondly remembered and lovingly told. *Holy Cow* is a delightful book but like so many travel accounts of India it portrays an environment so forbidding that only the hardiest of travelers, it would seem, should venture there. But as that tired cliché suggests—'no pain, no gain,' India is frequently characterized as the ultimate gauntlet of travel challenges, one of Himalayan proportions that if journeyed and endured, disburses a travel experience payout unlike any other.

Earlier twentieth century travel writers also represented India in familiar images of poverty and despair. Yet, it is my perception that their accounts indulged in such characterizations with less frequency—some omitting any references at all. When they did, trains and train stations were often the site of their descriptions, perhaps because it was there that Westerners were forced to view, if not encounter, masses of people in close, inescapable proximity. Louis Hagan, who typically wrote with sensitivity and perceptiveness about India, found himself overwhelmed by what he characterized as gangs of naked, lice-infested children cluttering railroad platforms, begging women carrying children, barking out "backsheesh, Sahib"—"plucking at you with greasy claw-like hands until you are ready to vomit." Then there were "the crippled, the blind, and the syphilitics" transported about by a guild of beggary promoters. Hagen told his readers, "the first time you see this sort of thing, it leaves you stunned. Although it was happening in front of our eyes and under our noses, one just couldn't take it unless one used one's imaginations. The utter degradation of these human beings was almost too exaggerated; it has a fantastic quality like the madhouse scene in *Peer Gynt*." At first, pity was the overwhelming emotion. But as the assault on his person and senses intensified, Hagan saw his emotions transformed from pity to irritation to near hatred and then back to irritation—but an irritation directed at himself for reacting with such pique at the sights before him.[4]

George Johnson, writing in the late 1940s when air travel was an option to train journeys, was advised to skip his rail itinerary and opt for air connections across the subcontinent. Johnson told his readers that "for some reason the Indian railways have an evil reputation with Westerners, who, over cocktails, will talk for hours of the grim horrors of the trains." He described scenes at Calcutta's rambling Howrah Station as filled with "whining beggars, emaciated, blinded, and crippled with revolting elephantiasis. There were lepers and syphilitics, their faces loathsomely eaten away." Although warned not to yield to the endless beggary, he found himself unable to resist dispensing coins to many supplicants that surrounded him. Johnson rationalized that such was India—as much a part of the subcontinent as the "colourful whirl of saris . . . or the jewel coffers of Hyderabad."[5]

For Frederick Muehl, the American who traveled extensively and wrote several books on India, rail encounters also afforded distinctly uncomfortable memories. One memory was of a train stop where a leper woman "approached the track on all fours, like a sick beast too weak to raise its head.

Her hand and one arm had been eaten away, so she crawled on the putrid stumps of her elbow." Muehl went on describing in increasingly depressing yet descriptive prose how the woman poked her deformed arm through the train's window, placing a hand on Muehl's shoulder while pleading for handouts. Startled, Muehl grabbed a rolled-up newspaper, fending off the arm and bolting to the other side of the coach. Finally, Muehl informed his readers," we are moving again, thank God. The shades have all been drawn, we can hear occasional scratches outside. What I feel is not simply fear, it is a disgust, a revulsion as at a rat or a fat grub worm."[6]

It is easy to criticize this type of descriptive rendering of India as horror-house of the East. In many ways it simply reaffirms long-held perceptions of a place that struggles to shed its image as the traveler's ultimate freak circus. Nonetheless, it is a familiar image that appears in various literary forms, including works by Indians writing of their native soil. In Rohinton Mistry's novel, *A Fine Balance,* one finds an India circa 1975 filled with characters struggling to survive a never-ending cycle of unrelenting poverty, absurd politics, and senseless violence. In one scene two tailors, forced to sleep on the streets, are rounded up by the "beautification police," boarded onto trucks and shipped out of the city (ostensibly Bombay) to meet pre-arranged work quotas for government "facilitators." There the tailors meet a legless beggar who tells them a few things about the art of begging. When challenged about his occupation, the beggar states simply: "without beggars how will people wash away their sins"?[7] Which takes us back to Naipaul's characterization of Indian poverty being of a special kind—one with persistent spiritual sensibilities that dissolve efforts to eliminate it as an impediment to human progress.

Of course, lepers and legless beggars hardly constitute the full panorama of poverty's reach. They are but several forms of India's image as the most impoverished site on the globe. How does one write about such conditions without reverting to the tired 'rumor of India'? If one were to assign the task of re-writing, for example, Frederick Muehl's encounter with the leprous woman, insisting upon ten distinctly different accounts, could one be produced that escaped time-worn clichés about the essence of India? There were travel writers of the Gandhian age who referenced lepers, beggars, and general conditions of poverty without adjectival flourish. Thus, the reader was left to her or his own translation of what such terms mean. Yet, however rendered, the words themselves are intrinsically loaded with negative imagery without added rhetorical embellishment. One minimalist approach might simply state that Muehl, while traveling on a train in India, frequently encountered people requesting money. Accurate to be sure, but its skeletal nature would distort in its own way. An alternative would be to dispense with negative descriptions entirely focusing instead on positive representations of sights seen and people encountered, not unlike a glossy travel brochure or ideological sound bite. In other words, the leper or beggar as colorful adornment to an Oriental Indian bazaar; or as fading remnants of a bygone age, currently being extinguished by the new, progressive India en route to becoming a major world power.

Or, as one Gandhian Age traveler experienced it, one could essentially ignore harsh external realities by cocooning oneself within a specialized tour where traveler and companions are generally shielded from unpleasant sights. Jane Tracy's *See India With Me* approximated such an account. Tracy and friends traveled through India for five months during World War I by private railway car with occasional excursions to local sites in the course of their journey. In a tribute to India's railway workers, Tracy, in the preface of her book, expressed these sentiments for their many efforts on her behalf:

> Sincere appreciation is here expressed for the kindness shown us by the many Station Masters. Often the car would remain several days in some stations, a week or more in others. These gentlemen were untiring in their effort that all sanitary laws should be complied with and our creature comforts well looked after. Every window and door was screened and curtained, tanks kept filled, and electric bulbs frequently renewed. From eleven to three o'clock each day the car was run into the station to avoid the heat, and later placed outside in the quiet of the train yard for the night.[8]

Although it sometimes appeared otherwise, to be fair, Tracy's journey did include some excursions from the train out into the streets and bustle of every day India. In Srinagar, for example, she and her companions rowed along its many canals, observing their beauty and the lovely balconied houses above them. Nonetheless, she commented, the "countless canals intersecting the city are its menace . . . filth breeds disease and death on every side." In Bombay, she noted the incessant stares from observing crowds, how the staring custom is omnipresent wherever one goes in the East. Along a pier she saw a throng of Hindus, whom she described as oddly dressed and groomed, having a "starved appearance" that was eerily distressing. However, she confided to her readers, "later when we learned something of their religion, we were not so horrified at their emaciated faces and bodies."[9] What initially might suggest the first awakenings of cultural empathy was ultimately little more than a dismissive barb conveying the negative effects of Hinduism on India's masses.

Tracy's book is at times gallingly touristic—at others a pleasing narrative chronicling a most enviable journey. The early twentieth century has been characterized as the 'golden age of travel.' Tracy's trip to India represented the quintessential model of the age; where travelers journeyed by ocean liner to the far ends of the earth, disembarked in exotic ports where prearranged contacts shepherded them through winding, twisting streets and markets; where luxury hotels or clubs awaited their tired, thirsty bodies with attentive, swarming teams of servants; and where special rail coaches were lined up for a leisurely morning launch into the interior. And of course there were the Station Masters: protective shields from the 'great unwashed' or the 'greatly deformed' that Muehl, Hagen, and Johnston encountered, so disturbingly, in their train station experiences. It is too easy to criticize Tracy's narrative, even with its at times arc condescension of Indian peoples, ways, and sanitary conditions. Like that side-of-the -barn sized target of European intellectuals, aristocrats, political radicals, and romantics—namely, the bourgeoisie—Westerns tourists or travelers are the recipients of never-ending critiques by post-colonial theorists and literary critics. And, much of it is deserved. Nevertheless, travel writing is inherently problematic. To describe, with particularity, scenes of beauty or ugliness, requires imagination. And imagination calls for descriptive rendering that descends ever so easily down the path of cultural chauvinism. Travel writing also demands that the scrivener operate from some sort of principled center that recognizes pain and suffering or political and social abuse, described as such even at the risk of making cultural judgments or perpetuating the 'rumor of India.' In addition to unpleasant visual sights, there are the pushy crowds, grasping beggars, clever con men, and difficult sanitation and hygiene problems that confront the Indian traveler. Many Westerners struggle mightily with guilt at what they are seeing, burdened with a "useless compassion" from which they never escape or from which they retreat to indifference. Except for extraordinary people like Mother Theresa who purposefully confront them daily—few Westerners could endure for any extended period of time the India of rail stations or other locales where the human condition is so alarmingly displayed and aggressively intrusive upon one's person.

In Aldous Huxley's account of his India travels, he described a leisurely drive out of Bombay and into the countryside, observing the squalor along the route. He told his readers, "I felt (but more acutely) that amazement which often overwhelms me when I pass through the sordid fringes of some European city—amazement at my own safety and comfort, at the security of my privileges, at the unthinking and almost un-resentful acceptance of my less fortunate fellow-beings of my claim to be educated, leisured, comparatively wealthy."[10] To ignore such conditions speaks poorly of our humanity; to write about it can feel like a case of literary numbness—that one is making "an observation of no value." Agnes Burr, writing in her *India, The Land that Lures*, described her first day in India as "rather staggering, it is so complex, so varied, so multitudinous." For Burr, India was more than Huxley's ironic reflection on poverty and privilege, it was a site inhabited by disturbing, pervasive threats as well. She described India as the "original *verboten* land . . . don't drink water that is not boiled . . . don't eat ice cream . . . don't visit bazaars on foot." Fear was pushed at her with every conversation—fear of contracting diseases, fear of venomous snakes, fear of scorpions or centipedes, fear of tigers or crocodiles, or fear of being knocked off by Hindu-Muslim riots. Even fears of lesser, non-life threatening events, such as watching servants precariously unload her trunk from her ship, envisioning its plunge into the bay below.[11] But of course, that is precisely what made and continues to make India so fascinating to travelers. India was 'off the beaten path'—not the path off into the hinterlands of the remote places of the world (although some sought that in the Himalayas and other locales)—but rather a journey into a fearful place, one filled with unsettling rumors that enticed travelers even as it repulsed them. For some travel writers, the greatest fear was facing that certain 'rumor of India'—the fear that one's conscience would be forced to travel down the most forbidding of paths—the path peering straight into the depths of India's human pain and suffering.

## NOTES

1. V.S. Naipaul, *An Area of Darkness: A Discovery of India* (New York: Vintage Books, 1964), 41–44.
2. John Hutnyk, *The Rumour of Calcutta: Tourism, Charity, and the Poverty of Representation* (London: Zed Books, 1996), vii, viii, 1.
3. Sarah MacDonald, preface to *Holy Cow, An Indian Adventure* (Mission Point, Australia: Broadway Books, 2002).
4. Louis Hagan, *India Route March* (New York: Pilot Press, 1946), 12–13.
5. George H. Johnston, *Journey through Tomorrow* (Melbourne: F. W. Cheshire Pty., 1947), 13–14.
6. John Frederick Muehl, *American Sahib* (New York: John Day Co.), 58.
7. Rohinton Mistry, *A Fine Balance* (New York: Vintage Books, 1995), 323.
8. Jane Tracy, preface to *See India With Me* (Boston: The Stratford Company, 1928).
9. Jane Tracy, *See India With Me* (Boston: The Stratford Company, 1928), 11–13, 73.
10. Aldous Huxley, *Jesting Pilate: The Diary of a Journey* (London: Chatto & Windus, 1948), 10.
11. Agnes Rush Burr, *India: The Land that Lures* (Boston: L.C. Page & Co., 1929), 5–6.

# Chapter Seven

# The Search for the Elusive Indian

Beverley Nichols, in his *Verdict on India*, devoted an entire chapter to the notion of the "elusive Indian." He had traveled for a year across the subcontinent when one day in a conversation with a Darjeeling physician he was asked the question: "have you ever met an Indian?" The query baffled him, so pondering its intent, he wondered whether it was facetious or serious, finally settling on the latter. He then thought of the many Indians he had met, concluding that taken as a whole they constituted "a pageant of astonishing diversity and color."[1] Like many travel writers, Nichols then launched into a demographic summary of India's complex mass of religious, ethnic, and social diversity.

Identifying the "typical Indian" was an elusive proposition—not unlike the attempt to identify the "typical European." Was the "elusive Indian" a Brahmin priest, babu clerk, peasant farmer, Congress party intellectual, bazaar merchant, wandering holy man, or was it sequestered behinds doors somewhere in feminine form? There may indeed be certain Indian sensibilities, forged through centuries of shared traditions, but articulating its true nature was another matter. Nevertheless, many travel writers during the Gandhian Age attempted to do so. They usually began by acknowledging India's different religious and ethnic groups; however, the more they honed in on specific Indian characteristics the more apparent it became that Hindus ultimately stood for the essence of India's cultural identity. Muslims, Sikhs, Parsees, Jains and others were part of the human parade, but Hindus dominated India's human imagery even in greater proportion to their numerical majority. Characterizations of Hindus were not only more plentiful, they were also more negative. For some travel writers, the Indian character was intrinsically flawed by the historically embedded beliefs of Hinduism, what Lowell Thomas referred to as "a library of travel stories in the trackless paths of speculative inquiry rather than a guide-book to bliss." Thomas found Brahminic literature impenetrable, comparable to futile efforts at summarizing the thicket of Baedecker volumes devoted to world travel.[2] Not infrequently, Brahmins stood in for the "elusive Indian." Travelers often complained about encounters with them, irritated by their arrogance, their dismissive attitude, and their belief system that viewed contact with Westerners as simply another form of potential defilement. Those not of the Brahmin caste were pitied for their subjection to Brahminic demands—slaves to their spurious claims to superiority and authoritarian religious tenets.

Western prejudice against Hinduism and Brahiminic authority was hardly new to the Gandhian Age. Two texts from 1888, one American and the other British, illustrate that deeply embedded and troubling representations of Hindus had a long history. Texts from the Gandhian Age rarely rose to the demeaning caricatures that at times marked some accounts written a half-century earlier; nevertheless, racial bigotry did surface in travel literature from the 1920s through the 1940s. One of the 1888 works, written for a younger audience, told readers that the Hindu boy "has not some of the good traits that you American boys have. For instance, he has no idea of truthfulness. To tell a falsehood is not the unmanly, mean thing it is it to you." The Hindu boy was credited with admirable qualities, but they were largely of the passive, subservient kind, what the writer referred to as the "mild Hindu." In short: the ideal colonial subject.[3] The other 1888 text also utilized the capsule term "mild Hindu" as the essence of what constituted the Indian character. The chapter headings revolved significantly around that term of disdain—"Babu." A Babu was the quintessential Indian low-level clerk or official—at times obsequious, at others obstinate and deliberately disingenuous in manner and conduct. Some of the book's chapters are most revealing: "Babudom–The Western Veneer . . . Babudom—Vapour and Gas . . . Babudom—What's Bred in the Bone will not out of the Flesh . . . [and] The Sub-Babu."Here we are informed that "oriental courtesy is associated with oriental shiftiness, insincerity, and craft . . . nothing could be more unlike the sturdy manliness and the reckless justice which are part of the best side of the British character." Easterners were generally described as sycophants, "servile, cringing and treacherous." But the Babu, suggested as a type of cultural mongrel exhibiting the worst traits of Western and Eastern influences—part ill-behaved barbarian and part sycophantic panderer—was particularly distasteful. In fact, Babu behaviors, notably their oily supplications for favors and childish aping of British customs, were invariably comic if not always irritating.[4]

J.F.C. Fuller, known in Britain at the time as a controversial military theorist, traveled to India in the 1920s to study the independence movement. Attempting to determine the root causes of India's nationalist revolution, he concluded that he had "no radical solution" nor "logical account" to explain its challenge to the Raj. On the other hand, as he phrased it, he did not "intend to kick a goal"—leaving his *India in Revolt* with a rambling set of conclusions that were full of contradictions—for after all, did not Gandhi himself once utter, "India is a country of nonsense?" Western minds might recoil at his unorthodox methods, Fuller warned, but that was the India he encountered. Fuller was harsh on British rule but he reserved his more distasteful characterizations for Indians. Babus, he contended, "breed like mice, one finding a job for another, and so on until hordes scribble to hordes, backwards and forwards, and all reality is lost in the mountains of files which clog every government office." Like his nineteenth century predecessors, Fuller characterized the "normal Oriental" as "cringing," cowards by nature and it was because the British had been "brave and strong" that India ultimately fell into their hands by weak and bickering natives yielding ultimately to the superior race. To Fuller, the Oriental (meaning the Indian) always settled for second best. He believed that the British never understood the Indian; but then again, he concluded, the British never really tried, content to make money and frolic mindlessly in British clubs. Nonetheless, he argued, Britain had provided the best rule that India had ever experienced.[5] Fuller, like other Britishers, exhibited a persistent compulsion to be even-handed, to dispense criticism and compliments to both sides of a civilizational equation, even if at closer inspection the equation was often titled heavily in favor of British superiority. Like the imperial cliché that one must be a good fellow and thus 'play the white man,' balancing East and West was a required feature of one's writings if it were to be taken seriously as a work of cultural description or analysis. A further example is represented in this quotation by another British travel writer:

> It is an unfortunate thing for India that the foreigner in this land comes into direct contact with more irritating people than in any other country on earth. This does not apply exclusively to Indians, of course, but they happen to be much numerous than the British irritants, and much more frequently encountered. He seldom, if ever, meets the backbone of India—the industrious, friendly, likeable, humorous *ryot*, the peasant farmer—and as a result he is inclined to judge all India and all Indians by the few infuriating *babus* and petty officials, the hordes of whining beggars, and obsequious servants who are always along his path.[6]

Here we have "irritating people" on both sides of the racial divide—subdivided again based upon different types of Indians the traveler would encounter on his or her journey. The traveler's complaint about bureaucratic officialdom is representative of so many travel narratives over the past century, perhaps summed up by that other timeless straw man of travel lore—'the French customs officer.' The "Babu" was an even more despised Eastern equivalent of his French counterpart. India, then and now, harbored an army of such officious characters, lurking behind piles of paper and desktop debris, guarding their micro-kingdoms with jealous ferocity. It was as if the gods had posted them there to impede and test the hapless traveler. One rarely sees the term "Babu" in post-Raj travel literature, but the obstinate, obstructionist Indian official is perhaps an even more common feature of recent India travel narratives. V.S. Naipaul, in the opening chapter of his first work of travel to India, *An Area of Darkness*, appropriately titled "A Little Paperwork," described a Kafkaesque-like ordeal of mind-numbing bureaucratic circularity. Naipaul arrived in Bombay with two opened-bottles of liquor. Two customs officials, working in perfect tandem, seized the items declaring that Naipaul could retrieve them only upon obtaining a liquor permit. The next day he went to the Tourist Office, where surprisingly, he was able to secure the permit fairly quickly by filling out a form. The following day he returned to the docks (as Naipaul put it, "to be in Bombay is to be exhausted"; hence, one bureaucratic enterprise per day) only to be informed that liquor is not retained there—he must make for the Customs House to reclaim his two bottles of spirits. At the Customs House he learned that he needed a transport permit in order to transport the liquor from his ship to his hotel, whereupon he was forced to return to the Old Customs House where he learned that there was no form but a simple letter would be required stating his situation. With transport permit in hand, he returned to the Customs House to be informed further that the transport permit was insufficient—Naipual had to go to a Mr. Kulkanrin to determine what warehouse charges had been assessed. Once that matter was settled, it was back to a blue-shirted clerk, then pay the cashier, and then back to Mr. K to retrieve the bottles. Naturally, Mr. K could not be found. A temper tantrum later, Mr. K was produced, Naipual wrapped up matters only to be told that the warehouse would close shortly and he must hurry if he wanted his liquor before the day's end.[7]

The experience of Naipaul and others suggested that India's fondness for officious habits was a mirror reflection of Hinduism's elusive and amorphous spirituality. In other words, entering the realm of India's bureaucracy in search of specific and immediate responses was a corporeal equivalent to entering the incorporeal realm of Hindu theology in search of quick and specific answers to one's religious questions. Thus, Hindu habits of mind were replicated within the framework of an exasperating bureaucratic maze—much like the complex pantheon of Indian gods and Hindu spirituality. Of course, one could argue that the world of officialdom was hardly the essence of a travel site as complex and diverse as India. The elusive Indian was more than babu bureaucrat or frustrating merry-go-round with customs regulations.

Such was the case with Cecil Beaton, a British photographer who traveled through India the 1940s. He observed that unlike in the West, Indians chose colors for their clothing as an "uncompromising personal preference." Writing in painterly tones, Beaton described one woman as a "walking rainbow; a ragamuffin had staked all on a surprising dark-red coat of the finest quality velvet." Delhi streets were adorned by "enormous edifices of colored paper" with Beaton being "constantly amazed by the beauty of the people themselves." Beaton's India is a kaleidoscopic wonderland. His artistic sensibilities were constantly stimulated by the images that surrounded him: "everywhere one found unexpected sequences of color—no gorgeous oriental riot but an extraordinary jumble of apparently inharmonious colors, harmonized nevertheless by some unknown law." Through Beaton's eyes, tedious Babus were hardly to be found, bureaucratic complexity replaced by visual complexity of astonishing beauty. Yet, as he attends a dinner party one evening, the politics of the era intrude upon his artistic vision. He is informed by an "intellectual lady" that India, once a great country, no longer produced writers or painters, spawning instead a new generation of Congress politicians who would make a bloody mess of the country. An elderly industrialist informed him that "India is a feminine country, all her faults are feminine ones," to which an Indian woman replied, "whatever those faults may be, let us make them. Please allow us our own headaches. India for Indians, please." Beaton was clearly uncomfortable with the attitudes of many British residents in India. He refused to see India as a "first-rate country for second-rate people," preferring instead to believe that not all peoples of the world have to live by the same civilizational standards to be considered civilized.[8]

One travel writer, John S. Hoyland, presumed to title a book chapter the "Indian Personality" as if it were a traceable phenomena across India's large population, multiple religious and social groups, and various regional differences. Hoyland emphasized the Indian capacity for friendship, chronicling memorable encounters with assorted individuals with whom friendship blossomed. Westerners, he claimed were of two minds about Indians and both were inevitably flawed. One viewed Indians from the perspective of the "superior white man"; the other saw them in "gushingly sentimental" terms, believing that the "Oriental view-point is always right." The more useful approach, he contended, was to be fair and to cultivate sensible and useful friendships. Moreover, he argued, the "average Indian is psychologically much more sensitive than ourselves." Spiritual awareness, tact, courtesy, modesty, and goodwill were Indian virtues in abundance, traits in which they excelled far more favorably than Westerners. As Louis Hagan observed, "whatever you are to the Indian, political enemy, hated rival or intimate friend, he is always polite." Moreover, he contended, Indians may hate the British as a race or nation, but it was an impersonal emotion based upon principle and never directed at the Briton as individual. Like Hoyland, Hagan was impressed by the depth of Indian friendships. Moreover, Hagan believed that if an Indian were to become a friend, a prospect arising solely from a well-earned, deep-seated trust, he would develop "a deep, sentimental, almost dog-like attachment for you." Yet, Hagan also characterized Indians as "fundamentally lazy . . . [that] they have no pride and little conscience where work is concerned." Moreover, he contended, "more irritating than anything is their masterly way of playing dumb," a tactic, Hagan complained, deviously designed to evade anything unpleasant.[9] Noted British travel writer, Eric Newby, in his travel memoir of a trip down the Ganges, echoed similar complaints. Newby recounted a confusing series of misunderstandings concerning the departure of a guide at one stage of his journey, grumbling that he could not receive a direct reply to a question he posed to sort out what had happened. Newby: "It was too logical and would therefore cause great offense." Later, while touring a temple, in a miscommunication with an Indian acquaintance-guide, Newby once again expressed frustration at what he perceived to be Indian equivocation: "I felt depressed. In India even the most mundane inquiries have a habit of ending in this way. There may be two answers, there may be five, a dozen or a hundred; the only thing that is certain is that all will be different. Usually it is because one is misunderstood."[10] The last sentence is quite revealing. It is as if he had caught himself in a traveler's complaint of political incorrectness. Clearly exasperated by the exchange, Newby vented his annoyance to readers, but he fears it is expressed in condescending, Western terms. By concluding the recollection as a misunderstanding, Newby sought to balance what he believed to be a specific Indian trait with a commonly expressed cultural offset—it was only a misunderstanding. Nearly every late twentieth or early twenty-first century traveler, at least those conversant with cultural sensitivities, has experienced similar moments and emotions. The "local" tactic of pretending not to understand or evasively responding to inquiries was and continues to be a common complaint of Westerners about non-Western peoples across the globe. Hagan's and Newby's characterizations are but two more entries into that voluminous yield of complaints in the annals of Western travel writing.

Gertrude Williams, referenced earlier in this work, also sought to identify those qualities intrinsic to the "Indian personality." She wrote that

> There is a simplicity about Indian men and women, a modesty, almost diffidence, that has great charm. Their voices are softer than ours, their manner more

gentle. They live at a slower, more graceful tempo. They have the ceremonious consideration and courtesy of an old civilization. The poise and dignity of the older people is impressive. The women carry themselves like queens and, in their homes, they give the passing Western woman a dazzling glimpse of the possibilities of the Eternal Feminine. The masses have better manners than ours. I watched them wandering through old palaces, gardens and tombs. A group of young men, squatting to enjoy a view were quiet and decorous. There was none of the wild and strident horseplay of our holiday crowds.[11]

Indians, by these travel accounts, projected a most positive profile. If we are to take Williams' and Hoyland's characterizations at face value, placing a premium on the qualities they admire, the "Indian personality" was surely one to emulate—East or West. However, the qualities are notably passive ones. Hoyland, mindful of Indian independence aspirations, suggested that if Indians were to be "led" it would have to be "from alongside," not by authoritarian colonial policy. Post-colonial sensibilities would note the term "led" as perhaps the operative expression of this solution. The travel writer's elusive search for the "Indian personality" finds an empathetic voice in these passages, eager to embrace Indians on what are perceived to be their own terms. Although clearly somewhere short of the dichotomous "superior white man" or "gushingly sentimental" perceptions of Indians, a softer "Peter Pan" syndrome re-appears here, the presumption being that India was yet unprepared for self-government but could be "led" down that path through friendship, goodwill and tact. Hoyland lamented the "commercial odor" of Britain's colonial system. He cautioned those who would seek to embrace the "Indian personality" in openness and friendship to beware of "unconscious" urges to simply reassert the Western impulse towards "dominance-drive." If one pursued a more gracious and sympathetic course of action, Hoyland assured his readers that Westerners could learn from Indians "things quite inexpressibly important and delightful."[12]

In reading Hoyland today it is difficult escape the conclusion that the "sentimentality" he sought to escape appears comfortably ensconced within his travel memoir. Yet, there is something admirable about his efforts to view Indians more openly—to engage them on what he perceived to be their own terms—namely the "Indian personality." If his project to find the "Indian personality" was culturally naïve, tainted by paternalistic sensibilities and inherently fraught with representational hazards, Hoyland is nevertheless sensitive to Britain's troubling legacy in India. He sought to locate East-West meeting points compatible to the age, where certain features of Gandhian politics and British policies sincerely, if not problematically, desired to reach mutual accommodation through friendship, tact and courtesy. In that regard, Hoyland was clearly a product of his times. His effort to locate the "Indian personality" was also a product of the times, derivative in part from nineteenth century traditions intent upon categorizing racial and ethnic types into some type of neat, systematic order. Travelers see *difference* everywhere. They marvel at what they encounter and those that pen their experiences inevitably attempt to describe that *difference*. Doing so means entering the minefields of cultural representation, leading invariably to representational traps where writers spew regrettable gaffes from which there are seldom escapes. It is a relatively easy project to detect flaws in how travel writers characterize the peoples and cultures they encounter—no less so today than in the Age of Gandhi. Finding accurate and insightful ways in which to write travel accounts is a far more difficult enterprise. Indeed, post-modern thought would tend to view terms such as "accurate" and "insightful" as subject to a "pre-interpreted context" where the knowledge the travel writer seeks to convey is burdened by a deeply embedded cultural memory, deterministically routing the observer to represent the "truth" of the object perceived in pre-ordained interpretational and rhetorical patterns. In short, the travel writer may be physically mobile as he or she roams the earth, but is ultimately mentally "caged" within culturally induced travel writing prescriptions. Richard Tarnas, writing on the post-modern mind, suggests that it recognizes human knowledge as something "subjectively determined by a multitude of factors; that objective essences, or things-in-themselves, are neither accessible nor positable; and that the value of all truths and assumptions must be continually subjected to direct testing. The critical search for truth is constrained to be tolerant of ambiguity and pluralism, and its outcome will necessarily be knowledge that is relative and fallible rather than absolute or certain."[13] The post-colonial critique or "testing" of Hoyland's (and others) efforts to locate the "truth" of India or the "truth" of the "Indian personality" might either be condemned to the waste-heap of early twentieth century Western arrogance, or more graciously, recognized as a small but flawed contribution to ongoing efforts to grapple with the *difference* peoples of the world find in each other. However, contrary to Hoyland's efforts, there was no "Indian personality." The multi-millions of Indians existing in the Raj during the Gandhian era represented innumerable religious, ethnic, and cultural ingredients—not to mention diverse individual personality traits common to all peoples—that were impossible to summarize. The traveler "catches" or senses something distinctive from his or her own traditions but rendering "truths" from such *difference* is risky territory indeed.

Are we then left with little more than neutered banalities so as to avoid a linguistic free-fall down the slippery slope of Western representational modes? Are adjectives such as "sensitive," "gracious," "simple," "quaint," to name only a few, inherently doomed as problematic vocabulary? Does it matter, for example, whether the words are applied to villagers in India or Europe? There are many Hoylands traveling the globe today, seeking open and constructive dialogue with peoples from non-Western traditions. The adjectives they use to describe the people they encounter frequently reveal more about themselves than about those they seek to understand and characterize. But that "insight" has been stated many times before and in many different ways. It has become another travel cliché, or like in the words of V.S. Naipaul (here, in a different context), "an observation of no value"—or certainly one of diminishing value. The best that a travel writer can do is to "write away," hopefully with openness, tolerance, and cultural sensitivity. For as the post-moderns have suggested, our observations never rise to the level of "truth" but rather are subsumed by socio-cultural shifts that render them part of the ever-changing "rumor" of places and peoples perceived. And of course peoples and places are never static in themselves. They mutate with time and circumstance, leaving representational projects like the "Indian personality" as elusive today as it was in the Gandhian Age. As Arundhati Roy has suggested, "there's no such thing as an Authentic India or a Real Indian. There is no Divine Committee that has the right to sanction one single, authorized version of what India is or should be. There are, and can only be, visions of India, various ways of seeing it—honest, dishonest; wonderful, absurd; modern, traditional; male, female."[14]

## NOTES

1. Beverley Nichols, *Verdict on India* (London: Jonathan Cape, 1944), 9-11.
2. Lowell Thomas, *India: Land of the Black Pagoda* (New York: P. F. Collier & Sons, 1930), 50-53. In spite of Lowell's criticism of the Brahmins and their teachings, he credited them for preserving religious belief in India, and like so many other travel writers, paralleled India's caste system with Britain's own and American racial segregation.
3. Olive Thorne Miller, *Little People of Asia* (New York : Dutton, 1888), 130-131.
4. Alfred J. Bamford, *Turbans and Tails; or Sketches in the Unromantic East* (London: Sampson, Low, Marston, Searle, & Rivington, 1888), table of contents, 2-8. Bamford's work covered both India and China. Whereas the Indian was referred to as the "mild Hindu," the Chinese were titled "the Man of Han." Both groups fared badly in Bamford's account; however Hindu's suffered the worst treatment.
5. J.F.C. Fuller, *India in Revolt* (London: Eyre and Spottiswoode, 1931), 10-12, 25, 30-31.
6. George H. Johnston, *Journey Through Tomorrow* (Melbourne: F. W. Cheshire Pty., 1947), 29.
7. V.S. Naipaul, *An Area of Darkness: A Discovery of India* (New York: Vintage Books, 1964), 9-17.
8. Cecil Beaton, *Far East* (London: B.T. Batsford, 1945), 5-7, 38, 49-51. Cecil Beaton was a celebrated fashion and society photographer who dabbled in set designs

for plays, film, ballet and opera as well during a long and distinguished career. His photographs of the famous were very popular, including a notable set of the young Princess Elizabeth in 1939. As stated in the National Portrait Gallery website, "with his immense style, extraordinary visual sense, fascination with new ideas and boundless energy, he is regarded as a seminal arbiter of 20th century taste." See National Portrait Gallery, "Cecil Beaton," http://www.npg.org.jk/live/beatondrawings2.asp.

9. Louis Hagan, *Indian Route March* (New York: Pilot Press, 1946), 56-61.

10. Eric Newby, *Slowly Down the Ganges* (Melbourne: Lonely Planet Publications, 1966), 127, 130.

11. Gertrude Marvin Williams, *Understanding India* (New York: Coward-McCann, 1928), 73.

12. John S. Hoyland, *Indian Crisis: The Background* (New York: Macmillan Co., 1943), 21-22, 27.

13. Richard Tarnas, *The Passion of the Western Mind* (New York: Ballantine Books, 1991), 395-399.

14. Aurundhati Roy, "Introduction," in *India: A Mosaic*, ed. Aurundhati Roy (New York: New York Review Book, 2000), xxxii.

## *Chapter Eight*

# The Search for an Elusive Spirituality

For many Western eyes, the bizarre was never far from Hinduism's wheel of influence. Hinduism's other side—the street festivals, the colorful garb, and the bustling bazaars were welcome visual delights reflecting India's kaleidoscopic variety. As such, they were uniformly noted and appreciated by travel writers. But most of India's "dark side"—the poverty, the begging, the disease, the fakirs—were seen as directly attributable to Hinduism's destructive theological system and its consequential practices. Fakirs and sadhus[1] were seen as particularly symptomatic of the Indian propensity for deceit, laziness, and parasitic tendencies. There were astounding estimates of how many of them actually existed in India. If Katherine Mayo's government-derived estimates were to be believed, "saints and fakirs living by beggary" totaled 1,452,174 in 1921.[2] Calculating saints and fakirs with such exactitude, given India's human landscape, was inevitably suspect. Nevertheless, it conformed to a general perception that they were ubiquitous to India, sprouting like weeds amidst India's human landscape. Constance Sitwell[3] came upon a temple filled with them, what she referred to as a "resort of the Fakirs . . . the Fakirs of travelers' tales—mis-shapen fanatical men" with hair matted, eyes glazed, bodies emaciated—all calculated for saintly effect. Sitwell was particularly struck by one fakir, what she described as the "the most grotesque object in the place." Upon seeing Sitwell and her group, the man hurriedly pulled a pair of gold pince-nez (eyeglasses clipped to the nose by a spring) from a tin box, donning them with triumphant delight. Sitwell remarked, "no one smiled. We stared as if awed, and indeed we were almost awed; for could anything more fantastic have been done? There he lay proudly on his nails, clothed only in ashes, a pale wig, and pince-nez that glittered in the sun."[4]

Some writers acknowledged that a few sincere sadhus existed, but they were a rarity. One author described them as a "huge conglomeration of unwashed, ignorant workshy-willies, trafficking and battening upon their credulous and superstitious followers." He particularly noticed them around train stations where they attempted to freeload their way about the country by sneaking onto trains. One sadhu, he observed, clung tenaciously to a rail car's doorway while a railway official physically sought to eject him. After a lengthy impasse, several people grabbed the sadhu by the loincloth, yanking him back to the platform and leaving the man naked in the glorious moonlight. Later, after hours of curses against the official's family, cow and crops, the official fed the sadhu and sent him on the next train—acknowledging defeat. For the police would never come. Ultimately, the sadhu could out-endure his adversaries, granting him railway privileges by default.[5]

Sadhus and fakirs were symbolic emblems of an India filled with spiritual mysteries and wonders on the one hand and good old-fashioned deceit and fakery on the other. The legendary Indian 'rope trick' was one such legacy of the late Victorian age enduring through the Gandhian era. Peter Lamont, a practicing magician, parapsychologist and historian at the University of the University of Edinburgh, wrote a book on the phenomenon titled *The Rise and Fall of the Indian Rope Trick*.[6] Lamont's work successfully discredits the legend while demonstrating how it originated and why it was successfully perpetuated in the West for decades. The trick involved throwing one end of a rope skyward as it stretched tautly in a straight vertical line. A boy then climbed the rope to the top when suddenly he disappeared before a stunned and appreciative audience. Once the legend circulated among Westerners and was picked up by numerous press accounts it became in some people's estimation an Indian sight that equaled or excelled in wonder that of the Taj Mahal. Lamont shows how late Victorian fascination with the paranormal facilitated the rope trick's popularity, and in some quarters its credibility as a legitimate manifestation of one of the East's great mysteries. The emergence of the Theosophical Society in the late nineteenth century was one of many developments of the times that helped feed the paranormal frenzy. The Theosophical Society was founded in 1875 in Britain but soon after moved its headquarters to Madras, India. Madame Blavatsky, the Society's founder, authored several voluminous works blending elements of Hinduism, Buddhism, and aspects of Western philosophy in a murky mix of religious teachings. Blavatsky believed firmly that proving miracles was critical to authenticating Theosophist objectives. Thus, supernatural manifestations presumably evidenced in various forms of magic, clairvoyance, or similar 'events' were commonly reported by the Theosophists and were essential to the movement's identity and aspirations for credibility. India proved a fertile environment to advance their claims.

Several travel writers were intrigued by the Theosophist movement and managed a visit to its compound in Madras. Annie Besant was its central figure during the Gandhian era. A convert to the Theosophist faith who later moved to India to promote the movement's goals in addition to championing the Indian independence cause, Besant was a larger-than-life character who commanded a great deal of respect or disdain, depending upon the writer. One described her as "kindly, dignified, [and] gracious"—a white-haired reformer intent on spreading the Theosophist faith while at the same time contributing to the shaping of India's future:

> She, too, believes that India has a spiritual message for the world but that it cannot express itself while in bondage to a Western nation, that while in this condition, it cannot bring out national Indian traditions. The recognition of the unity of life is the great truth which India would teach the world and this life is the life of God. That this life permeates everything, literally *is* everything, is the essential idea of India.[7]

Others were not so receptive to Besant or to others in the movement. One writer characterized them as neither "meat nor fish" expressing unease at "these half-Hindus." To his mind, the Theosophists failed to understand Hinduism's ethic that the material world was to be renounced—a concept he believed to be "outside their comprehension."[8] Another writer, disdainfully recounted a day's outing to a Theosophist convention. To get there he shared a two-wheeled taxi with an "expensively dressed" widow and a gray-haired gentlemen who conspicuously quarreled when the transport ran into problems en route, prompting the observation that Theosophists succumbed like the rest of us to "matter over mind" in spite of the philosophy's claims to transcendence. The convention featured a lecture attended mainly by Indians. It provided a brief history of the movement, its basic religious tenets, and claims by the speaker that he was "able to communicate with spirits." The writer dismissed it all as subjective blather no doubt "satisfying to those who have not been taught the virtue of skepticism and the meaning of scientific evidence." Although disappointed by Theosophist philosophy, he did find aspects of the day's outing rewarding, commenting that nearly "every face I saw was worth looking at twice, and some many times." In other words, he was fascinated by the female attendees, arrayed as they were in beautiful costumes and adorned with exotic Asiatic features. They, he contended, would create a photographer's dilemma between "sensuousness and spirituality." He concluded his observations with this cynical reflection: "One longs to know what the psycho-therapy and the religions of the twenty-first century will have to offer to the descendents of these gropers."[9]

As Lamont suggests, "India was regularly presented as the most magical of lands"—a most likely site to locate and explore the types of claims advanced by the Theosophists. It was in this mystical milieu that the rope trick emerged as a legendary phenomenon. By the 1930s it had gained notoriety as "the world's most famous illusion." Many Indians and Britishers claimed to have witnessed it, or at least had supposedly talked to credible witnesses who had. But as Lamont concludes, "though this was a legend about the East, it was one that was fabricated in the West." In the end, it was simply one more example of an Orientalist construction that bi-furcated East and West along rationalist-primitivist lines or a variation of the divide; namely, the West as spiritual failure looking to the East's more profound engagement with ever-elusive notions of spiritual fulfillment.[10]

Floating fakirs, buried yet resurrected fakirs, snake-charming fakirs, and other creative expressions of the "craft,"[11] were part of the exotic imagery of India's kaleidoscopic spirituality. To what degree a Gandhian era public bought into the rope trick legends or other alleged exhibitions of Eastern magic is hard to determine. Surely, Peter Lamont's scholarship on the subject reveals a clear fascination with the topic. As for travel writers of the era, fakirs were usually written about with disdain and only occasionally with respect—typically reserved for the rare fakir or sadhu who appeared to be involved in a genuine search for truth. Travel writers surveyed for this work rarely referenced the rope trick. The fact that they generally viewed fakirs as pretentious panderers disguised as holy men evidenced their skepticism of rope tricks or similar magical or paranormal exhibitions. However, several writers did subscribe to the theory that there was something to such manifestations. Sir Henry Sharpe, in a kind of farewell tour through India towards the end of the Raj, informed his readers that he had never seen the "famous rope trick" and he had never believed in it until he met a man who, by his account, had actually witnessed its demonstration. Sharpe claimed to have witnessed unexplainable events during his time in India. An orderly under his hire developed a malignant growth on his neck necessitating several surgeries, none of which were successful, for the growth continued to reappear and fester. Sharpe arranged for one more surgery but the orderly went off to a "doctor of the Ayurvedic School" instead, where he was treated with the *Vaid's* special salve. According to Sharpe, the growth disappeared never to return. He was astonished by what occurred, suggesting that it "seemed to me a miracle." Sharpe contended that Westerners confused the ordinary Indian juggler with Indian magicians, the latter, in his opinion, having "remarkable hypnotic powers."[12]

Lowell Thomas' account of India travels included a chapter on a sadhu in Puri who it was claimed had remarkable powers, including the power to raise small creatures from the dead. The sadhu, as the story went, had been bitten by a mad dog at the age of thirteen, whereupon his mother took him to the

Ganges for burial, a common practice for those understood to be on the verge of death. There along the Ganges the boy's mother and others witnessed water sinking and rising around him, a sign to those present that he was destined for great things. An old sadhu provided him with a salve-curative; the boy healed and then went off to Tibet to study the "science of solar energy" for three decades. Eventually settling around Benares, he then embarked upon a career as a guru to a host of disciples, enjoying several residences and a "laboratory" to conduct his mysterious experiments. One involved the healing of sparrows that were "carefully and completely strangled" and then left for dead for several hours to make sure they had truly expired. The sadhu then focused sunlight upon them using a small magnifying class. Reportedly, "the rumpled feathers stirred, their beaks opened, and with a shake and a hop and a chirrup and a flutter, the sparrows flew away, praising the Lord of birds and men." The hope was that such "laboratory" experiments would eventually result in the raising of the human dead.[13]

Hearing of the sadhu, Thomas and his companion headed off to his compound armed with a camera and considerable skepticism. Although Thomas refused to draw any definitive conclusions concerning what he encountered, he nevertheless teased his readers with the remark, "what follows we saw with our four eyes." With that tantalizing bit of phrasing, Thomas proceeded to relate several demonstrations of the sadhu's powers, who turned out to be quite warm and welcoming and more than willing to exhibit his mysterious talents. According to Thomas, the mahatma (the term used by his disciples) directed the sun's rays upon a piece of cotton several times, each occurrence producing the smell of violets, then roses, and then a native scent. Thomas claimed to have been within a few feet of the sadhu observing his every movement but could not detect any sleight of hand or obvious human trick to produce the odors. Thomas concluded his tale appearing to suspend his skepticism, stating, "we felt that Mystery had been brought close to us, and that we touched her garment's hem." He offered no explanation for the exhibition, allowing it to dangle elusively as simply one more of India's great mysteries. "Only one thing is for sure," he stated, "there are more things in Heaven and earth than are dreamed of in travelers' philosophy!"[14] The capitalization of "Mystery" and "Heaven" was noteworthy. It bestowed supernatural qualities upon the sadhu's actions as Thomas ended the chapter on a note of hazy mysticism. A more skeptical sensibility would no doubt dismiss the sadhu's multiple smell production as sleight-of-hand trickery. By Thomas casting a mysterious aura over the event, India's exotic religiosity was perpetuated once more by traveler recollection, providing readers with yet another captivating tale about the strange powers of India's holy men.

The West's fascination with India's menagerie of mahatmas, fakirs, sadhus, gurus, yogis and other holy men is well known. From Herman Hesse's *Siddhartha* to the eastward wanderings of the Beatles, India has often been perceived as the ultimate destination for the spiritual aspirant, an exotic alternative to the presumed spiritual decay of the West. Stories of spiritual enlightenment, or at least spiritual quests, have been generously represented in the annals of short stories, novels, memoirs, and travel accounts. Arguably, India has carved out an identity as the quintessential spiritual bazaar. Some accounts relating religious quests to the East stem from the Gandhian period. One, by Paul Brunton, titled *A Search in Secret India*, is such an account. It is an unusual story of a journalist in search of spiritual meaning. Brunton told his readers "I feel quite humbly that I have been privileged to see a remote aspect of India seldom seen and less understood by ordinary travelers." That line was common to travel literature lore but Brunton put a different spin on it, focusing his tale on travels to the sacred and secret heart of India's spiritual realm where it is the geography of the soul that is sought, not that of landscape, peoples, and related physical features of the traveler's itinerary. Yet, as Brunton saw it, he embarked on his quest armed with the "scientific training" of the West and his years as an experienced journalist, assets that in his mind would assist him in sorting out the variant claims of India's yogis "by the method of first-hand investigation."[15] These remarks exemplify his approach to his search; one that is skeptical of what India has to offer *except* for its spiritual offerings:

> That the West has little to learn from present-day India, I shall not trouble to deny, but that we have much to learn from Indian sages of the past and from the few who live today, I unhesitatingly assert. The white tourist who 'does' the chief cities and historical sights and then streams away with disgust at the backward civilization of India is doubtless justified in his deprecation of it. Yet a wiser kind of tourist shall one day arise who seek out, not the crumbling ruins of useless temples, nor the marbled palaces of dissipated kings and long dead, but the living sages who can reveal a wisdom untaught by our universities.[16]

In retrospect, Brunton's words seem prophetic when one considers the trail of Western pilgrims, the famous and not so famous, that traipsed off to India later in the century in search of spiritual wisdom from a variety of gurus and like-holy men. Brunton's journey interacted with a variety of Indian magicians, fakirs, assorted men. It is apparent from Brunton's text that he met up with the same sadhu that Lowell Thomas wrote about while in Benares (they traveled in India within a few years of each other). In Brunton's account the scent of violets, roses, and jasmine were created out of Brunton's handkerchief with the sadhu ending the exhibition with a fragrance from a Tibetan flower. Again, the demonstration was conducted with the sun's light refracted from a magnifying glass. Brunton was invited back for another exhibition the next day. Unlike Thomas, he actually witnessed the killing of a bird, its motionless state for an extended time, and then the bird's "resurrection" and flight into the air. The yogi attributed his magical feats to Tibetan "solar science." Brunton had a much more extended interaction with the man than Thomas. When Brunton sought answers to his "experiments," the yogi's explanations became increasingly cryptic, suggesting paradoxically that they "can be studied in exactly the same way that any of your Western material sciences are studied" yet concluded that such things can only be attained to by a serious and extended commitment to yoga practices—something which the yogi intimated was most likely beyond Brunton's Western sensibilities. Brunton eventually moved on, intimating to his readers, "my welcome is but a surface one; Western investigators and Western disciples are not wanted here."[17]

Brunton then experienced a series of evening sessions with an Indian astrologer, absorbing the lessons of the 'Brahma Chinta.' Brunton warned his readers that the 'Brahma Chinta' system was beyond the capabilities of the average European, that it involved Tibetan meditative practices directed towards an esoteric state best described as "the vacuum mind." If indeed they were to undertake the meditations, Brunton declared that "insanity lies around the corner for Western amateurs who dabble in such practices." For to achieve its purposes, one lapsed into a catatonic-like state giving the appearance of death. The heart stopped, blood no longer flowed, but the spiritual effect was one of intense happiness. Brunton did not claim to have entered such a state. Ever the reporter, he continued to question the astrologer until the pursuit reached its end with few answers, only vague pronouncements that the West would someday embrace the East's mysteries. But until then, Brunton queried, would the astrologer mind having his photo taken?[18]

Brunton's spiritual quest continued on throughout India as he visited various spiritual colonies and holy men. In the end he declared "that my battle for spiritual certitude had been won . . . but without sacrificing my dearly held rationalism for blind credulity."[19] To Brunton, East and West—mystic mysteries and rational inquiries—had met in mutual harmony. Reading his work from the distance of nearly a century one is not so sure. Brunton experienced some remarkable encounters, including witnessing a number of unexplainable phenomena. Nevertheless, the encounters, interesting reading on their own terms, resembles a quest-like search for a spiritualized 'rope trick.' He was essentially on the road in search of 'holy grail' East. What he found were some extraordinary experiences, most of them explainable upon rational review. Indeed, the creation of floral odors or resurrected birds seem in retrospect to be little more than a magician's tricks. Brunton's claim to strange auras and mind-body spiritual sensations appear to be self-generated, momentary submissions to a strange and exotic 'other,' yielding states of mind unfamiliar to him but never beyond rationalism's pale. Moreover, the journalist's scent for a good story inhabits Brunton's account. His search for the "secret India" produces the spiritual bizarre, or perhaps one could say the Eastern bazaar of a journey across India to sample its spiritual wares. Ever exotic and strange to Western eyes, Brunton recounts travel experiences of a different order. Nonetheless, the unexpected is expected when traveling India. Brunton gave his readers a glimpse of the exotic-spiritual where the reader was free to suspend the rational from the comfort of an armchair's grounding. Although Brunton's travels were extraordinary in many ways, he was never more than an armchair's distance from mental luggage carried with him from his native England.

Many Westerners have replicated his journey in variation as the twentieth century wore on, suspending their rationalism as it suited them. Clearly, India as a type of Mecca further east but focused instead upon holy figures or gurus, has been well-chronicled over the years. Sara MacDonald's popular Indian adventure, *Holy Cow,* contains several such spiritual quests with twenty-first century twists to them. She pays a visit to an ashram near Bangalore where a self-proclaimed holy man named Sai Baba and his followers make extraordinary claims about him. For MacDonald, like Brunton, visiting the ashram is more than a curious side trip. She informs her readers that unlike her husband who is in India to report on more prosaic matters, she has been "indulging in the boundaries of belief and the unbelievable." MacDonald is disappointed in what she finds. The ashram is cluttered with uniformed staff, crass commercialism and crazed followers. Sai Baba Inc., as it were, includes Sai Baba music shops, restaurants, and gift shops carrying lockets, bracelets, watches, postcards, and many like items with Sai Bab's photograph prominently featured. When she queues up to meet him, the lottery-like prospects of her ever having an encounter with the man quickly fades as hordes cluster everywhere and only a select few are plucked from the crowds. She does manage to get a glimpse of the man but he seems frail, sickly and unimpressive. But Indian gurus are rarely noted for their physical virtues. The fact that Sai Baba claimed twenty-five million followers, including a number of public figures, attests to his appeal. For MacDonald, she leaves the ashram "without seeing his divinity," but departs with encouragement from a Swedish devotee who tells MacDonald that "it's not too late, that the great one comes to those who ask."[20]

Stories seeking the divine within India's lush spiritual traditions abound. The Travelers' Tales Series includes a volume titled *The Road Within, True Stories of Transformation and the Soul*, containing several stories of such searches—in and out of India. One by Mark Seal concerns an Indian transplant from the subcontinent to a village outside of Frankfurt named Mother Meera. Like Brunton and others, Seal is a skeptic who manages to wrangle an interview with Meera, a considerably more modest and toned down version of Sai Baba and his commercial exploits. Her devotees appear more dignified and well-heeled but like Sai Baba she had become a kind of international celebrity, drawing followers and the curious from around globe. Seal's skepticism eventually melts as he experiences "some strange energy playing with me, teasing me, seducing me. It seems to flow through my body, bulging out my shoulders, then bubbling up in the middle of my forehead, making my brain feel like it is going to burst." Onward the experience rolls, as Seal sees visions of hallucinatory images fleeting before his eyes, only to emerge from the vision to witness the hall he is in "pulsating with a blizzard of white light." He then kneels before Mother Meera who, he exclaims, "holds my head for an eternity." When Seals returns to his seat, he describes the experience as "my soul swimming towards heaven." Seals clearly believed that he experienced something extraordinary but like many such accounts by Westerners he doesn't know what to do with it. So, he makes his way to a bar hoping that a few stout German beers will help him sort things out. The reader is left to do with the account what he or she will.[21]

Nilla Cram Cook, referenced earlier in this work as the delightfully eccentric American traveler to India during the 1930s, followed and became attached to an Indian figure named Gurudev. According to Cook, "everyone knew that Gurudev could read minds and see what happened at a distance." Cook portrayed him as a Christ-like figure dispensing 'turn the other cheek' and similar advice bearing a distinct resemblance to New Testament passages. Many flocked to him seeking practical answers to everyday dilemmas. Cook was especially impressed with the Nationalist workers who had sacrificed home and family for extended incarcerations—but never becoming embittered over their experiences. One woman, old and sickly, had come to Gurudev to extend her final good-bye after years in a jail for making political speeches and leading political processions. She had contracted tuberculosis, presumably in jail, but in her shyness before Gurudev could only express joy for the opportunity to serve the Nationalist cause. Although Cook's experiences with Gurudev fell far short of Brunton's and other writers' suspended rationality in the face of the unexplainable, she did subscribe to a belief that Gurudev possessed unusual powers. Clearly, he exerted a powerful influence upon her. In one rapturous recounting, she told her readers that "one night when Gurudev had been talking of love, great love, I saw doves rise up from their dreams in the moonlight and circle around the star-crowned altar, calling softly to each other . . ."[22] The line reads more like poetry than visionary experience; either way, Indian spiritual gurus, for the few that sought them out in earnest aspiration, inevitably had such an effect upon Western travelers.

Another form of the bizarre was strange, unexplainable manifestations—large disappearing acts set against India's vast landscape. Sir Walter Lawrence, recounting district travels in Rajputana, frequently heard tales of strange societies and mysterious happenings. One evening he went out shooting only to experience a "curious illusion." A part of the excursion involved getting into a small boat where he paddled out to a small green promontory. There he saw a lovely girl, sitting by the edge of the lake. He inquired as to her name and village, but she only brushed off his questions with laughter and silence. Lawrence paddled on to the shore and returned home. He returned to the site a few days later but the lake, the boat and the girl were gone. Moreover, none of the locals knew anything about the lake, the boat or the girl. Lawrence, in a effort to explain the occurrence to his readers, concluded that "I have seen so much in India of what we in England call the supernatural, that I have an open mind, and I think that if we lived with the Hindus, apart from the influence of our own people, we should soon find that in that land of enchantment there is indeed more than is dreamt of in our philosophy."[23]

## NOTES

1. The term "fakir" variously means Hindu or Islamic holy man, ascetic, or one that performs feats of magic. Winston Churchill's famous reference to Gandhi as that "fakir" contributed to its pejorative understanding, suggesting what the term commonly refers to in English—one who is a "fake." Notably, it generally does not appear in the glossaries of more recent books about India. However, the term "sadhu" does, variously described as "holy man", "ascetic", or "mendicant", often as a wanderer seeking spiritual truth.

2. Katherine Mayo, *Mother India* (New York: Harcourt, Brace & Co., 1927), 406.

3. Manuscript Register, Mount Holyoke College Archives and Special Collections, www.mtholyoke.edu/lits/library/arch/col/msrg/mancol/ms0021r.htm. Constance Sitwell was a cousin of Edith Sitwell, the noted British poet. Constance's travel memoir of India was based upon a visit to India to see her brother. The foreword to her book, *Flowers and Elephants*, was written by E.M Forster, who trumpets the author's unique vision of India, someone graced with a "gift"—a dream-like image of India not to be confused with the ordinary "travel impressions of a young lady."

4. Constance Sitwell, *Flowers and Elephants* (London: J. Cape, 1927), 75–77.

5. John W. Mitchell, *The Wheels of India* (London: Thornton Butterworth, 1934), 56–59.

6. "Every Culture Believes in Some Sort of Magic," rediff.com/news/2004/aug/17inter.htm.

7. Agnes Rush Burr, *India: The Land That Lures* (Boston: L.C. Page & Co., 1929), 441.
8. Maaraten Matisse, *Wanderer from Sea to Sea* (New York: Harcourt, Brace and Co., 1936), 34–35.
9. Richard Maurice Elliott, *The Sunny Side of Asia* (New York: Century Co., 1928), 170–173.
10. Peter Lamont, *The Rise of the Indian Rope Trick: How a Spectacular Hoax Became History* (New York: Thunder's Mouth Press, 2005), xxi–xxiii, 64–69, 93, 173, 208.
11. Ibid, 22–26.
12. Sir Henry Sharp, *Good-Bye India* (London: Oxford University Press, 1946), 60–61.
13. Lowell Thomas, *India: Land of the Black Pagoda* (New York: P.F. Collier & Sons, 1930), 289–292.
14. Ibid, 293–296.
15. Paul Brunton, *A Search in Secret India* (London: Arrow Books, 1934), 9–11.
16. Ibid, 13.
17. Ibid, 192–203.
18. Ibid, 208–225.
19. Ibid, 317.
20. Sarah MacDonald, *Holy Cow, An Indian Adventure* (Mission Point, Australia: Broadway Books, 2002), 238–242.
21. Mark Seal, "Meera Gazing," in *The Road Within, True Stories of Transformation and the Soul Eye Witness Travel Guides: India*, eds. Sean O'Reilly, James O'Reilly, and Tim O'Reilly (San Francisco: Travelers' Tales, 2002), 299–314.
22. Nilla Cram Cook, *My Road to India* (Boston: L. Furman Inc., 1939), 190–197.
23. Sir Walter Roper Lawrence, *The India We Served* (London: Cassell & Co., 1928), 42.

## *Chapter Nine*

# The Paradox of Caste: East and West

When travel writers wrote on the issue of caste the most striking feature of their coverage was the tendency to compare India's caste system with what they perceived to be rough equivalents within Britain's social structure. This penchant for representational balance, for "playing fair" in their efforts to portray Indian culture, could result in some rather creative analogical illustrations from historical and contemporary models. The notion of "caste" was universally abhorred by almost all travel writers, but by emphasizing cross-cultural parallels, East and West, the critique of India's system was noticeably softened. Some writers were the exception, using "caste" as a way to highlight Indian culture as fundamentally dysfunctional. Most, however, found East-West comparatives of "caste" to be a most useful device to showcase their openness and perceptiveness as observant travel savants, a means by which they could contribute insightful depth to the travel writing enterprise. Moreover, the subject of "caste" was rich with interpretative possibilities. As one travel writer put it, "the social structure of the Indian Empire is an unsolvable maze, a pathless forest of unlimited areas and innumerable flora."[1] With that sort of complexity, matching European social codes with Indian ones not only provided interesting parallels, but also gave writers a topic with which to think of East and West, however different, as conspicuously similar in their social behaviors.

On writer, Robert Blackham, devoted a chapter of his book on India to explaining the origins and character of "caste." He informed his readers that the term "caste" originated from Vasco da Gama's voyages to India during the sixteenth century, derivative of the Portuguese word "casta" meaning "purity of breed." Although its origins in Indian history are rather murky, it is believed that the custom of caste was legalized formally several thousand years ago, supposedly by ancient Aryan invaders who ultimately found the dark-skinned Dravidian and aboriginal populations too "dusky in hue" for suitable marital unions. Blackham's, like several other accounts of the Gandhian era, laid out the basic structure of caste. There were four main divisions: the priest, the warrior, the husbandman, and the artisan. Springing from the four divisions were thousands of sub-divisions. For example, only a minority of Brahmins functioned as priests. Most others engaged in the professions such as medicine and law and yet others worked as clerks, agriculturalists, soldiers, or policemen. Drawing parallels to English society, Blackham suggested that "the Englishmen who bear such names as William Priest, John King, Edward Farmer, and James Smith are but the survivals in England of the four 'varnas' of Manu." Yet, Blackham's taxonomic analysis of "caste" divisions, East and West, clearly revealed an Indian construct significantly more complex and restrictive. To be a barber or carpenter, for example, required that one's parent be born of the respective caste. And each province had its own subtle variations on being barbers or carpenters so that intermarriage between people of the same trades was impossible even though by all appearances (to an outsider) the union was essentially a parallel match.[2] Blackham then applied the principle to the imaginary "Smith" clan in England, borrowing from an earlier British commentator on the subject:

> First of all, the entire caste of Smith would be split up into an indefinite number of in-marrying clans, based upon all sorts of trivial distinctions. Brewing Smiths, Smiths with double-barreled names and hyphens, Conservative Smiths and Radical Smiths, these, and all others imaginable varieties of the tribe Smith, would be, as it were, crystallized by an inexorable law forbidding members of these groups to marry beyond the circle marked out by the clan name . . . Thus a Hyphen-Smith could only marry a Hyphen-Smith, and so on.[3]

Blackman added religious differences to his analysis, stating that women of certain religious persuasions could marry up but not down if courted by someone of a different sect. A male Anglican could marry someone of any religious group but a female Anglican could not. Although Blackham characterized the differing gradations of the Smith clan as a "parable" on Indian forms of caste, it nevertheless revealed certain caste-like qualities in English society. By doing so, he muted the stark East-West antithesis so often summed up by that imperial cliché—'East is East and West is West and never the twain shall meet.' One writer suggested that the I.C.S. (Indian Civil Service) corresponded to the *Brahman* class (except they did not perform any priestly functions); the British army was the *Kshatriyas* or warrior class; the *Vaisyas*, or trading class, corresponded to the British business elements in India; and the *Sudra* or servant caste represented transplanted British servants to the Raj.[4] Once again, the travel writer's quest to find civilizational parallels was clearly at work here.

Comparative analogies sometimes originated from conversations with Indians. A merchant of Agra declared to one travel writer that "you're lucky in Europe—you ignore the castes!" He responded by telling the merchant that caste was very much alive in Europe even though it was absent from the teachings of Christianity. A different kind of religion, "the most terrible tyrant on earth: Public Opinion" dictated a less formalized caste structure; nevertheless, he contended, "it is as inconceivable to see a dinner in Benares where Brahmins and Sudras eat at the same table as it is to see a dinner of fashionable people on Park Lane in London where a plumber counts among his guests." Occidentalized forms of caste, the writer argued, were as prevalent and binding as one might find in the East. Only love, he conceded, could break the bonds of caste. Thus, the "amorous Lord marries a chorus girl" or the Emperor Jahangir married Nur Jahan, a little Persian girl abandoned on the highway and taken in by a charitable merchant." Of course, this argument was a stretch since whether in England or India love was easily as subject to the strictures of caste as occupation and other aspects of human existence. As for "untouchables," the claim was made that the English coal miner rising from the filth and debris of the mines was no less an "untouchable" than his Indian cousins to the East.[5]

The East-West "caste" comparatives included the structure of the British army. Frederick Muehl argued that it revealed a caste system "as rigid as Hindus' own." It had separate messes for separate ranks and rarely would enlisted men or officers eat with soldiers far from their status in rank. If they did, contended Muehl, they would be demoted in line with the ranks of those with whom they socialized.[6] Gertrude Williams echoed Muehl's observations. She claimed that "English colonial society is organized into compartments almost as water-tight as the Hindu's." On her way to India she traveled on a P. & O. liner that observed strict social distinctions that if not silly were surely comic. At the top of the pecking order were a traveling Prince and Princess who lounged lazily and alone on deck chairs never to be spoken to unless they spoke first. Apparently, they did not. Williams commented, "for most of the voyage the Prince sat and smoked and looked bored and sad; and the Princess sat and looked like a pretty pink and white china doll. She did not read, she not sew, nor play cards, nor talk. She just looked out across the water." The next social layer down, the I.C.S. clan (Indian Civil Service), enjoyed a certain prestige as the ruling elite of India, followed by British army personnel, frowned-upon tradesmen, working down to the lowest ranks of nurses, servants, mechanics, and laborers. Each group kept to themselves, divided by clearly delineated rules of social interaction.[7] Once on shore, social stratifications continued in earnest, perhaps exemplified most sharply by the ritual of British club life.

The clubs designed policies specifically aimed at excluding those deemed inappropriate for the establishment's social standards. This observation by Robert Bernays exemplified the exasperation some travel writers experienced in watching the absurdities of club insularity:

> Amongst their own people there is the most ludicrous snobbery in social relationships. I heard more talk in Bombay of men who had "accents", or were not "sahibs", than I have heard since boyhood days in a London suburb. The conditions of admission to some of the clubs are preposterous. At one of them it is necessary to be personally interviewed by members of the committee. Absurd tales are told of wholly eligible young men being turned down because the name of their public school is unknown to the chairman of the committee. There is a fantastic line drawn between commerce and trade. If a man in commerce he is eligible to be a sahib; if he in trade he is in outer darkness. A man may sell wine from an office. All is well. That is commerce. He hands it over the counter. That is trade. He is an outcast.[8]

Bernays provided numerous examples to push his point, one being young English males who spent their school days in India—not England. Having missed the homeland's public school experience, albeit similarly educated in India, usually meant denial of club membership once they were of age for admission. Bernays quoted an Indian who quite marveled at the disingenuous peculiarities of British social life, stating: "We know that you English have in your society as many 'untouchables' as we Indians do. We often talk about it amongst ourselves." Bernays commented that it was hardly surprising that overwhelming barriers existed between the British and Indians since a deep chasm dominated intra-British social relations as well.[9]

It is interesting to note that twenty-first century observers, commenting on the continuation of British traditions in India, have remarked that Indians have maintained them in perhaps greater elaboration than the British have today. "One such aspect was the mania of India's Anglophone elites for belonging to exclusive clubs."[10] Yet, the divide is one of economics and education, not one sustained by India's ancient caste system that has been impressively dismantled in contemporary India. Opposed by Gandhi and Congress Party during the independence era, the new Indian state legislated it out of official existence even if caste practices lingered on, particularly in rural India. However, as India has rapidly become more urban, it is argued that "the stigma of caste is disappearing more rapidly in Indian cities than that of race in the United States." As one Indian sociologist suggested in an interview, "Your Blacks are visible. Ours are not." Thus, in India's cities one can ride in busses, eat from the hands of restaurant cooks, and otherwise mix in close proximity with untouchables without being aware of their traditional identity. Moreover, caste traditions have been further eradicated by affirmative action legislation. In today's India, Dalits ("the Oppressed" or those generally known as "Untouchables, "Harijans" and related designations) and aboriginals are guaranteed admission to higher educational institutions, are entitled to 22.5% of all government jobs, and are assured 85 of India's 545 parliamentary seats. Although largely positive, some of these developments have witnessed troubling trends. Lower-caste politicians often profoundly corrupt and given to violence have dominated state and local politics in recent years, raising concerns about the fate of Indian politics.[11] But as all of this shows, both historic and current, caste can take many forms and express itself in endless variations, including hybrid East-West institutions and modern affirmative action programs that can turn caste-like traditions on their head.

Perhaps one of the most commented upon social barriers by travel writers during the Gandhian era was the great gulf between Eurasians and the rest of Raj society—whether British or Indian. Depending upon the author, they were sometimes referred to as Anglo-Indians (a phrase reserved in certain quarters, more typically in pre-Gandhian India, for long-time British residents in India). It was estimated that by the 1930s there were more than 130,000 Eurasians in India created by mixed unions of Indian and various European origins. A large segment of them served in clerical positions for the government, in business operations, or on the railways; many others became tradesmen. Whatever their occupation, they were seen as "neither fish nor foul"—ostracized by both the British and indigenous Indian society. Travelers commented upon the beauty of many Eurasian women. Yet, no matter how elegant, mannered, or educated, they were barred from European social life. Many became mistresses. Some British males married Eurasians, and if they did, were required to hand in their club registration upon taking a Eurasian bride.[12]

Travel writers might project progressive sensibilities but when it came to mixed unions of European and Indian descent the Eurasian offspring they produced were universally viewed as sad commentaries on colonial life. Often guised as genuine sympathy, travel writer remarks could not conceal thinly veiled prejudices against Eurasians. Some noted their tendency to mimic English manners and ways, inferring that they were pathetic social climbers aspiring to a status they could never achieve—'true' Europeans. They were, in eyes of many observers, the ultimate wanna-be Europhiles. Gertrude Williams referred to them as "the most pathetic of India's minority's groups." She noted that they were once designated as "Eurasians" but by 1920s "coveted the name Anglo-Indian"—a name traditionally reserved for British-born residents of India. Williams noted as well that they referred to

England as "home" even though few had ever traveled there. When she traveled the trains many of them observed Williams closely and some would engage her in conversation, quick to emphasize their common origins as "we English" and frequently speaking disparaging of fully indigenous Indians.[13] Generosity and affection for Indians was common; the same sentiments were rarely if ever applied to Eurasians. To the twenty-first century mind, such racial attitudes are difficult to comprehend particularly in view of the fact that so many travel writers sought to cross the great cultural divide between Europeans and Indians. One could argue that Eurasians were a natural bridge between two civilizations if only the obvious were acknowledged—not necessarily because of Eurasian physical characteristics but rather deriving from their determined effort to absorb Western values and customs.

It has been stated that the British Raj could not eradicate "untouchability" because "it belonged to the very foundations of Indian society—the caste system." "Caste" was quintessentially Indian and so deeply imbedded within that cast of mind that it would forever impede progress towards twentieth century notions of social and political equality.[14] To travel writers, indeed even to Indians, "caste" at greater inspection was intrinsic to the human experience. It may find variable expressions depending upon religion, custom, and locale, but nevertheless persisted as a kind of "original sin" of social interaction—socially constructed perhaps—but nevertheless omnipresent wherever one traveled the earth. The concept of "caste" as universal phenomenon did not entirely minimize Indian caste traditions as simply an Eastern variety of the practice. Some travel writers may have blurred the lines between traditional East-West distinctions; nonetheless, the Indian tradition of caste was generally acknowledged as more profoundly prejudicial and socially disastrous to millions of people. Barring admission to British clubs was one thing; the more pervasive forms of exclusion, abuse and violence based on caste was quite another. Yet, the fact that travel writers sought out civilizational parallels spoke to their ambition to locate commonalities fundamental to all peoples. They believed that the travel experience widened their cultural apertures, providing a field of vision that British expatriates within the Raj could never obtain because of the cloistered insularity and inter-dependency of their social relations. A traveler, by contrast, could observe, record, and synthesize—independently—from a distance. Or at least they believed it was possible.

## NOTES

1. Albert Farwell Bemis, *A Journey to India, 1921-1922* (Boston: Privately Printed, 1923), 43.

2. Robert J. Blackman, *Incomparable India: Tradition, Superstition, Truth* (London: Sampson, Low, Marston & Co., n.d.), 48-51.

3. Ibid, 52. Blackman took this "parable" from Sir Herbert Risley's analysis of India's caste system.

4. Gertrude Marvin Williams, *Understanding India* (New York: Coward-McCann, 1928), 11.

5. Maurice Dekobra, *The Perfumed Tigers Adventures in the Land of the Maharajahs* (Oxford: Brewer and Warren, 1930), 176-178.

6. John Frederick Muehl, *American Sahib* (New York: John Day Co., 1946), 109-110.

7. Williams, 10-11.

8. Robert Bernays, *"Naked Faquir"* (New York: Henry Holt & Co., 1932), 25.

9. Ibid, 26.

10. Edward Luce, *In Spite of the Gods: The Strange Rise of Modern India* (New York: Doubleday, 2007), 91.

11. Shashi Tharoor, *India: From Midnight to the Millennium* (New York: Arcade Publishing, 1997), 103-111, 365.

12. E. Alexander Powell, *The Last Home of Mystery* (Garden City, NY: Garden City Publishing Co., 1924), 106-107. Powell observed that all young British men were required to turn in their club registrations upon marriage. However, if the young man married a suitable European he was immediately re-admitted; if a Eurasian he was barred for life. According to Powell, the policy was specifically designed to filter out those intent upon marrying either Indians or Eurasians.

13. Williams, 167-169.

14. Jeffrey Paine, *Father India: How Encounters with an Ancient Culture Transformed the Modern West* (New York: HarperCollins Publishers, 1998), 16. Paine quotes political scientist Partha Chatterjee's point that "all arguments . . . about the inherent incapacity of Indian society to acquire the virtues of modernity and nationhood, tended to converge upon this supposedly unique Indian institution" (meaning caste).

## *Chapter Ten*

# From Bazaar to the Bizarre: India as Terra Exotica

One of my favorite travel stories concerns an avid bird enthusiast who goes to India on a quest to locate the legendary "pink-headed duck" of Calcutta. The bird, a gorgeously plumed creature of exquisite beauty, had not been officially spotted since 1935. Since its native habitat in the environs of Calcutta had been drastically reduced over the course of the twentieth century and it did not reproduce in captivity, many ornithologists believed the bird to be extinct. Undeterred, our enthusiast (designated Duck Man by the locals) embarked on a mission to somehow locate one, believing that the Calcutta fowl market was a promising place to start. Duck Man spent days in around the market and on the Hooghly River aided by a clinging guide by the name of Babba. Babba knew an easy mark when he saw one. Before long, "sightings" were rumored and "ducks" appeared from enterprising locals in the form of chickens, doves, and other sundry fowl. Three pink ducks do eventually appear; however, a suspicious layer of fresh pink paint betrayed their false identity. One local delivers a turtledove, claiming that it *was* a pink-headed duck but unfortunately like all pink-headed ducks it became a dove once it emerged from water. The quest continued for days. Before departing Calcutta to continue his search elsewhere, Duck Man shelled out a tidy sum of money to locate the rare creature—but all in vain. Babba, in tribute to his mark (now dubbed the "Searcher of the Duck"), decided that a party should be given in his honor to celebrate his departure from Calcutta. Nothing was too good for the "Searcher of the Duck." A band of musicians was hired, many locals were invited and a merry event was had by all. Our bird enthusiast had a wonderful time even if he was by evening's end obligated to pick up the tab.[1]

Stories like this abound about India. It is the ultimate travel fantasia, filled with such wondrous yet often disturbing sights that travelers frequently experience sensory overload. The editors of *Travelers' Tales Guide: India* have summed it most appropriately: "India—monsoon and marigold, dung and dust, colors and corpses, smoke and ash, snow and sand—is a cruel, unrelenting place of ineffable sweetness."[2] For travelers to India during the Age of Gandhi, no less than today, India was an assault on their senses, wonderfully magical in one moment yet profoundly disturbing in another. The turn of a corner could open up to a bright and colorful bazaar; the turn of another corner could present sights of the most bizarre and shocking variety. Most writers, somewhere in the body of their travel narrative, indulge in bouts of descriptive excess in trying to articulate what they feel and think about India. One writer, exemplifying this trait, recounted this day on the streets: "I prowled the bullion bazaars of Bombay all day feeling alternately creepy, astonished, frightened and shocked. Such a fabulous, hideous country. No man can picture it. Write what you really see in this impossible country and at once your stuff is thrown in the wastebasket."[3] Another writer stated the point even more enigmatically: "every scene in India is produced as if by the stereopticon apparatus for dissolving one view into the next, showing at the moment absurd juxtapositions of the high lights of each."[4]

For some, visions of India began with Kiplingesque memories implanted by family memories or evenings curled up with *Kim* and other classic tales of the Raj. Leila Hadley, in her *A Journey with Elsa Cloud*, wrote of a grandmother's summer readings filled with enchanting images of India, "dazzling my imagination . . . with the glitter of India's bazaars and the wonders of its temples and magic mountains." Hadley later traveled through India during her mid-twenties "to discover India for myself and, by writing about it, to make it my own." And by doing so, she claimed in typically sensuous prose, "I saw India through all my senses in a tumultuous assault of sight and sound and smell and taste and resonating color." *A Journey with Elsa Cloud* was about a later journey—a quest in the 1970s to re-connect with her estranged daughter, Veronica, who had taken up Buddhism with a Tibetan lama in the Indian Himalayas. Hadley's India is the India of the bazaar. It is a wonderland that foregrounds painful recollections of family memories and the uncertainties of re-establishing a relationship with a daughter who has rejected nation and family in favor of a land and culture that promises, at least in Veronica's mind, something far better than that which she left behind. So much of the work is personal; but India is ever-present in the story, nourishing Hadley's weary soul as she tries to keep pace with her daughter's energetic search and contend with an India without the creature comforts to which she has become accustomed.[5] There are many passages like the following in her book, excerpts that burst into expressive rapture about what she sees around her, and like many India travel accounts, appear suddenly at the turn of a page, as if spontaneously uttered:

> In India more than anywhere in the world, I am aware of hands graceful in motion, gracefully poised with beautifully shaped nails and delicately spoked tendons. Here in the market, hands silent as paintings, hands stretching, reaching, holding, hands pinching vegetables and fruit for the feel of freshness, these hands posses the sensuality that the faces lack. Everywhere gestures are visible harmonics, vanishing as they happen, as ephemeral as music.[6]

Women travel writers tend to capture such India-moments with more regularity and sensitivity. Patricia Kendall, writing during the mid-1930s in a style reminiscent of so many of her travel writing contemporaries, beckoned readers to *See India with Me*, where "her revelations sometimes seem to come from a magic world, sometimes from Pandora's Box; some will inspire your soul, some will wrench your heart, but all will stir your thoughts."[7] In these and many other statements, prose becomes poetry. India as wondrous bazaar dominates the imagery—but the bizarre, frequently disturbing, usually lurked nearby. One's soul may be inspired, but one's heart would invariably be wrenched as well.

A site of continuous wonder and delight to Westerners was the Taj Mahal. Built in the seventeenth century by Mughal ruler Shan Jahan for his beloved wife and palace favorite, Mumtaz, the structure was an elegant mausoleum to her memory. Mumtaz died in 1631 giving birth to her fourteenth child. Started within a year of her passing, the Taj took approximately twelve years to complete whereupon it was immediately deemed a masterpiece, retaining that tribute continuously to the present. Kipling described it as "the ivory gates through which all dreams pass;" Tagore contributed a similar accolade, that it was "a tear on the face of eternity."[8] Most travel writers were no less astonished by its architectural splendor and ethereal qualities. Nearly all paid an obligatory visit, for to have traveled to India without having visited "that bubble of beauty" was to somehow have missed the quintessential romantic symbol of the East—perhaps not unlike a Parisian visit without having seen the Eiffel Tower. A few writers were somewhat indifferent to the monument or were fearful of penning yet another tiresome piece of architectural flattery. Aldous Huxley confessed, uncomfortably so, that he found its wealth-laden picturesqueness to be most unattractive, and its four minaret towers as "among the ugliest structures ever erected by human hands."[9] But most travel writers were captivated by its grace and beauty and wrote gushingly of its aesthetic qualities. This quotation, reminiscent of Kipling's and Tagor's eulogies, effectively illustrates the point:

> When the guide has finished, you feel more than ever that here is a living spirit, a voice of love and devotion. You see again those apartments at the Fort in which the little lady who lies here lived, the slender, graceful figure, the gentle

> features, the big dark eyes, the rich dress of silk, brocade and jewels. You see the prisoner in those same apartments gazing with dying eyes to this tomb of her he had so loved. You listen again to that echo floating, floating, floating, like that universal cry of the heart, "Beloved, where art thou?" And Taj ceases to be a building—it becomes the voice of a soul.[10]

When in Agra, the railway tourist Jane Tracey and friends visited the Taj "all hours of the day or night." Whether by dawn, midday, dusk, or moonlight the Taj exhibited unique expressions of light and color that greatly inspired Tracey. By moonlight, for example, the Taj became as "a phantom of silver, mystic in form and beauty, floating in air." In a tour inside the dome, she related to her readers the marvel of its acoustics, where sounds loud or soft echoed and re-echoed in haunting waves. One of her companions began singing the hymn "Nearer My God to Thee" mesmerizing the entire party and the building's guards. The way it was sung, claimed Tracey, had the effect of "each note repeating itself and gaining sweetness in its ascension until, perhaps, it was caught and re-chanted by the angelic choir." Critics, she argued, might find minor flaws, "but all in all, the Taj is the most perfect and beautiful building, architecturally and artistically, ever erected."[11]

Hindu temples evoked more varied responses than the Islamic Taj Mahal. They could charm travel writers or horrify them, depending largely upon the sensibilities of the writer. Lowell Thomas, like others, found the Black Pagoda a temple that combined the qualities of both grace and repulsion—a place where "the most beautiful and most obscene" rose to "the uttermost pinnacle of bafflement." The Black Pagoda was filled with sculptures depicting every variety of sexual expression. Westerners frequently found it shocking and foul. Thomas described it matter-of-factly, reminding his readers that sexuality and religion had a long and storied symbiotic relationship and that contemporary America had its love and tantric cults not unlike the Black Pagoda's orgiastic imagery.[12] Again, that predisposition for travel writers to smooth the edges of civilizational disparity by locating comparable practices East and West.

One of the most humorous accounts of Hindu temple expositions was Maurice Dekobra's encounter with 'the puritan lady at Benares." Miss X, as he referred to her, was newly arrived from Boston via Calcuttta, decked out in a Colonial helmet, tailored khaki outfit, and looking lost in the train station. Dekobra approached her, engaged her in conversation, establishing a rapport while assisting her towards her hotel destination. Dekobra told Miss X that he, like Sinclair Lewis and others, had had their books banned in Boston. Miss X demurely informed Dekobra that she had been a member of the association that had initiated government action against such writings. Dekobra, as he put it, then devised "an inoffensive and at the same time Machiavellian vengeance"—a sightseeing trip to a Hindu temple filled with erotic images. Dekobra described Miss X in stock anti-Puritan condescension: she was forty-ish, she was a spinster, she disapproved of vaudeville if there was "anything French connected with it," and "thought less than nothing of erotico-scientific German essays" and the "recent audacities" of certain English writers. Given those cultural sensibilities, Miss X was in for a big surprise. Dekobra and Miss X first visited a temple dedicated to Shiva where a guide expounded upon a statute where god and sacred bull kneeled before the *lingam*. Miss X, attempting to figure out its meaning, inquired as to whether the object was "God's finger." When informed of its reproductive function, she quickly averted her gaze and exclaimed, "Oh!—It's an outrage—Oh! Never would I have believed . . . " In the next touristic sequence, they visit a miniature temple where "an enormous phallus, painted a brilliant red, stood up, still wet with the ritual water which the faithful had sprinkled on it." Once again, at first perceiving a different meaning, Miss X upon learning that it was yet another *lingam*, turned to the guide and inquired, "Can't you show me a temple where that horror is not offered to the eyes of decent people?" The guide attempted to shift the tour's routine itinerary in order to honor Miss X's wishes, but the temples of Benares afforded scant relief for eyes resistant to sexual imagery. Miss X determined to head back to the hotel. However, yet another offense to her moral proprieties awaited her. They passed a street celebration of the Hindu holiday known as *Holi*. Young people were spreading red liquid around them in riotous celebration. When Miss X learned that the red liquid symbolized spurts of blood from young virgins, for her it was "the last straw." Off she went in a rush to the sanctuary of her hotel, angrily telling Dekobra that the "League of Nations should intervene and put a stop to these scandals!" Dekobra, gleefully sensing a *coup de grace*, remarked to Miss X what a shame it was, however, that United States would have nothing to do with the League.[13]

One travel writer, E. Alexander Powell, devoted a considerable amount of coverage to the temples, essentially echoing Miss X's complaints, yet acknowledging that they were nevertheless worth seeing. Powell's descriptions at times read like purple-prose travel musings. In one segment he quoted Pierre Loti's adoring remarks about the Temple of Madura, but thought that the temple's "marvels" would be "more aptly described as horrors, the effluvia of diseased brains and a debased religion." Interspersed between pages of general description were phrases of revulsion, like "nausea of the soul" or "spiritual cesspool." Hinduism, according to Powell, "is the only religion in the modern world which actually wallows and glories in the unnatural, the degrading, and the obscene." It was, to his, mind, and un-reformable religion.

Powell was aware that others saw Hinduism much differently, that he could be accused of not being fair to his subject; nonetheless he concluded: "It is (Hinduism), when all is said and done, nothing but a form of phallicism . . . no religion which tolerates any of these monstrous customs . . . is fit to serve as a spiritual guide to more than two hundred million people."[14]

The sight of cows roaming endlessly about contributed as much as anything to the notion of an un-reformable Hinduism. Although some writers wrote fondly of their symbolic importance and leisurely loitering, many saw the cow as a representative source of India's problems. Cows had free rein of the streets, dropping their dung gratuitously about, contributing to the filth and stench of Indian cities, towns and villages; cows, if eaten, could help resolve India's recurrent waves of famine and starvation, arrest malnutrition, and rid the nation of a public nuisance; cows, holy and sacred as they might be, were nevertheless a neglected and abused animal, with innumerable examples of starving, crumpling creatures milling about hopelessly and uselessly, a testament to a kind of benign, passive cruelty India inflicted upon its honored species. Lowell Thomas claimed that "the cow *is* India." Its languid, patient qualities mirrored the Indian people. To kill a cow was to commit an "unspeakable crime" warranting tortures worse than death and in some native states punished as a capital crime, although rarely so in the twentieth century.[15] If indeed "cow protection is the dearest possession of the Hindu heart"[16] some wondered why it simultaneously remained an object of such neglect. Yet, neglect was a constant in India—a leisurely, languid neglect writ large across nearly every aspect of its landscape. Why, some inferred, should it be any different for the cow?

If India was the land of the bizarre, no other tourist site symbolized that characterization more than the famed Towers of Silence on Malabar Hill in Bombay. The Towers are cylinder-like stone structures approximately twenty feet in height that house the funerary rites of adherents to the Parsee faith, refugees to India from the Muslim conquests of Iran during the ninth century. As Zoroastrians, they were deemed infidels and of those who resisted conversion to Islam, some fled to Bombay and surrounding areas to escape persecution and carry on their religious faith. The Parsees were particularly successful in commerce and proved to be an influential force in Indian life that far outweighed their estimated 60,000 in number. They were particularly adept at adjusting to European ways. When the British arrived a significant number of them made fortunes in industrial and commercial enterprises. Although noted for such accomplishments, the Towers were clearly of greater interest to travelers. They were comprised of three layers—one each for men, women and children. The bodies of the Parsee dead were brought to the Towers where vultures picked them clean, as it were, so as to ensure "that the sacred earth is guarded from defilement."[17] The idea of bodies being ritualistically devoured by vultures high on a tower overlooking Bombay's metropolis was a most striking image to travel writers. If the Taj Mahal symbolized grace and beauty, the Towers represented the morbid and grotesque. Most tourists who went to Bombay went to see the Towers just as they would visit the Taj Mahal in Agra. Although they couldn't enter the Towers, they were allowed to approach in sufficient proximity to view, as one writer put it, "vultures sitting in a row like sentinels, peering down into the Tower in an expectant attitude."[18] Reportedly, the bodies were devoured within half an hour, leaving nothing but skeletons, which were left to dry in the sun before being deposited into a well to complete the ritual cycle.[19] It is interesting to note that there is currently a serious vulture shortage causing consternation among traditional Parsees and debate as to the future of the Towers' rituals. However, during the Age of Gandhi they were numerous and voracious, providing yet another example of India's claim to being "the best show on earth."

## NOTES

1. Rory Nugent, "The Calcutta Fowl Market", in *Travelers' Tales Guides India: True Stories of Life on the Road* (San Francisco: Travelers' Tales, 1998), 51-64.
2. James O' Reilly and Larry Habegger, eds., introduction to *Travelers' Tales Guides India: True Stories of Life on the Road* (San Francisco: Travelers' Tales Inc., 1998), xx.
3. Gordon Sinclair, *Foot-Loose in India* (New York: Farrar & Rinehart, 1933), 175.
4. Richard Maurice Elliott, *The Sunny Side of Asia* (New York: Century Co., 1928), 129.
5. Leila Hadley, *A Journey with Elsa Cloud* (New York: Penguin Books, 1997), 7-9. Hadley informs her readers that the name "Elsa Cloud" came from an experience she had with her daughter Veronica during visit to Iceland. Standing by the harbor's edge, young Veronica told her mother, "Mummy, I'd like to be the sea, the jungle, or else a cloud." Thereafter Veronica was "Elsa Cloud." Hadley has had a colorful life and was an established travel writer by the late 1950's. Among other works, she wrote *Give Me the World*, *Tibet: Twenty Years After the Chinese Takeover*, and *Fielding's Guide to Traveling with Children in Europe*.
6. Ibid, 164.
7. Patricia Kendall, *Come See India with Me* (New York: Charles Scribner's Sons, 1935), 3.
8. John Keay, *India, A History* (New York: Grove Press, 2000), 335-336.
9. Aldous Huxley, *Jesting Pilate: The Diary of a Journey* (London: Chatto & Windus, 1948), 57-59.
10. Agnes Rush Burr, *India, the Land that Lures* (Boston: L.C. Page & Co., 1929), 103.

11. Jane A. Tracy, *See India with Me* (Boston: Stratford Co., 1929), 141.

12. Lowell Thomas, *India, Land of the Black Pagoda* (New York: P.F. Colliers & Sons, 1930), 330-331.

13. Maurice Dekobra, *The Perfumed Tigers: Adventures in the Land of the Maharajahs* (Oxford: Brewer & Warren, 1930), 123-131. The Benares guide, according to Dekobra, complained that he could never figure out how to please Western visitors. Miss X found temple images shocking horrible; the previous month an aristocratic woman found everything ho-hum, complaining, "Is that all you have to show us?"

14. E. Alexander Powell, *The Last Home of Mystery* (Garden City, NY: Garden City Publishing Co., 1924), 44-60.

15. Lowell Thomas, *India: Land of the Black Pagoda* (New York: P.F. Collier & Sons, 1930), 135.

16. Burr, 431.

17. John A. Hutchinson, *Paths of Faith* (New York: McGraw Hill Publishing Co., 1981), 285-287.

18. Charles M. Hendley, *Trifles of Travel* (New York: Rider Press, 1924), 271-272.

19. Kendall, 300.

## *Chapter Eleven*

# Benares: Journey to the Soul of India

Benares is India's Mecca.[1] It has also been described as Buddhism's Jerusalem.[2] No other site in India engaged travelers' imaginations or repulsed them more than this sacred city along the Ganges—or elicited as much colorful prose as writers struggled to articulate what they encountered. As India's "holiest of holies," Benares housed more than two thousand temples and uncountable shrines to go with upward of thirty thousand priests, fakirs, and other assorted holy men. For Hindus, dying in Benares was a ticket to eternal life. The Ganges River, which flowed through it, is lined with hundreds of ghats (stepped embankments) on which pilgrims cremated the remains of their beloved relatives before depositing them into the river, or where bathers dipped their souls as much as their bodies into its flowing path. For two to three miles along the river pilgrims performed their ablutionary rites, principally between seven to nine in the morning. For some the sight was horrific; for others it was an inspiring spectacle. Lowell Thomas remarked that there were "few sights more beautiful in all the world than the crescent sweep of the Ganges" displaying early morning washing ceremonies. Yet, he admonished Westerners to capture the sight from the distance of a telephonic lens, not as peering voyeurs invading the sacred space of devout pilgrims.[3] Agnes Burr issued the same advice, remarking that the sight of pilgrims on the river was novel and lovely—one of the most beautiful yet strangest sights in the world. Yet, she cautioned, "a 'close-up' is not so entrancing"—that the traveler would be better served viewing ceremonies from a distance—by boat in the middle of river.[4]

Indian mythology places the Ganges at the earth's center where the Hindu god Vishnu formed the world at creation's dawn. Hindus believe that Lord Shiva dwells in Benares where the "Ganges washes away the sins of a myriad of lifetimes, and Shiva whispers a sacred mantra in the ear of those who die here, ensuring *moksha*—instant union with the Universal Soul and freedom from the painful cycle of rebirth and death."[5] In the eyes of Gandhian age travel writers Benares was so saturated with religiosity that one writer mused: "there is almost nothing in Benares—apart from sacredness."[6] Another writer remarked after witnessing Benares' wretched poor: "I felt I had never seen anything so near to heaven come so close to hell."[7] Nearly every travel writer paid the city a visit; many of them devoted entire chapters to its role in Indian history and life. For Western observers traveling through India, Benares was the ultimate expression of Hinduism, "a plunge into that real India of which Calcutta gives no foretaste."[8] Their reactions often generated melodramatic prose, as this statement illustrates:

> Once in the nightmarish labyrinth of passages and tunnels and narrow alleyways that run under and between and behind the temples, you feel there is no escape. Thousands of people are milling to and fro in the gloom and filth. Most of them are mumbling and spitting. You push past the beggars, the mutilated and diseased; past food stalls and vendors selling flowers to offer to the gods; you in your turn are pushed and elbowed and breathed on; you step on a pie dog and it yelps, or your foot sinks into the droppings of a sacred cow. Through a small grille in a wall, you catch sight of a temple prostitute, squatting on the bare floor of her empty cubicle, waiting to accommodate worshippers.[9]

Portrayed here is the "rumor of India" in its claustrophobic whirl of desperate masses, filthy streets, and frazzled commotion. In today's travel writings, Benares is simply one expression of that 'rumor.' In the age of Gandhi, Benares was, more than any other Indian location, *the* quintessential representation of the image.

Benares lay along the famed Grand Trunk Road, a 1,500 mile military route (now National Highway Number 1 in India) that stretched between Calcutta in the east to Delhi in the north to the Khyber Pass leading northwest to what is now Afghanistan. The British utilized the road to control India's most traveled route, lining it with imperial towns, military camps, police stations and similar control points in order to monitor the most traveled route within the Raj.[10] The city was ceded to the British in 1775. By possessing it, the British were then burdened with supervision of the city's annual march of religious pilgrims that numbered more than a million visitors to go with its 700,000 inhabitants. Benares had been an important center dating back centuries before Christ. Buddha had arrived there from Gaya to teach his religious concepts, continuing on in the region until his death in 483 B.C.[11] As one writer expressed it, "My first, my last, my most abiding feeling concerning Benares was the sensation of its antiquity."[12]

The Ganges River, inextricably bound to the city's image, evoked considerable fascination among Westerners. Robert Bernays wrote of a brief jaunt to Benares where he hired rowers to take him on a boat excursion to view the pilgrim throngs carrying out their ritualistic duties. Inadvertently rammed by a vessel crammed with American tourists, Bernays quipped that "the whole river was covered with them . . . they were all wedged four deep on to the top of their barges and I in my solitary grandeur must have looked the embodiment of the reserved Englishman taking his pleasures alone and sadly." Of course, he had the rowers to propel him along the river in comfort, but as in so many travel writings from the age, the "solitary" Western traveler discounted the presence of indigenous guides or assistants; they were rarely referenced as fellow travelers, portrayed instead as little more than a landscape feature in human form. Bernays luxuriated in his perceived traveler versus tourist superiority. Feigning indifference to the sights of the river, Bernays told his readers that even though he was anxious to return to shore his rowers were "very reluctant to let me go without tasting the full ghoulish horror of the ghats." Bernays, evidently yielding to the rowers' pleas, lingered on as the reluctant traveler, disdaining the eager clicking sounds of touristic Americans snapping away with their cameras. Bernays then commented sardonically that the photographs would most likely end up on the screen of a ladies' club slide show in some small, provincial American town. He also wondered, as tourists clicked away, how they would react to "snaps of themselves at Holy Communion transported back to the Oriental clubs in Calcutta and Bombay."[13]

Tourists were especially attracted by the river's burial ceremonies. Families brought their dead to be cremated on designated ghats—the stair-step pathways leading down to the river. Typically, the body was wrapped in a sheet, placed in the water momentarily for purification, and then hoisted onto a bamboo frame readied for burning. Prior to that, however, the family would take water from the river, sacramentally pouring it into the mouth of the corpse, followed by the eldest son "cracking the skull with a club to free the spirit." The bamboo frame, with body, would then be set on fire and its remains deposited into the Ganges—sometimes accompanied by jewelry or other valuables—depending upon the family's wealth.[14] Aldous Huxley, having also observed these scenes, was astonished at what he saw:

> For it was not to look at the moon's silhouette that we had rowed out that morning on the Ganges; it was to look at the Hindus looking at it. The spectacle was vastly extraordinary. There were, at the lowest estimate, a million of them on the bathing ghats that morning. A million. All the previous night and day they had been streaming into town . . . the ghats go down in furlough-wide flights of steps to the river, which lies like a long arena at the foot of enormous tiers of seats.

> The tiers were thronged today. Floating on the Ganges, we looked up at acres upon sloping acres of humanity.[15]

Huxley went on to describe crematory and burial ceremonies in addition to other spectacles displayed by the river's activities. To Westerners, there was no sight like it in the world. And, surprisingly, some seem to subscribe to the notion, held by the Hindu intelligentsia and masses alike, that the Ganges had magical qualities. Along with the river's sacred powers, it was believed that the Ganges had extraordinary purifying effects, one writer contending, "the strangest part of it is that scientists *have* discovered the presence of a powerful antiseptic in the water."[16] Another writer told this story:

> A few years ago an experiment was made by a government analyst. Water was taken from the main sewer of Benares containing not unnaturally millions of cholera germs. These were emptied into a tank containing Ganges waters. In six hours the germs, instead of multiplying of their kind, died! The analyst then took ordinary filtered water and emptied into it cholera germs. They multiplied exceedingly.[17]

In referencing these antiseptic qualities, writers tended to straddle the line between belief and disbelief, fascinated by the river's alleged powers but reluctant to buy into Eastern "superstitions" that would insult the presumed skepticism of their readers. Nonetheless, like the famed rope trick and other legends of the supernatural or unexplainable in India, the belief that the Ganges flowed uncontaminated water enjoyed wide circulation among travelers. Others, however, noted the morass of dead bodies, raw sewage, and strewn garbage that millions of pilgrims inevitably left in their wake—severely challenging the notion that the river could sustain its antiseptic qualities.

> The multitudes continue to bathe and bow and make offerings. Waist-deep in the stream they stand and pour the water over head and neck and breast, their dripping locks and wet bodies shining in the sun like bronze. Some are aged, and shiver in the cotton garments that cling to their emaciated limbs. Some are sickly, and hands tremble as they pour the purifying liquid over their shaking figures. But nothing chills the fervor of their faith. The river, close to shore, is not so sparkling. It is covered with a scum of garbage, dead flowers, dead animals, leaves, orange and banana skins. Sometimes corpses float by. Yet the pilgrims bathe and drink and depart happy. At last your boat goes back to its landing place and you clamber off, dazed and somewhat staggered by "god-intoxicated India."[18]

Nonetheless, this author as well referenced the experiments of "sanitation experts" puzzled at the river's purifying properties, where normally proliferating bacteria was eliminated shortly after contact with Ganges water. Thus, the story of the river's extraordinary powers continued to circulate, even as it does today, although skepticism abounds as well. In January of 2007, thousands of sadhus, or holy men, protested against the government's inability to address the river's rampant pollution. One sadhu threatened to commit "jai Samadhi," or ritual suicide by drowning, if the authorities failed to clean up the industrial pollution, municipal sewage, and pilgrim garbage that are incessantly dumped into the river. The protest coincided with the arrival of "Ardh Kumbh Mela" (Half Grand Pitcher Festival), a 45-day event where it is estimated that seventy million Hindus would ceremonially bathe in the river's waters.[19]

Norah Rowan Hamilton, purveyor of the "government experiment" tale referenced earlier, went on to write that Benares, in spite of its locale on the Ganges, its eager pilgrims, and other remarkable features, "seems to me indescribably evil." In characterizing Benares in that way, she did so in striking contrast to other Indian cities she visited: Delhi was described as "pre-eminently masculine"; Agra with the Taj Mahal and its lovely gardens as engagingly "feminine"; Jaipur "joyous as a laughing girl", and so on. But Benares was burdened with the descriptive—"indescribably evil."[20] Even though many writers harbored moments of unease if not disdain for Benares, particularly its ancient ties to Hindu rites and ceremonies, the city amazed every traveler in some fashion. "One could prowl about Benares for many days. Its temples, and there are literally thousands of them, its narrow streets, with their high, overhanging houses, its spectacular river front, its shops gleaming with brass and silks . . . never cease to fascinate."[21] The temples were an especially interesting part of the traveler's itinerary. One, the Temple of Love devoted to the Hindu god Siva, was frequently referenced because of its erotic images. Travelers described small shrines laden with phallic sculptures and various forms of orgiastic imagery. To Western eyes, the sculptured scenes of bodies entangled in contorted and exotic sexual positions made for delectable bits of travel writing. Authors varied in their descriptive renderings of what they saw—some were amused and others scandalized. However they covered it, one senses that the images were a revelation, even if they had been forewarned or had witnessed similar scenes elsewhere in India. One writer commented: "the entire temple breathes pornography," a typical perception and one invested with moralistic sensibilities sure to resonate with many Western readers of the times. Even the guides were depicted as sensuous. One's description rivaled that of the sculptures, his physical features detailed in equally lascivious adjectives even if less specifically sexual than the images themselves. He was summed up as "the ideal minister for the Goddess of Sex."[22]

Benares' Monkey Temple was also frequently remarked upon. It was described as one of the largest in India, overrun with thousands of perky monkeys enjoying the run of the temple's premises and the pilgrims' largesse. Travelers would tempt them with nuts and grains, the monkeys approaching and retreating in fits and starts, ultimately scurrying off to nearby tree branches and precarious temple ledges. They could be seen as well all over the city bouncing along rooftops and scavenging amidst the gardens, verandas, and houses of Benares residents. They were left to their own devices, surprisingly so to Western observers, who seemed amazed that their irksome intrusiveness could be so easily tolerated by humans. But this was India. Such sights, although striking to many travel writers, was typically characterized as the norm. In the topsy-turvy world of India—what would be considered bizarre elsewhere was standard for a place like Benares. After all, this was the land of the sacred cow. They, like the monkeys, enjoyed the run of the city, wandering aimlessly through streets alleys, poking their heads into doorways, and mingling casually amidst the bustling crowds and activities of the city. Even the crows were sacred, hovering brazenly about travelers' feet in search of food, hardly having the symbolic stature of cows, but clearly its equal in having the run of the city. Travel writers frequently commented upon Hindu vegetarianism and its relationship to how they perceived and treated the animal world. One guide told his client that if he were so much as to eat an egg, family and friends would immediately ostracize him. Generally, authors had mixed reactions to Hindu vegetarianism, sometimes admiring the practice and its attendant laissez-faire approach to creaturely freedoms, but at others harshly critical of what they perceived to be animal neglect.[23] Cows, for example, were free to roam. But they were also free to starve in the streets no less than humans were.

Benares, in addition to being the ultimate pilgrim's site, also enjoyed a reputation for religious and educational cosmopolitanism. One writer remarked that the city served as a magnet for philosophers, theosophists, educators, and like personages who were nearly as fascinating as the city itself. While visiting Benares, he spent time with a Hindu art historian, a Hindu political theorist, a Unitarian clergyman, to name only a few. As he put it, "the manifestations of Brahma are nowhere more diverse than at Benares." To his mind, there was no place in the world quite like Benares to study religion.[24] Another author was deeply moved by what he saw and experienced in Saranath, the section of the city where Buddha had once lived and taught, and where a German Buddhist had embarked upon restoration efforts in 1932 to restore Buddhist holy sites. He found assistance, from among various sources, a wealthy Hindu who donated funds to establish a pilgrim hostel. There, among the ruins to be restored and beneath the shade of a descendant of Buddha's sacred

Bo tree—the site of his received enlightenment—travelers could experience another side of Benares' rich religious heritage. The city also housed a Hindu university. There, the author met with professors and students, enjoying tea on the lawn and shared experiences with a man who had studied under the same Oxford don back in England. He also gave a lecture to students titled "Youth, the Dictators, and the World Crisis," a timely subject of the 1930s. He was extremely impressed with the students' knowledge and lively interest in his topic and world affairs in general. The entire experience was an eye-opener into what he termed the "progressive wing of Hinduism." From there, the author moved on to a "sensational adventure" into a new temple of Mother India, where "one looks down on surely the strangest object of worship that the world can afford." The object was a huge relief map sculptured out of Italian marble, scaled perfectly to India's size and geographic features. The temple was characterized as a device to lure Hinduism's prodigal sons back to the fold—those who had wandered off in pursuit of the subcontinent's new religion—nationalism. It was seen as a progressive alternative to the pot-bellied, monkey-headed, Kali-like excesses of traditional Hinduism: an iconic feat to modernity, Hindu style. Since Hinduism's eclecticism housed many mansions, this was but one more expression of the trait. It even welcomed outcastes who were usually banned from most Hindu's temples.[25]

## NOTES

1. Madhur Jaffrey, "Stairway to Heaven," in *Travelers' Tales Guides India: True Stories of Life on the Road*, James O'Reilly and Larry Habegger, eds. (San Francisco: Travelers' Tales, 1998), 165. Benares was the name and spelling used by most travelers to India throughout most of the twentieth century and is retained for this work. It is currently spelled Banaras as well, with "Varansi" (its ancient name) having been adopted more recently. It can be found under that spelling on most contemporary Indian maps. Kashi, a name favored by the more religious, has also been used.

2. Patricia Kendall, *Come With Me to India* (New York: Charles Scribner's Sons, 1935), 321.

3. Lowell Thomas, *India: Land of the Black Pagoda* (New York: P.F. Collier & Sons, 1930), 253.

4. Agnes Rush Burr, *India: The Land That Lures* (Boston: L.C. Page & Co., 1929), 68.

5. Jaffrey, 165-66.

6. George H. Johnston, *Journey Through Tomorrow* (Melbourne: F. W. Cheshire Pty., 1947), 48-52.

7. Basil Mathews, *India Reveals Herself* (London: Oxford University Press, 1937), 69.

8. Burr, 61.

9. Louis Hagan, *Indian Route March* (New York: Pilot Press, 1946), 71.

10. Peter Hopkirk, *Quest For Kim: In Search of Kipling's Great Game* (Oxford: Oxford University Press, 1996), 107.

11. Kendall, 320-321.

12. Norah Rowan Hamilton, *Through Wonderful India and Beyond* (London: Holden & Hardingham, 1915), 194.

13. Robert Bernays, *"Naked Faquir"* (New York: Henry Holt & Co., 1932), 99, 102.

14. Charles M. Hendley, *Trifles of Travel* (New York: Rider Press, 1924), 240.

15. Aldous Huxley, *Jesting Pilate: The Diary of a Journey* (London: Chatto & Windus, 1948), 124-125.

16. Hendley, 238.

17. Hamilton, 193.

18. Burr, 71.

19. Biswajeet Banerjee, "Hindu Holy Men Threaten Ganges Boycott," *Associated Press*, January 8, 2007, http://news.yahoo.coms/a/sp/200070109/ap_on_re_as_/india_hindu_festival.

20. Hamilton, 195.

21. Burr, 73.

22. Hagan, 72.

23. Hendley, 238-240.

24. Richard Maurice Elliott, *The Sunny Side of Asia* (New York: Century Co., 1928), 167-171.

25. Basil Mathews, *India Reveals Herself* (London: Oxford University Press, 1937), 70-72.

## *Chapter Twelve*

# Calcutta, Delhi and Bombay: Urban Itineraries

The three great cities of India—Calcutta, Delhi and Bombay—frequently surfaced in travel writer accounts. Madras and other urban sites also merited comment, but they never rose to the prominence or stature of the Raj's imperial triad—urban centers that more than any others (Benares excepted) dominated writers' imaginations. For travelers, it is the great cities of the world that typically symbolize a civilization's grandeur whether a Paris, Venice, Beijing or Bangkok. In India's case, the stature of India's symbolic trio of Calcutta, Delhi and Bombay was problematically fused with Britain's, its European identity inevitably usurping the Indian one. Travel writers often noted the fact that Calcutta and Bombay were quintessentially European in origin and design, even if their bold imperial face functioned solely as grandiose foreground against the more dominant reality of their Oriental background, teeming with swarming multitudes, squalid buildings, and overwhelming poverty. Delhi, even with its *New* Delhi of British imperial grandeur, enjoyed a far richer native heritage, a city estimated to have had eight layers of civilizational legacies to boast of, extending back millenniums in time. Yet to travelers' eyes Delhi, like Bombay and Calcutta were at first blush British settlements. Typically, it was Britain's imperial presence, most visibly expressed in its architecture, that generated initial impressions. Once remarked upon, most writers would then describe their forays into the far more dense and diverse reality of their native quarters. Writers often referenced the fact that Bombay and Calcutta in particular were not the real India. That could only be found in the interior, far from imperial influence and restraints. Nonetheless, the great urban triad remained obligatory travel destinations for nearly all travel writers, particularly in this Gandhian age when the politics of a changing India was never far from their thoughts. After all, India's independence movement was spawned principally from its urban intelligentsia, even though the countryside was pulled into the movement as well, particularly with Gandhi's increasingly prominent role from 1919 onward. But, it was the cities, especially Calcutta that signified rebellion against the Raj. Moreover, it was within Bombay, Calcutta and Delhi that travel writers most consistently and conveniently found Indian politicians, intellectuals, and ordinary Indians to interview concerning questions of independence and aspirations for a nation free to chart its own future.

## CALCUTTA

Calcutta. It's very name stirs troubling images of urban chaos, poverty, and human suffering—and of course Western impulses of curiosity, repulsion, and the urge to rescue. As discussed earlier in this work, John Hutnyk's *The Rumour of Calcutta: Tourism, Charity and the Poverty of Representation*, surveys a range of images embedded firmly in the West's perception of the city; namely that it is "an overcrowded place of poverty, despair, of desperation and decline." The *rumor* of Calcutta circulates in perpetual disparagement of the city's identity, an "imperialism of meaning" as it were, lodged so deeply in Western consciousness that alternative images and realities can seldom surface with any degree of prominence. It suggests how difficult it is to challenge or reinvent the city's essentialized persona.[1] This holds true for my own experience as well. When I was a teen my father took me to see a film called *Mondo Cane* (meaning crazy or insane world), a voyeuristic documentary that toured some of the globe's most disturbing images and practices. The most memorable ones, permanently encoded in my consciousness, were images of India, particularly a scene of a brothel with caged prostitutes set out in row-like despair while roaming Indian males luridly eyed the wares. Childhood symbols of elephants, snake charmers, and the Taj Mahal were quickly displaced by *Mondo Cane's* more sensationalistic representation of India, particularly that of Calcutta which was to linger for a lifetime. A number of years later I ran across Geoffrey Moorhouse's *Calcutta* in a bookstore. I immediately purchased the book because the *rumor* of Calcutta had preceded it, and I wanted to see if the city, as characterized by Moorhouse, was as bad as its reputation suggested. It was. For reasons better known to psychologists, humans are often captivated by cataclysmic disasters, horror films, tales of human woe and the like. Moorhouse's depiction of Calcutta certainly lived up to my expectations as a gritty read, filled with the most horrific accounts of human poverty, suffering and despair—a sequel to *Mondo Cane*. What Moorehead delivered was amply reinforced by the emerging legacy of Mother Teresa's work in the city. Hutnyk, I should add, cites Moorhouse's urban biography as one of many exemplars that create and perpetuate Calcutta as *the* obscene situs of urban despair.[2]

A more recent publication about the city, Simon Winchester's edited volume *Calcutta*, offers a diverse array of writings from authors such as N.C. Chaudhuri, William Dalrymple, Gunter Grass, and inevitably, Geoffrey Moorhouse's 1971 work. Interestingly, Winchester's introduction to the volume, titled "The Scent Behind the Smell," essentially replicates much of Moorhouse's descriptive essence and tone. Its opening line, "the hot stench of the slow-decaying poor," is but a foretaste of the *rumor* of Calcutta to be recycled once again, a metropolis that Winchester characterizes as "a truly infernal city . . . .a city that has, perhaps, a more grim reputation than any other major conurbation on the face of the planet." The litany of pejorative terms and phrases continue: "sudden disaster"; "spectacular mayhem"; a city that is a "curious amalgam of the wholly delightful and the half insane"; and capped off by this opprobrium, "this dreadful, dreadful, town." To cite any more examples would find one complicit with the *rumor* enterprise; indeed, it is arguably so anyway—a perverse conundrum that travel writers frequently inhabit. To be fair, for all of Winchester's gloomy prose, he expresses a clear affection for Calcutta, its wonderful surprises, and its engaging residents. And, like so many writers on India in the past, he tells his readers that he cannot find the words to capture what he truly thinks of the city.[3]

Calcutta was founded circa 1690 (the dates vary by author) by an agent of the British East India Company in search of a permanent trading center on the Hooghly River, a large distributary of the Ganges River along India's east coast. There was a small hamlet on the site named Kalikata from which Calcutta's current name derives (Kolkata). The site has often been disparaged for its unhealthy, swamp-like conditions, but it was ideal for the fast burgeoning cotton, tea, rice and jute trading posts scattered along the river to serve Dutch, French, Prussian, Portuguese and other European trading interests. From those humble beginnings Calcutta would eventually emerge to become Britain's chief imperial city in the East. Before that stature was obtained the city's notoriety, or more precisely its *rumor*, would achieve its first mark of distinction. A local nawab (Mughal governor) named Siraj-ud-daula inherited his title in 1756 and immediately set his eyes on the rich trade the British were doing out of Calcutta. He took the city that same year with an army of 50,000 soldiers and four hundred battle elephants. By one contemporary account 146 captured Europeans were detained in a small cubicle of a room, later coined the "Black Hole of Calcutta." The following morning, only 23 were found alive. Scholars have disputed the account, suggesting that among other discrepancies the actual number incarcerated was more like 65 or 70. Nonetheless, not unlike events surrounding the Rebellion of 1857, the Black Hole incident fired European imaginations and a thirst for revenge.[4] The image of suffocating Caucasians dying horribly within the confines of the "hole" confirmed the perpetrators barbarity requiring only one response—quick action to re-take the settlement and punish the offenders. The East India Company enlisted Robert Clive for the task. He completed it within a year, shortly thereafter defeating Siraj-ud-daula not so much by military means as through secret pacts with the nawab's commanders that emasculated his forces, clearing the way for an easy victory and British domination in the region. By 1774, Calcutta, subordinating the Madras and Bombay administrations, became the chief administrative center of the East India Company. Its governor, Warren Hastings, assumed the position of governor-general of the Company's operations in India.[5] Calcutta would become the capital of the British Raj only to relinquish that role in 1911 when the government moved to New Delhi.

To travel writers in the Gandhian Age, Calcutta was indeed known as the site of Black Hole notoriety; it was at times also characterized as the infernal city of poverty and despair. But perhaps more than those identities it had the reputation of a metropolis that housed terrorists, political malcontents, and dull-minded Babus. To be sure, Calcutta laid claim to primacy of place as quintessential urban horror story, one writer remarking that it had long been known as "the Cesspool of the Orient"[6] and another summarizing it as "an evil city and a dirty one, where the rich are callous and poor are legion, a place of many gods but little godliness."[7] Yet, Calcutta was a site of fond travel recollections as well, many writers relishing its storied imperial past and its rich native bazaars, customs and peoples. Jane Tracey found it a "charming English city," focusing on its government architecture, cathedrals and churches, educational institutions and other imperial influences.[8] Her visit to Calcutta, however, much like her rail journey across India by separate train, concentrated on European quarters and sights. Maarten Matisse's travel mode was the polar opposite of Tracey's. A wanderer across India, upon arrival in Calcutta he immediately began exploring its native quarter, informing readers that it made "an extraordinary impression on me." He strolled through slums and alleys fascinated by Calcutta's colorful humanity. Women in saris, long-haired Brahmins, scurrying children, ambling water buffaloes, and much more, constituted a wonderland of astonishing variety and interest. Maarten gushed: "At every step fresh surprises greeted me. I was like a child picking flowers in a field." His upbeat account did not preclude writing about troubling images. He noted, among references to human suffering, an urdhabahu (translated as arm-raiser) whose withered arm was tied to an extended stick that prompted some to kiss his feet and others to collect the dust from his footprints, seeking spiritual solace if not reward for coming into contact with this deformed holy man.[9] Generally, however, Maarten concentrated on positive imaging, even if it reads at times as the stereotypical account of the wide-eyed Westerner mesmerized by the exotica of an Eastern urban bazaar. Gordon Sinclair's more sensationalistic *Foot-Loose in India* was more the travel account equivalent of *Mondo Cane,* focused on the odd and bizarre. He roamed Calcutta's native quarter with the rather transparent purpose of searching out the most grotesque or troubling of images to pass on to his readers. One sample was his description of a Calcutta baby brander. According to Sinclair, the baby brander tattooed an image on a baby's stomach with a red-hot needle, serving roughly fifty infants per day. Sinclair: "This probably sounds barbarous and fiendish and full of voodoo, but remember these bare-legged Bengalis shave their heads, wear war paint and crimson teeth, drive rings through their noses and sport slave bangles on their legs." Sinclair noted that the ritual was done to scare off devils and that he only saw females branded. He passed on a missionary's statement that one out of every four babies died from the ritual.[10] But Sinclair's account of the city, like most of his book, revealed the workings of the ugly travel writer of the East—Orientalism at its worst—where Calcutta's slums and India's problems were requisite fodder for constructing an essentialized "other."

Peter Pinney's characterization of Calcutta in many ways replicated that of Sinclair's but added a political dimension as well.

> The poor live on the west bank and in suburbs encircling the city center, amid festering slums and simmering hate rising regularly to a froth of riot and turmoil. Bengalis are a volatile people, and Calcutta has ever been the flashpan of Indian unrest, a barometer of coming trouble. In the stench of the unsewered alleys and rat-infested basements are born the social movements and accompanying riots of all India; cholera, typhus, and dread plague which the Bengali is wont to treat with fatalistic indifference; and here too is the seat of the outlawed Communist Party, inflaming the poor with fact and fraud against the criminal rich.[11]

Pinney's Calcutta was a hotbed of political radicalism, a sentiment that frequently surfaced in contemporary travel accounts. Basil Mathews devoted a chapter in his work to what he titled "The Bengal Cauldron." Its epicenter, according to Mathews, could be found at Calcutta University, from whence came a continuous flow of revolutionaries nursed on the writings of Mill, Burke, and others—the "British apostles of freedom." In their Indian form, Mathews saw little more than unemployed Bengali intellectuals with too much time on their hands—endlessly spouting spurious rhetoric derived from presumptuous analogies from English history. For example, one discussant suggested that there were lessons to be learned from the execution of Charles I; that perhaps aspects of that historical drama could be applied to conditions in India swirling about the *Swarjist* movement. In short, Charles' stubborn, reactionary policies towards a Parliament bent on reform and liberation from monarchial whim bore an eerie resemblance to twentieth century India. The *Swarajist* movement, contemporary stand-in for England's seventeenth century Parliament, was determined to convince the British that they were no more destined to preside over India by imperial rule than was Charles I to rule England by the guiding principle of divine right of kings. Mathews expressed alarm at the restless numbers of unemployed graduates "with nerves exasperated by the febrile atmosphere peculiar to Bengal." Clearly, he pointed out, British officialdom was faced with a serious threat. Students joined armed robber bands to fund their political movements, assassinated officials, and committed other offenses against the state in an effort to advance their cause. Mathews and others noted that the Bengal region had an "historic reputation as the home of secret societies," originating from reaction to Lord Curzon's decision to partition the province in 1905. Yet, even as Mathews expressed disdain for Calcutta's student revolutionaries, he also voiced concern for the government's practice of arresting and detaining large numbers of young men, reportedly a thousand or more in Calcutta, for periods extending into six years. Mathews believed that as subjects of the British Empire even young revolutionaries deserved better.[12] Such notions of fair play frequently surfaced in British travel writings—even from those exhibiting racist sentiments. There is a British expression, politically incorrect today, where one is admonished "to play the white man." Largely an orphan in the twenty-first century, the phrase remains a telling expression of not only imperial racism but also the burden upon the colonist to live up to British standards of justice and fair play—wherever the call should be heeded.

A Frenchman, Maurice Dekobra, was warned similarly by an Englishman from Delhi that Bengal was "the hive from which escape most of the politicians who annoy us." Sikhs had cautioned him that the Bengalese were "Big talkers! Bluffs! Degenerates!" Dekobra's expectations were inverted. Instead of finding Calcutta's Bengalese despicable rascals as he had been forewarned across the Raj, he found them to be charmers, exclaiming to his readers: "I saw them and they won me over to their cause." The negative characterizations, according to Dekobra, were to be expected when one considered the enormous diversity of the land—where so many tongues, sects and interests had collided through centuries of warfare, conquest, strife and racial and religious enmity. Thus, the *rumor* of Calcutta was dissolved—at least for this travel writer.[13] J.A. Spender likewise found Calcutta to be a hub of frenetic political activity and still "so much the center of India." Having first traveled through India fourteen years earlier, his return in 1926 presented him with numerous surprises about how the country had changed. He found Calcutta, like the rest of India, full of eager, hopeful anticipation that political change was possible. And not just for Indians. He noted that British officials, unlike before the Great War, now encouraged contact with "extremist politicians," reaching out as it were in search of some middle ground upon which they could all agree. The "extremists," by contrast, were more cautious about crossing the divide, worried, according to Spender, that they would lose favor with the *Swarajist* movement's elite.[14]

Urban identities, like people, are seldom frozen in time. Aspects of Calcutta have been resistant to changing perceptions, but others dissolve, blend, or change significantly with time. In the Age of Gandhi, Calcutta, less so than today, conjured images of the worst conditions India, indeed the world, could produce. But it was less the singular image of its present *rumor* of the globe's ultimate urban blight. The city's reputation for political agitation, for intellectual activity, for richness and diversity of culture, shared a prominent place in the Gandhian Age as well. After all, Calcutta was the city of Nobel Laureate Rabindranath Tagore, of universities, of publishing houses, of elegant palaces and government buildings, of beautiful parks and gardens, and streets buzzing with the best that an Oriental bazaar could provide. Cecil Beaton, who spent time in Calcutta during World War II, marveled at the city's electric environment, a cherished haven for soldiers on leave.

> Air Commodores, Generals, and celebrities of every kind and race spend the night at one of the overcrowded hotels or at the vast Caravanserai of Government House. Most of the men of the Fourteenth Army spend their leave here. In their bush-hats and shorts they crowd out the hostels, canteens, air-conditioned cinemas, cafes, milk-bars and "attractions along the Chowringhee." It is a thrilling experience, after years in jungle foxholes, to walk along stone pavements, to gaze up at tall jostling buildings and to sleep all night in solidly constructed edifices. After listening to the whispers of the jungle, the violent noises of the town come as a relief.[15]

Beaton marveled at Calcutta as Oriental bazaar: its junk stalls with carved ivory "by the ton"; silk kimonos embroidered with dragon lore; markets filled with second-hand furniture, including old Victorian bedheads coated with "treacly gilt"; flower stalls abundant with roses and "bundles of white daisies like clouds"; long-haired monkeys running about with "eyes like wallflowers and the dignity of saints"; and, for the British, American and Polish soldiers milling about, semi-pornographic literature stalls with titles like "Erotic Edna" or storefront signs like that in the Bow Bazaar that announced "Specialist in Wet Dreams." For Beaton, Calcutta was an "Oriental Clapham Junction." Everyone and everything seem to converge upon its throbbing streets and exotic array of beckoning goods and activities. Yet, Beaton, like others, was fully cognizant of Calcutta's dark side. He related to his readers that one could not walk about without "encountering the most shocking objects, the poor starved people lying dead and dying in every street and road." Beaton wondered how such masses of people did not suddenly rise up and assault the city's houses or go-downs, pilfering at will to satisfy their pangs of hunger. But Beaton believed that such was the Indian nature, gentle and stoic, resigning itself to an inevitable fate, accepting death without protest. Only an "absolute Bonapartist," Beaton contended, could witness such horrific scenes without desiring to somehow alter Calcutta's wrenching suffering and poverty.[16]

To some, the war clearly revived Calcutta's fortunes. Perched on the east side of the subcontinent in much closer proximity to the Burmese theater and other Japanese occupation sites than other Indian cities, Calcutta regained its preeminence, momentarily, as *a* center of Empire if not *the* center of Britain's flagging imperial domain. But, as the war ended and independence loomed shortly on the horizon, the focus shifted back to Delhi. Calcutta was increasingly viewed as a decaying remnant of an earlier age, retaining that image into the twenty-first century. Shashi Tharoor, author of a recent work chronicling India's progression from independence to its current status as an emerging superpower, contends that India, in the words of E.P. Thompson, "is the most important country for the future of the world" because it serves as the quintessential exemplar of the four central issues facing the globe at the turn of millennium. But, Calcutta, in his estimation, "has become a backwater . . . for all its achievements, Calcutta has been reduced to a provincial capital." It is now a "second-rate Bombay" of diminishing commercial, political and intellectual importance. Tharoor recalls another Calcutta of his youth, when he moved there with his parents from Bombay as a twelve-year old in 1968. The city was, perhaps more by adolescent reminisce than actual realty, a place "that still had the lingering aura of the former First City of the British Empire," an urban site buzzing with commercial vitality, intellectual discourse, and diverse forms of entertainment, including India's first disco. But today's Calcutta, according to Tharoor, has been "overshadowed by power cuts, poverty, potholes, pavement-dwellers, political violence, paralyzed industry."[17]

Thus, the *rumor* of Calcutta lives on. Tharoor, like others, cite the role Dominique Lapierre's 1986 novel, *City of Joy*, has played in sustaining the city's image as a site of desperation and despair. The book was made into a film of the same name by Director Roland Joffre, starring Patrick Swayze. It generated a host of rabid protests that included everything from stinging editorials to book burnings to lawsuits—even one incident where a bomb was heaved at the set. According to Tharoor, for many the film insured that "Calcutta will become the favorite pinup of the pornographers of poverty. Westerners are going to munch popcorn in air-conditioned theaters as they stare at flickering images of dying Indian babies." Tharoor notes that *City of Joy* reminds him of Mahatma Gandhi's 1920s reference to Katherine Mayo's *Mother India* as "a drain-inspector's report," covered earlier in this work. Tharoor laments *City of Joy's* Western voyeurism of India's poverty and despair, but takes the position that such is the necessity of artistic freedom, that sentiments bellowing "this is *our* poverty, *you* can't depict it," is trumped by larger considerations than efforts at image-control by Third World protectionists, even if their outrage is perfectly understandable.[18]

## DELHI

In 1911 India's capital was moved from Calcutta to Delhi—a twenty-four hour train ride to the northwest. Delhi was steeped in Indian history, a natural site for re-invigorating imperial rule, even if, as some surmised, transferring the capitol to Delhi was as well a natural demise for the Raj since it had been the graveyard for many of the subcontinent's imperial reigns. Thus, the reasoning went, the Raj was simply moving there to meet its imminent and fated end—as seven previous capitals had reaching back into the deep mists of Indian history. For Delhi was a museum of imperial memorabilia dating back millenniums. Its most recent pre-Raj legacy was that of the Mughals, who like many invaders from the west, could not resist the city's wealth and fortified position along the banks of the Jumna River, seizing Delhi and launching its rule in 1526.[19]

To Western travelers, Delhi was the "Hindu Versailles." It was the capital of the "Vice-Roi Soleil" who presided over the British army, the Raj's administrative apparatus, and where the hosts of maharajahs, rajahs, nawabs, nizams, emirs, and other assorted Indian dignitaries came to court, as it were, in Versailles-like homage to courtly power. Delhi was graced with magnificent forts and other architectural splendors to go with its lovely gardens, impressive boulevards, and exotic bazaars.[20] It was for many Gandhian Age travelers their favorite city, but not necessarily the one most written about. Jane Tracy, in one of her many private train stopovers across India, wrote, "Delhi had long been anticipated (by her group) as one of India's richest treats." And it was more than just government buildings and ruins. The city was alive and bursting with exotic sights and happenings. Among several guided tours through the city, she and her entourage were taken to Delhi's great mosque, reputedly the largest in the world. They observed thousands of worshippers from the private box of a Maharajah. Tracy remarked to her readers: "it was an astounding thought to me that this service was taking place all over the Mohammedan world the same day, the same hour." She also attended a Muslim wedding. She marveled at the filmy gauze of colorful gowns and jewels dangling discreetly but beautifully about the female guests, the exotic ceremony, the snacking on nuts, cardamon seeds, tea, and small cakes while they waited for the event to commence. Tracy and her friends, dressed in Western attire, marveled as well at the casual manner in which guests approached them to examine their clothing, checking beneath their skirts looking for jeweled anklets and "handling our person as they pleased."[21]

Yet, for all of the exotica of local customs, it was the British imperial New Delhi that was most often the focus of traveler perceptions. It was approximately three miles from the old city. The route from old to new could be traveled down a long avenue lined with newly planted trees and electric light posts, which Maurice Dekobra quipped was "the Sacred Way of the English conquest." Nearby were numerous palatial residences of India's princely elite that dwarfed in style and wealth any counterparts in New York, London or Paris. Dekobra noted that when a session of the House of Princes opened, "the quarter of the rajahs of New Delhi will be a field of gold and pearls and sapphires." Nearby as well were the elegant bungalows of British high functionaries.[22] All in all, New Delhi, although seemingly always under construction, was clearly meant to impress residents and visitors alike that its stately government buildings, grand residences, and beautifully coiffed landscaping constituted an imperial order that would more than rival in time and grandeur those which had preceded it.

The British imperial city was dominated by three government structures: the Legislative Building, the Secretariat, and the Government House. They were constructed of local red sandstone, blending indigenous elements with British design in a landscape littered with Indo-Saracenic monuments to past empires—what Lord Curzon had called "deserted cities of dreary and desolate tombs." Old Delhi formed a dramatic, Rome-like backdrop to the Raj's nouveau imperial structures, lending historic depth to an otherwise presumptuous Western upstart—piling on one more civilizational center to the many layers that preceded it. One historic landmark, the great Fort from the days of Mughal emperors, was one of the city's most imposing structure, rivaling its cousin in Agra. Its impressive gateways, vaulted arcades, graceful courtyards, emerald lawns, and decorative shrubbery were evidence of a time when princes and dignitaries of an earlier magnificence were the equal of India's British imperial rule. Delhi's extensive environs were no less complemented by cities, palaces, temples, mosques and tombs of the past so that "almost wherever the eye lights are domes, cupolas, arches, columns" scattered about in whole or in fragments, remnants of a past that now served as an open-air museum for curious travelers.[23]

Not all travelers found New Delhi to their liking. Peter Pinney viewed it as a flamboyant expression of "frustrated Westernism . . . a spreading and ornate metropolis, a gilt-edged paradox where one might be in Washington or Canberra, but surely not in the capital of India."[24] Maarten Matisse, a Dutchman writing in the 1930s, was no less cynical of its intrusion upon Indian soil: "in the midst of this miraculous chaos of Eastern structures and ruins, the British have built a massive, ungainly parliament building, a monument to ugliness for centuries to come that will bear witness against them when the murder of Amritsar and the imprisonment of Gandhi have long been forgotten." Matisse was a harsh critic of British rule. From their initial coastal conquests to their divide and rule tactics in taming the interior, Matisse told his readers that British rule had been one long epoch of misrule. The Mutiny of 1857? It was provoked by the East India Company's policies. The Company's successor, the British crown? It generously produced a series of famines decimating the lives of millions of Indians, each year listed by Matisse in numerical series for dramatic effect. To push his point further, Matisse related a conversation he had with a Delhi beggar, one claiming to be a descendant of the Mughals that the British had usurped. Matisse queried to his readers: "somewhere in this immeasurable land, after all, descendants of the great emperors must still be living—why not he?" Matisse threw him a few coins in pity, contrasting his fallen state against the "fairy princes of my youthful dreams" whose luxurious palaces, elegant tombs, and powerful rulers were now eclipsed by the ugliness of the Raj.[25] Matisse was of the traveler breed that came to India searching for spiritual meaning and life alternatives. They seldom had use for Western influences, often viewing them as intrusive transgressions of all that was sacred in India.

William Dalrymple, author of a recent impressionistic study of Delhi titled *City of Djinns,* and a far more insightful and measured observer than Matisse, has suggested that Edward Luytens magnificent Rome-like creation in the new city was perhaps most reminiscent of Nuremberg than any other architectural legacy. He describes how this revelation seized him one evening while strolling about its environs: "with this great imperial mass of masonry towering all around me I suddenly realized where I had seen something similar, something equally vast, equally dwarfing, before: Nuremberg." Acknowledging the considerable differences between Luytens talent to that of Albert Speer, of the Third Reich to that of the Raj, Dalrymple nonetheless contends, "Imperial India, Fascist Italy and Nazi Germany all belonged to comparable worlds. All were to different extents authoritarian; all made much of magnificent display; all were built on a myth of racial superiority and buttressed in the last resort by force."[26] It's a stunning comparison. Many would argue it is an unfair one given the extraordinary excesses of the Third Reich, the hallow pomposity of Mussolini's Italy, and the broader perception that perhaps all empires are built on myth, display, force, and in variant forms, racial if not religious superiority. Yet, from one side of the imperial divide, particularly that of the *Swarajists*, the Raj and its last great imperial enterprise, New Delhi, were but a more genteel variation of the German experiment in Europe. From the other side of the divide, one thinks of the haunting observation, one that repeatedly surfaced in books and conversations in the twentieth century: would Gandhi have been able to pull off his independence movement if the Third Reich were in power in India, not the Raj? In short, would Gandhi have been quickly eliminated before his name ever reached the crescendo of devotion and fame that it eventually attained? Probably not. Which proves little; it only demonstrates how endless the debate has been and will be regarding the legacy of Britain's imperial order in India.

There is an elegant nod to Delhi in the prologue of William Dalrymple's book, inspired by his first encounter with the city when he was seventeen years of age, and one reminiscent of the sometimes luxuriant forms of travel expression that travel writers in the Age of Gandhi frequently indulged in. It bears repeating here because it captures Delhi so well, transcending historical epochs, and serves as a reminder of why we travel:

> From the very beginning I was mesmerized by the great capital, so totally unlike anything I had ever seen before. Delhi, it seemed at first, was full of riches and horrors: it was a labyrinth, a city of palaces, an open gutter, filtered light through a filigree lattice, a landscape of domes, an anarchy, a press of people, a choke of fumes, a whiff of spices.[27]

These words could serve to capture India in general, not just Delhi. But Delhi had its own particular urban identity. It was a specifically imperial one, suggestive of empires come and gone, and perhaps of a new one, an eighth one, emerging as India lunges towards major power status in the twenty-first century. Shashi Tharoor, comparing Calcutta to Delhi, suggests that today the capitol's inhabitants represent the city as being unlike the rest of India, that it is a successful urban experiment that points to a new era, where graceful late-colonial architecture and broad, expansive boulevards dwell amidst new highways and tourist hotels, a complementary fusion of new and old emblematic of what a great world capitol should be. But Tharoor also suggests that there is a dark side to the equation, that in Delhi's new-found celebration as a rising model of twenty-first century power and wealth, that it "has lost its soul," that it is "the epitome of a new concrete culture of 'black money' and five-star hotels divorced from tradition, the arts, or the refinements of the higher life"—qualities that residents of Calcutta assure others remain in abundance in their great city to the east. Tharoor notes that such culture wars, those that pit historic nostalgia against the rise of new societal forces, is nothing new, that it echoes debates circulated in the Magadhan-Mauryan period from the sixth to third centuries B.C.[28] And it circulated freely among travel writers in the Gandhian Age as well. Some yearned for a timeless India, one where the intrusions of modernity and the tentacles of the Raj would remain forever distant, leaving the traveler with an oriental dreamscape in which to journey, absorb and describe. Many others, however, were fascinated at this particular historical junction where old and new clashed, where democratic political ideals and technological progress could be tested outside of European influence and control; whether "Peter Pan" India was up to the challenge of a new societal vision, and if so, what form it would take. Delhi, more than any other city in India, represented this historical junction. Its storied past and its newly minted imperial present clashed with dreams and aspirations of a future India retentive of its religious and cultural traditions, but surging forward with the democratic ideals of a new age.

## BOMBAY

For most travel writers, Bombay was all light and color and a most curious yet satisfying mélange of orient and occident. As the gateway to India, particularly after the Suez Canal opened in 1869, cutting the distance from London to India in half, Bombay was often the tourist or traveler's first exposure to India. Cecil Beaton described it as "less artificial than Delhi, less dirty than Calcutta, beautifully situated on the sea."[29] Indeed, the city's legacy as a cosmopolitan port had defined its identity, as least for visitors, for many centuries. As far back as the third century B.C. the West had encountered Bombay, naming it Heptanesia, a reference to a group of seven islands that later were fused to the mainland as the site expanded and grew. The Portuguese arrived in the sixteenth century, much impressed by the bay's beauty, designating it Bom Bahia or "Good Bay," from which it longstanding name Bombay derives.[30] The British assumed control a century later, having received it in a royal transaction between Portugal and England's Charles I. The city's second governor, Gerald Aungier, was responsible for igniting a population surge borne of sponsored commercial ventures and other deliberate efforts to grow the city to prominence. Augnier was also responsible for ceding land to the Parsees on Bombay's Malabar Hill, a contributing factor to their emergent role as a dynamic player in the city's commercial life and as a prominent fixture of Bombay society. As cited earlier, the Parsees emigrated to India from Persia, fleeing Muslim persecution in the wake of Islamic conquests in West Asia twelve centuries before. As discussed further below, a part of Malabar

Hill became the location for the famed Towers of Silence, the site of Parsee burial ceremonies that so many travelers sought out and covered in their travel accounts.[31]

Travel writers have the quirky trait of designating foreign cities as analogous exemplars of urban locales back home. Thus, to American writer Patricia Kendall, Bombay is "Chicago on the Arabian Sea"[32]; to Englishman Robert Bernays, it is "the Piccadilly Circus of India" because for a traveler in India "everybody worth meeting could be found there." Bernays told his readers, "if I had to live in India, it would be Bombay that I would choose." Compared to other cities in the Raj, he found it most reminiscent of Europe and far less provincial in its sensibilities. Bernays relished the fact that to his mind Bombay conversation was about substance rather than the customary expatriate gossip about one's neighbors.[33] And Bombay lent the appearance of being a metropolis on the move with its busy harbor laden with ships from about the world, wharves piled up with every variety of goods, and its large assortment of indigenously-manned vessels or large fleet moored at the local Bombay yacht club. The city's dramatic imperial arch graced the harbor's approach, lending substance to the characterization that Bombay was the "gateway" or "front door" to the subcontinent, not unlike, according to one author, the Arc de Triomphe's as entryway into the city of Paris.[34] The arch was the official landing spot for imperial officials, built to commemorate the royal durbar of 1911 when King George V and Queen Mary passed through a temporarily constructed mock cardboard and pastiche structure while en route to Delhi. The arch of honey-colored basalt was not completed until 1924, but once erected it became for travelers the city's dominant architectural icon. The Taj Mahal Hotel, situated nearby, also faced the harbor, commanding a stunning view of the sea and, dependent upon the traveler's aesthetic tastes, lending an imposing grandeur to the city's image. Aldous Huxley described its architectural character as a combination of "South Kensington Natural History Museum with that of an Indian pavilion at an International Exhibition."[35] It was built in 1903 by a Parsee industrialist, Jamshedji Tat, who, as the story went, determined to build his own hotel because he was refused entrance into the "White Only" Watson's Hotel—an establishment now long since closed.[36] In John Murray's 1933 *A Handbook for Travelers in India, Burma and Ceylon,* a promotional slot for the hotel boasted of 30 private suites, 350 double and single rooms, complete with all the modern conveniences, including electric fans, lights, clocks and telephones. Dinner and cocktail dances (three dance floors totaling 5,200 square feet), cabaret performances, classical concerts—even miniature golf was provided. Moreover, tailors, outfitters, jewelers, hairdressers, chemists, and railway book offices were all on call to accommodate travelers.[37] No wonder that Bombay's harbor, both as to its spectacular bay and portside grandeur, bustle and amenities, appealed to Western visitors. Eye-popping vistas were complemented with the familiar and exotic—a combination few travelers could resist. Patricia Kendall's description of the city's visual image was representative of various travel accounts:

> Color and commerce are two impinging impressions of this seething metropolis. Extraordinarily broad boulevards and spacious squares lined with imposing government buildings of Gothic architecture, massive, modern shops and clubs of Western design; congested thoroughfares teeming with luxurious Rolls-Royces and Packards intermixed with trucks (mostly Chevrolets) and brightly painted carts drawn by hump-shouldered bullocks, donkeys laden with huge loads or ridden by Mohammedan ladies enveloped in sack-like robes that cover them from head to foot with small veiled squares for their eyes; native traffic policemen clearing a one-way street for the bodyguard of the governor, giant Sikhs and Punjabi Mussulmans magnificent in crimson uniforms and towering turbans; smart-frocked Englishwomen coming out of "Liberty's" or other British shops or French "magasins" which are duplicates in buildings and in wares of their London and Parisian prototypes.[38]

Not everyone appreciated Bombay's architectural reputation, mostly Western, that graced the city's European quarter. Aldous Huxley relayed to his readers that "architecturally, Bombay is one of the most appalling cities of either hemisphere." Most of the city's public buildings were designed and constructed between 1860 and 1900, a fact to which Huxley quipped, "it is hardly necessary for me to expatiate or comment." Clearly, Huxley was no fan of Britain's late nineteenth century Gothic revival. Working through the local guidebook with his readers, he ticked off a list of various neo-Gothic structures, implying *ipso facto* that their medieval character was garishly awkward, redeemed only by certain buildings that incorporated some eastern elements to them. However, the Georgian Town Hall was an exception, exuding "an air of calm and quiet decency." Huxley stated further that its grace and dignity was a welcome sight "among so many architectural cads and pretentious bounders; it is almost the only gentleman. In Bombay, it seems as good as the Parthenon."[39] As for the villas of the rich on Malabar Hill, Maurice Dekobra, like Huxley's abhorrence of neo-Gothic structures, had little use for the architectural pretensions of their grand houses, built largely between 1870-1890. Dekobra's described them in the most disparaging of terms:

> Enlarge a hundred times or more the tiny feudal castle moulded in grease by an artistic pork butcher or, if it suits you better, the white, pink and yellow wedding cake designed by a pastry cook who is clever at manipulating nougat, cream and colouring matter, and you'll have a life-sized picture of the pretentious residence of a gentleman of Malabar Hill who has made a fortune in cotton or pearls.[40]

If travelers could not agree on Bombay's architectural qualities, most all expressed affection for the city's markets, particularly those set back into the interiors of Bombay's native quarters. According to one writer, Bombay had "the best native market in all India." Along with every type of commodity, one could find "every grade of humanity in that part of the world, not to mention numerous examples from other worlds."[41] Bombay more than other India cities tended to elicit positive reactions. Even descriptions of the native districts of the city tended to emphasize the positive, even when India's legendary poverty surfaced in the accounts. Eugene Wright, commented that upon entering Bombay, "India began to grow upon me." His Bombay tour was focused largely upon non-European sectors of the city. He roamed Bombay's native quarter for five days losing himself amidst the snake charmers, fortune tellers, beggars, bird-vendors, fascinated by the exotic bustle of India's street life.[42] For Agnes Burr, the streets of Bombay's native quarters were "enchanting." In her travel memoir of India, she recalled sections of the city in beguiling terms, much like the title of her book, *India, The Land That Lures*, suggested:

> Pale-green houses lean across narrow thorofares toward soft creamy ones. Blue domiciles are friendly with brown. Balconies, some daintily carved, projecting windows, house-tops high and house-tops low, lure the eyes upward, while below bob a million, one would think, of turbaned heads in white and yellow and red and green, like an animated flower garden. Saris are hung on balconies. Long pieces of cloth that have been dyed float in the air like banners, red, delicate blue, lavender. There is no order or neatness. Our good housekeepers would probably sniff at the disorder—and the smells. But there is color, glorious color everywhere.[43]

Although Bombay was noted for its ethnic and religious diversity, one sector of the city's multicultural character—the Parsees—dominated travelers' perception of the city. Their numbers varied, but were generally estimated to be about 60,000 strong, a small number when pitted against the city's projected population of one million. However, Parsee influence far exceeded their modest numbers, for they dominated much of the native population's business scene and were generally well-regarded by the British community in Bombay, and in turn, were strong supporters of British rule in India—even if the British never invited them into their homes. One writer went so far as to claim that "every public hospital, charitable institution, notable statue and drinking fountain is traced to their benefaction,"[44] a perhaps dubious exaggeration, but nonetheless suggestive of Parsee prominence in the city. But it was the ghoulish rituals of the Towers of Silence that most attracted travel writers (and tourists) to Parsee culture. No trip to Bombay was complete without a visit to the Towers. They were grouped in clustered prominence on the top of Malabar Hill, built within a park-like enclosure that housed a fire temple where religious services were conducted prior to placing a decedent in the Tower where the body was devoured by an eagerly awaiting band of vultures. The image of the beady-eyed vulture, lustily anticipating its meal of human flesh, was especially chilling to writers. This excerpt captures both the curiosity and repulsion of many writers:

> The cortege approached. The body, carried by four men dressed in white and wearing white skull caps, passed through the trees. The birds of prey soon became agitated. The ceremony was about to commence. Twenty minutes later the dead man was devoured. Only a skeleton remained. The most cunning of the vultures ate the choice morsels: the eyes, the nostrils and viscera. The rest contented themselves with the muscles and the tendons. In twenty-four hours—so my companion told me—the terrific sun would have dried the bones completely and the *de cujus,* safe in the birds' stomachs, would have regained the sidereal ether, the waiting room of Zoroaster's Paradise.[45]

As another writer queried, "the process is not pleasant to contemplate; but is it one whit worse than slowly to have one's flesh changed into a subsoil worm?"[46]

There was more to Bombay's image than its lovely harbor, architectural splendors, and colorful markets. Unlike Calcutta it was not caricatured as a hotbed of nationalist conspiracies and terrorists; however, a few writers saw Bombay in much the same terms. Patricia Kendall, so easily repulsed by things Indian, characterized Bombay as a "cauldron of clashing political interests." She saw the Swarajists, Nationalists, Unionists and Communists (described as closely tied to Moscow) as all competing for political control, Bombay being the center of party strife in India. Kendall wrote her travel account in the mid-thirties, thus her reference to Bombay as a "composite Madrid and Moscow." She concluded her comments on Bombay with this most appalling racist remark: "built by the brains and brawn of the Occident, Bombay vibrates with the blood and breath of the Orient."[47]

Today, Bombay continues to fascinate foreigners and Indians alike. To explore its current state, venture a read of Suketu Mehta's *Maximum City: Bombay Lost and Found*. It is an extraordinary look at the city's complex mix of radical politicians, organized crime bosses, callous hit men, colorful Bollywood characters, to name only a few, to go with the city's seemingly insolvable social, political, and infra-structure problems. Suketu was born, in his words, "in a city of extremis, Calcutta." He then moved to Bombay for nine years, to the U.S. and Europe for several decades, before returning to Bombay to do a contemporary study of the city. Mehta asserts that Bombay is the largest city on the planet, and if "Bombay is the future of urban civilization on the planet—God help us." In short, Bombay is the quintessential "urban catastrophe."[48] But beneath the catastrophic debris is a city teeming with vibrant human aspirations and activity, a kaleidoscope, as Gandhian travel writers would characterize it, of wondrous, colorful and ever-changing physical and human variety. Mehta's book at first blush reminds one of John Hutnyk's *The Rumour of Calcutta*, a study of Calcutta's caricature in inescapably wretched terms. But Mehta's work, in spite of its sometimes shocking and bleak character, is written by an expatriate Indian—one whose deep affection for the city never wanes regardless of what he sees and experiences. Somehow, like travelers who wrote of Bombay in the first half of the twentieth century, the city escapes the *rumor* of being the ultimate urban hell-hole, lifted perhaps by its Bollywood image, seaside magnificence, and vibrant hopes for a better future in spite of much evidence to the contrary.

If Calcutta was India's storm-center and quintessential urban cesspool, and if Delhi was a fated British Versailles or pretentious Graceland awaiting its demise amidst glorious historic ruins, then Bombay was in the Gandhian era, much like today, a seaside wonder of exquisite beauty and kaleidoscopic diversity—a site where dreams and hopes could be realized—even by society's dispossessed. Whether such perceptions conformed to reality is a different question. Closer observation revealed that Bombay, in terms of poverty and human suffering—then and now—differed little from Calcutta. Ranjee Shahani, an expatriate Indian returning to his homeland in the 1930's, remarked upon arriving portside that he immediately recognized the "Bombay-smell—dull, noxious, clinging, like a coffin by your side." Yet, the next morning Shahani was off to Bombay's bazaars and his writing style immediately shifted from one suggesting the *rumor* of India to one bursting with rapturous, almost tourist-like wonder at the colorful human characters and goods of the crowded squares and streets of the city.[49] Traveler descriptions and opinions, for better or worse, are frequently uneven if not distorted recollections, dictated more often by compelling motivations to construct images of color, distinction and contrast rather than by a desire to render accurate characterization. Nonetheless, how does one ever describe, accurately, the essence of a place? Whatever can be quantified or empirically written about a locale is usually subsumed by impressionistic renditions where certain images surface to the obscurity of others. Most Gandhian Age accounts portrayed much of what was true about Calcutta, Delhi and Bombay, even if frequently accompanied by editorial flourish, if not excess. And there is much evidence that travel writers constructed their accounts on writings and word of mouth information that preceded their own works. Add to that the issue of selective inclusions and omissions, inevitable in any writing project, and one has the making of a flawed travel account. But that is arguably what makes travel writing such a unique and pleasurable genre. Its unpredictable nature, perhaps essential to its enterprise, mirrors expectations of the journey itself—both as to the writer and reader. In spite of its deficiencies, something wonderful is wrought. One has to sift through, discerningly, in recognition of a book's limitations, but armchair travel accounts do bring the world to people. Calcutta, Delhi and Bombay inevitably looked and felt different to Western travel writers than they did to native residents, but such are the diverse perceptions generated by complicated and profound cultural differences, making consensus as to what constitutes the *real* nature of a place impossible to achieve. Travel writers can never capture the true essence of a place, because everyone turns the kaleidoscopic wheel to slightly different angles, altering images of a Calcutta, Delhi, Bombay—or any other Indian site to the patterns and colors selected by the viewer. Nonetheless, much of the essence is conveyed and perhaps *caught*—even if inevitably problematic.

## NOTES

1. John Hutynk, *The Rumour of Calcutta: Tourism, Charity, and the Poverty of Representation* (London: Zed Books, 1996), vii, 32.
2. Ibid, 9.
3. Simon Winchester, ed., *Calcutta* (Oakland: Lonely Planet Publications, 2004), 11-19.
4. Ibid, 31-40.
5. John Keay, *India: A History* (New York: Grove Press, 2000), 389-391, 393.
6. George H. Johnston, *Journey Through Tomorrow* (Melbourne: F.W. Cheshire Pty., 1947), 72.
7. Peter Pinney, *Dust on My Shoes* (New York: Bobbs-Merrill Co., 1951), 267.
8. Jane A. Tracy, *See India With Me* (Boston: Stratford Co., 1928), 192-196.
9. Maarten Matisse, *Wanderer from Sea to Sea* (New York: Harcourt, Brace and Co., 1936), 30-32.
10. Gordon Sinclair, *Foot-Loose in India* (New York: Farrar & Rinehart, 1933), 256.
11. Pinney, 267.
12. Basil Mathews, *India Reveals Herself* (London: Oxford University Press, 1937), 78-79.
13. Maurice Dekobra, *The Perfumed Tigers: Adventures in the Land of the Maharajahs* (Oxford: Brewer and Warren, 1930), 244, 255.
14. J.A. Spender, *The Changing East* (London: Casell & Co., 1926), 105-109.
15. Cecil Beaton, *Far East* (London: B.T. Batsford, Ltd., 1945), 15.
16. Ibid, 14-15.
17. Shashi Tharoor, *India: From Midnight to the Millennium* (New York: Arcade Publishing, 1997) 3-4, 308-309. Tharoor characterizes turn of the century debates as

"the bread-versus- freedom debate; the centralization-versus-federalism debate; the pluralism-versus-fundamentalism debate; and the Coca-colonization debate, or globalism versus self-reliance."

18. Ibid, 314-317.

19. Patricia Kendall, *Come With Me to India* (New York: Charles Scribner's Sons, 1935), 308-309.

20. Dekobra, 255.

21. Tracy, 115-117, 126,127.

22. Dekobra, 255-257.

23. Agnes Rush Burr, *India: The Land That Lures* (Boston: L.C. Page & Co., 1929), 133, 135, 145.

24. Pinney, 266.

25. Matisse, 277-299.

26. William Dalrymple, *City of Djinns: A Year in India* (New York: Penguin Books, 1993), 82-83.

27. Ibid, 7-8.

28. Tharoor, 310-311.

29. Beaton, 21.

30. Homi J. H. Taleyarkhan, *Roads to Beauty Around Bombay* (Bombay: Popular Book Depot, 1953), 11.

31. *India: A Reprint of the Special Number of 'The Times,'* (London: London Times, 1930), 175.

32. Kendall, 296.

33. Bernays, 273.

34. Charles Hendley, *Trifles of Travel* (New York: Rider Press, 1924), 268.

35. Aldous Huxley, *Jesting Pilate: The Diary of a Journey* (London: Chatto & Windus, 1948), 9.

36. *Eye Witness Travel Guides: India* (London: DK Publishing, 2002), 446.

37. Murray's Indian Handbook, *A Handbook for Travelers in India, Burma and Ceylon*, 14th ed. (London: John Murray, 1933).

38. Kendall, 296-297.

39. Huxley, 8-9.

40. Dekobra, 27.

41. Albert Farwell Bemis, *A Journey to India, 1921-1922* (Boston: Privately Printed, 1923), 29.

42. Eugene Wright, *The Great Horn Spoon* (Indianapolis: Bobbs-Merrill Co., n.d.), 62.

43. Burr, 186.

44. Tracy, 12.

45. Dekobra, 29.

46. Bemis, 32.

47. Kendall, 301.

48. Suketu Mehta, *Maximum City: Bombay Found and Lost* (New York: Alfred A Knopf, 2005), 3.

49. Ranjee G. Shahani, *Indian Pilgrimage* (London: Michael Joseph, 1939), 35.

## *Chapter Thirteen*

# Princely States and Pauper Villages

Paul Bowles, the distinguished American novelist, once remarked, "It is better to go to the villages of a strange land before trying to understand its towns, above all in a complex place like India."[1] This observation was common currency among travel writers in India during the Gandhian Age. Many may have focused their accounts on urban sites, issues of independence, and controversial social and cultural questions, but most yielded to the notion that the *real* India existed outside of the cities and beyond the reach of Western influence. This was equally true of the Princely States, that vast quilt of 562 kingdoms or principalities comprising forty percent of India's land mass and approximately 80,000,000 of its population. The Princely States were ruled by hereditary princes, who if Hindu or Sikh held the title Maharaja or Raja, if Muslim Nizam or Nawab. In some instances a ruler of one religious persuasion would reign over a population made up of largely another. The Princes ruled their territories essentially free of British control. They administered separate civil and criminal legal systems, civil services, tax and customs agencies, and were allowed to establish and maintain military forces of up to eight or nine regiments. They had direct access to the British Viceroy, in part through the Chamber of Princes, a type of House of Lords that met annually in Delhi, presided over by the Viceroy to engage issues of common interest to the States, including their relations with the Raj.

From time to time a Prince was removed for criminal conduct, financial mismanagement, or unusually harsh rule; the reign then passed on to another member of the ruling family. If a minor, a British Resident, the eyes and ears of the Raj, would serve as regent until the youth attained the age of majority. Such Residents had varying powers, but usually functioned chiefly as advisers, depending upon the specific arrangement the State had with the Raj and other considerations. It should be added that the States enjoyed the same status in the League of Nations as that of British India, but matters of external diplomacy and defense remained in the hands of the British.[2] Moreover, the Princes were restricted in other ways. Unless they first obtained the Viceroy's consent, the Princes were not allowed to travel outside of India, appoint foreign advisers, or name their successor. One Briton commented that the Prince's status in India was not unlike that of a young married man who shares a bungalow with his mother-in-law. She, "as sweet as honey and attentive as the devil," oversees the household, scrutinizes its checking accounts, and ensures that all is run properly, but does so most casually, as if she were a disinterested guest. By analogy, the British Resident was the Prince's mother-in-law, a genteel but omnipresent inhabitant of the Prince's court, keeping tabs on the kingdom's ways.[3]

Britain's relationship to the Princely States was constructed principally from parallel conceptions of "class," or "caste," as it were, where Britain's aristocratic traditions found remarkable commonality among India's hereditary elites. Thus, the Princely States with their rajas, maharajas, nawabs, and nizams represented a roughly equivalent aristocratic structure to that found in Britain with its dukes, marquesses, earls, viscounts, barons, and so forth. Moreover, British monarchs stood in for the vanished Mughal emperors, retaining the imperial banner but in Western form. The British found this elitist landscape a most compatible setting in which to promote their imperial ambitions, supporting indigenous rulers, permitting local sovereignties, and gracing their efforts with innumerable social functions and events to fuel and celebrate the symbiotic character of the Raj's system of correspondent elites.[4] Yet however chummy this system appeared to be on the surface there was a huge divide between the two realms. No one doubted that the real power in India remained in the hands of the British. Moreover, it was becoming increasingly evident that emerging democratic sensibilities would eventually turn the Princely States into obsolete relics of India's past.

A number of travel writers of the age visited the Princely States, hopeful that they might locate something of the *real* India they sought to discover. Richard Pym, an American journalist who traveled extensively throughout India in the late 1920's, noted how different the Princely States were from that of British India. There was no white Gandhian cap of the cities, the people were friendlier, the bazaars were cheaper, and in Pym's opinion, many of the towns were cleaner and more ably administered than those in British-run sectors. This was a common sentiment among Western travelers. They marveled at the States' distinctively Indian atmosphere, the glitter and wealth of their palaces, and the progressive infrastructure advances, particularly irrigation projects that laced the countryside. Some states, like Hyderabad in southeast

India, were large territorial realms. Hyderabad had square mileage equal to that of England and Scotland (some writers used Italy as the example) and a population comparable to that of Ireland or Belgium. Others were more reminiscent of old landed estates in Europe, relatively small in size, comprised of a palace hub and a cluster of local villages. The States possessed varying degrees of sovereignty; some having nearly absolute power over their subjects, others constrained by limited powers of self-rule. Pym and others contended that the most salient feature of their rule was their "intensely personal quality." That attribute, for some writers, led them to believe that many of the Princely States were fundamentally more democratic than British India because the exercise of power was more direct, immediate, and responsive to the interests of the States' subjects. Thus, as was true in many of the larger States, Indian princes abolished child-marriage while the British waffled on the issue for political reasons. Free and compulsory education was also instituted in numerous states. Travancore, that "great feminist State of India" according to Pym, enjoyed a constitutional system far superior to anything that existed in British India. Women could vote, manage their own affairs, and be employed in the State's civil service. To Pym's mind, the British knew very little about the Princely States, even the larger, more prominent ones like Hyderabad. What they did know was skewered by rumors of scandal, Hindu nationalist propaganda (Hyderabad, for example, was ruled by a Muslim prince with a majority Hindu population), and presumptions of exaggerated wealth set against a sea of impoverished subjects. Pym characterized Hyderabad as a "constitutional autocracy," combining the Nizam's absolute veto power over legislative actions with that of enlightened and benevolent rule. Among other examples, Pym cited two administrative experiments conducted in Hyderabad during the 1920's, one concerning financial management of the State's resources, the other heralding its impressive educational reforms.[5]

Cecil Beaton, the artist, remarked that Hyderabad's streets, in contrast to those in other Indian cities, were "extraordinarily clean and sweet smelling."[6] Henry Brailsford likewise hailed the progressive nature of certain Indian States, surpassing British reforms in many locales, but contended that most were "backward and reactionary," reminiscent of old European feudal states that forced peasants to perform obligatory services for local rulers and donate foodstuffs from their meager resources to supply the prince's many feasts and ceremonies. Brailsford maintained that only twenty-three of the 562 States had any kind of consultative council. Moreover, according to Brailsford, many princes were so hated by their subjects that only British troops could ensure their hold on power.[7] Like the Raj, they would ultimately fall victim to the new politics of India's independence movement, to be expelled from or absorbed into the new political order arriving on the heels of World War II.

Notwithstanding Brailsford and others, many travel writers emphasized the more benignly autocratic character of the Princely States, including the perception that their character was better defined as kingdoms of dazzling wealth and courtly splendor—fantasy realms worthy of the exotica and mystery of the East. Upon arrival, most writers, impliedly by prior arrangement, enjoyed remarkable access to the States' ruling families, palace life, and the four corners of the kingdom. Some, like Lady Lother, utilized their own aristocratic heritage as travel asset, enabling them to experience aspects of a Princely State others could only see from afar. In Lady Lother's travels through India, she journeyed to, among other places, the Princely States of the arid western region of the subcontinent, known for their fairy tale palaces, forts, lakes and remarkable histories. One of her travel destinations, Udaipur, lay in the heart of Rajputana, a legendary land of proud rulers and fierce warriors. It was founded in the sixteenth century, becoming a Rajput stronghold that remained defiantly resistant to Mughal control in spite of Mughal efforts to link their cultures through matrimonial unions. Udaipur is a magical city of marble palaces, beautiful lakes, and surrounding hills. It is dominated by a massive palace overlooking Lake Pichola, a body of water graced by enchanting island palaces, picturesque ghats and temples along its lake front, and lively bazaars inhabiting the old walled city situated nearby.[8] Lady Lother arrived in Udaipur with her maid and Hindu courier after two days rail journey, tired yet relieved that a palace official was there to meet and escort her to a guest house. The next day, escort in lead, she toured the city, marveling at its beauty and charm.

> My guide left a nice pair of patent-leather pumps at the bottom of some steps and pattered up the warm granite stairs in his socks along the corridors leading the way to what was apparently the roof of the sky! Up, up we climbed and then–all of a sudden–we stood upon a marble terrace–and the vision flashed before me which enchants one today as it enchanted the Oriental Princes of long ago. Below us, about us, above us, rose groups of airy pavilions and small domes upheld by splendor pillars; behind the open-work marble balustrades which surrounded hanging gardens green boughs drooped and water tinkled . . . It suddenly dawned upon me that this wonderland was alive! It was not a museum or a monument . . . I felt the East and its Romance still lived.[9]

Lother's continued on in this rapturous vein. Two days later she met the heir-apparent of the kingdom, sitting beside him, chatting amiably, exchanging compliments—"an audience much like many another in the East." Later she visited the Udaipur's European palace, to Lother a motley mélange of expensive furnishings from the West devoid of any beauty or taste—"simply luxury run wild, a debauch of upholstery and varnish from the Crystal Palace."

Notwithstanding Lother's scorching critique of the European Palace, she otherwise found Udaipur's architecture consistently beautiful, the city's design elegantly balanced between plain and decorated surfaces. Lother had a gift for description, making the palaces, the streets, and gardens of Udaipur come alive with detailed and sumptuous prose. She was, however, deeply entrenched in aristocratic airs, commenting in an audience with the Prince that she thought it "unwise to grant self-government to uneducated masses led by agitators, lawyers, and students." Rather, she contended, the future India would be governed by a council of Princes. The Prince replied that "if the English go—we all go!" Surprised by this retort, she found it insightful nevertheless. And of course, it proved to be ultimately prophetic. In addition to Lother's architectural and courtly observations, she was also fastidiously aware of her own "toilette"—how she dressed and looked and what impressions her couture made upon the princely clan. Called back later to revisit the heir-apparent, she remarked in parenthetical concern, "I wonder what he thought of my costume in the pale-mauve crepe-de-chine with floating folds from the shoulders and hips, a drooping straw hat also mauve, weighed down at the back and lined beneath the brim with orchid-pink velvet?" As it turned out her host hardly noticed, but much to her dismay, he did seem keenly interested in "my horrid little knitted coat and skirt."[10]

Nilla Cram Cook, featured earlier in this work as one of the more eccentric travel writers to India during the Gandhian Age, was also a great admirer of the Princely States, but experienced them much differently than Lady Lother. Lother was the quintessential British aristocrat right at home in the kindred pomp and luxury of Indian courtly life, reveling in Udaipur's glorious architecture, urban bazaars and the city's distinguished history. Although she saw reflections of her own world, India was forever the East, a land of sweet mystery and intrigue, but never to be engaged on a deeper personal level except where privilege and rank intersected with travel amenities. Cook was from another aristocracy, a less celebrated and less traditional one—America's literary aristocracy—which likewise granted her access to a princely court, that of the State of Mysore. In addition to invitations to durbars, parties and other celebrations, she was asked to lecture at the University of Mysore on the traditions of Greek theatre, philosophy and poetry. Cook fell in love with India, going "native" in her journeys and becoming fiercely pro-Indian and antagonistically anti-Western, particularly concerning issues of child marriage and other hotly debated socio-cultural issues prominent to India's identity for many Westerners. At one dinner party she attended, an elderly Englishwoman felt compelled to critique Indian marriage customs, proclaiming that twenty-five was the proper age to enter matrimony. This was clearly a reference to Katherine Mayo's diatribe on the Indian custom of child marriage, one of the most culturally contentious issues between Indians and Westerners during the 1920's and 1930's. Since nearly everyone at the table had married before the age of twenty-five (Cook had married at sixteen), Cook indignantly challenged the "sour old Englishwoman," chastising her for her crude table manners. The Englishwomen shot back with statistics, as Cook put it, "from the great standard pornographic book on India" (clearly a reference to Katherine Mayo's *Mother India*). A verbal brawl ensued with the Englishwoman droning on with statistics and declarations that those who married earlier in life were inevitably stricken with stunted mental and physical development. Cook, in turn, championed the cause of early marriage, vehemently challenging the English woman's assertions. It was not long, however, before the Prince began interrupting the argument with pleasant asides and inquiries about the table, eventually bringing the debate to a premature halt.[11]

While staying in Mysore, Cook was chaperoned about and afforded the most lavish of attentions, even though she was often ascetic in appearance and behavior, embarrassed at times at the courtesies and benefits bestowed upon her. By her own account she became something of a court favorite impliedly due to her adoption of Indian dress and ways, her charming eccentricities, and her pro-Indian stance on assorted issues. She also fell madly in love with the Maharajah. Although she kept her emotions publicly in check, her account was filled with love-struck prose proclaiming his extraordinary qualities—a devotional tribute not unlike those reserved for gurus—with a romantic twist. In a private audience with the Maharajah, he greeted her with the remark, "What are all the wonderful things I have been hearing about you?" Thunderstruck, she told her readers: "I talked only automatically. I was transfixed, and could not utter a coherent sentence. I could tell him nothing about myself because I loved him, and it made me tongue-tied." Shortly thereafter she received a special invitation to be the Maharajah's guest at the Government House for the upcoming Dasara celebration, an invitation she was told was quite remarkable given the fact that Mysore was "retrenching," intent on cutting back on courtly entertainments, greatly restricting the usual guest list. Cook was delighted with but fretted over the invitation. Toward the end of Dasara, in the European segment of the durbar, guests customarily filed pass the throne and the Maharajah presented each female guest with a host of flowers. Since Cook, by her own admission, had been living strictly on orange juice for six weeks, and Dasara was yet six weeks away, she wondered whether she could continue her regimen, but vowed to do so nonetheless. "I would not break my fast until I had taken the bouquet of flowers from his hand. That would mean three whole months on nothing but orange juice, six or seven weeks more. But to tell him I loved him, in the hidden world where speech is unnecessary and thoughts are realities, what could be better than to fast for three months for a flower from his hand? It was better to love him in that world alone, to enrich myself by giving than to impoverish myself by asking anything in return."[12]

For Cook, Mysore was a magical kingdom where religious quest meshed harmoniously with courtly splendors. It was an otherworldly experience, living up to her original, dream-like aspirations for touring India. Other writers were equally fascinated by the Princely States they encountered; however, they rarely produced anything approaching Cook's fairyland experiences and descriptions. Among them are a number of accounts and references to persons who were employed as advisors, tutors, private secretaries and in similar capacities for Indian courts. E.M Forster's *The Hill of Devi* was one such account. Forster served for six months as private secretary to the ruler of Dewas, a small state in central India on the Deccan plateau. His is an affectionate account of a place once referenced as "the oddest corner of the world outside of Alice in Wonderland."[13] Dewas was outside the usual tourist circuitry since it lacked notable antiquities, distinctive geographical features, exotic wild animals or other attractions. It even lacked a rail station. Its central feature was rolling fields of wheat, millet and cotton, an agriculture backwater of small notice among the 560 Indian States that spanned the subcontinent. But for Forster it was a memorable place filled with quirky characters, steeped in traditional customs, and prolific of interesting social events and courtly confidences. Once while traveling through India by train with a group of Indian nobles he spotted beef on the menu and proceeded to order it. The waiter replied that it was no longer available. Forster thought little of it and ordered something else. Upon his return to Dewas, the Maharajah politely took Forster aside to discuss "a very serious subject indeed." The nobles, seeing that Forster was about to eat beef, clandestinely instructed the waiter to claim it was not on the menu, because if the item had appeared on the table, the nobles would all have been obliged to absent themselves. In the Maharajah's words, the nobles "did this because they knew you did not intend anything wrong, and because they love you." For all of its rumpled charm (Forster noted, among many like observations, the palace's "warped pianos and broken telephones"), politically Dewas was of another time, a medieval kingdom clinging to the coattails of British rule and doing everything in its power to resist the rhetoric of Gandhi and others seeking a new India. In his final chapter, entitled "Catastrophe," Forster chronicled a series of personal tragedies that befell Dewas' ruling family. When the prince died in 1937, Forster seethed at the *Times* of London's demeaning obituary which caricatured the prince as a failure in marriage, administration, and diplomacy, leaving little else but a legacy of a self-indulgent, profligate ruler. Forster, in an effort to correct the record, stated that "he was lovable and brilliant and witty and charming" and a far more complex figure than history will ever give him credit for.[14] But the age provided scant sanctuary for the memory of deceased Princes or for their typically *ancien regime* governing traditions. Dewas, like other Indian states, was to be absorbed shortly thereafter into the new India, a fading memory of a time when Princely States were worlds unto themselves.

In Paul Scott's Booker Prize novel *Staying On* there is a poignant moment in the book when Lucy, wife of a retired British officer, reminisces fondly about their one assignment in a Princely State, that of Mudpore. Lucy and her husband, Tusker, have stayed on after independence, living precariously on their pension in an annex of an old hotel set within one of the hill station towns remaining from the days of the Raj. Reflecting back on their years in Mudpore, Lucy recalls how it was the only time that she and her husband were truly content in India. Tusker had believed that Lucy was happy there because the fairy tale world of India, its princes, palaces, and wondrous exotica conformed to the India she had hoped to experience. Rather, Lucy reflected, it was because her husband Tusker had been happy there, happy to be working with Indians, finding work that suited his solitary nature, and because he was absorbed and content in his work he had treated her well. No other English people lived and worked in Mudpore except for the rare visit of an itinerant Political Agent. Thus, for Lucy, Tusker's solitary nature became a mutually shared experience, one that suited their marriage. Nostalgia for the Princely State of Mudpore was linked to Lucy's lifetime frustration with Britain's own version of a caste system, its tedious class rituals, and the insularity of life within expatriate communities. She had been brought up in England to know her place as a vicar's daughter, but believed that by marrying Tusker she could escape the social rigidities of her homeland for the presumably more liberated air of the colonies. To the contrary, from the moment she arrived in India she found pecking orders so elaborate that it easily rivaled the complicated layers of India's caste system. Not only were there the usual officer ranks such as Generals, Colonels, Majors, and the like, there were also the sub-divisions of those ranks. Moreover, even a day's seniority within a rank affected social sensibilities—equally if not more so for soldiers' wives. Everyone was expected to know one's place in the social order, and pity the poor slacker who failed to studiously determine his or her place within it.[15] At parties, bridge games, committees, dinners, or in the town shops yielding to the incessant demands of minute social protocols was tedious, wearing, and withered the spirit. For Lucy, it was a never-ending cycle from which she could never escape. But there was Mudpore. Ironically, there in one of India's Princely States, known for their own regimented social hierarchies, Lucy could claim her individuality and self-worth in solitary removal from the burdensome social rites of the Raj. It was for her the real India, the India she believed she was marrying into when she left with Tusker for the East. Lucy's sentiments echo those of E.M. Forster, both in his acclaimed *Passage to India* and in his *The Hill of Devi*. Colonial expatriate life was so socially claustrophobic that only in the fresh air of the Princely States, far from the madding crowd of one's countrymen, could one claim one's identity, liberated from the insufferable vacuity of British caste.

If the Princely States symbolized havens from the claustrophobic world of the Raj to Lucy in *Staying On*, it was not necessarily so for those who were raised there. In Santha Rama Rau's *Home to India*, there is a revealing exchange between Rau and two Indian princesses during an off-season tour of the Taj Mahal. Rau, having spent most of her life in Europe, had recently returned to her homeland to discover an India in profound transition. One morning, while having breakfast in an Agra hotel, two princesses from a small eastern Indian state shared a near-empty dining room with Rau, her mother and sister. Rau recognized the two princesses from vacations in Paris, "two solemn children" who now exhibited extreme awkwardness at having encountered Rau in Agra. The younger Princess, much to the displeasure of the older, launched into a lengthy apologia concerning their attire and behavior, explaining that in off-season Agra, not unlike Paris, they were free to be themselves, out of the reach from wagging tongues regarding their foreign dress and activities. For at home the princesses were required "to be what people expect any member of the ruling family to be, correct in a thoroughly orthodox way." In fact, they maintained, there were no parties at home, only palace receptions. There were no dates, no riding, no dancing and gaiety—only the straightjacket of courtly rituals and obligations. Moreover, the jewelry they were wearing was state-owned, not their own. Rau was quite surprised at these confessions. She assumed that the life of princesses would be fairy-tale like, filled with glamour and absent of responsibilities. When Rau raised the notion that perhaps they could break free of their life and move elsewhere, the elder sister, shocked at the suggestion, blurted out, "goodness, we couldn't do that . . . what would we work at?" In short, their education thus far had been provided by palace tutors, dominated by training in palace etiquette and French finishing school traditions—all designed to match them with a proper husband. Rau, having spent most of her life in Europe, was surprised at this, but she shouldn't have been, even if the princesses had spent considerable time in Europe as well.[16] Arranged marriages were still very much in vogue during the Ganhdian Age.

Indian villages were the other side of the Princely State equation. For many travelers they represented the *real* India, even more so than the Princely States because they not only inhabited all of India's states and regions, they also most pervasively inhabited traditional Indian customs, mentalities, and life. Travel writers were often struck at how quickly "all pretence of European modernity ceases on the outskirts of the city." Mud huts, wood fires, dirt, dust, filth and abject poverty were immediately visible in a distinctly different way once urban sites were left behind.[17] Some writers, particularly those who had worked and lived in India for a time, viewed the timeless existence of the Indian village as a sacrosanct reality. Thus progress as Westerners understood it, would not necessarily be accepted by villagers nor would it be in their best interests. As one writer argued, "My conclusion was that the village is really happy when it is left to itself and its illusions."[18] Most travel writers were not so blunt in their observations, but many questioned the benefits of outside influences upon village life.

One of the more comprehensive travel studies on Indian village life was penned by John Frederick Muehl, an American who returned to India in the late 1940's after having written an earlier account several years before. Muehl had been present at India's Independence ceremony on August 15, 1947, noting how restive indigenous crowds were, annoyed that the ceremonial rites were articulated in Oxford English, not their own tongue. He noted that although India on that day was free, "it was an India of the past in which we were living. It was an India of the past and a feast of the past."[19]

Muehl's work *Interview with India,* chronicled an essentially rural trip across a large expanse of India. Like some British attitudes concerning Indian village life, he found, not surprisingly, similar ones among India's aristocracy. While in Janmnagar he attended a banquet hosted by its aged ruler, Jam Saheb, a man saturated with reactionary views about his state and its peoples. Saheb complained to Muehl that Western journalists failed to either to understand or tell the truth about Indian States. For example, Sahed contended that journalists assumed that because villagers were poor that they were obviously unhappy. Rather, Saheb went on, "the Western mind cannot comprehend them, for they are like children, accustomed to poverty and squalor." To Saheb the Indian peasant lived in the spirit, that he was indifferent to physical discomforts, that Western notions of progress and democracy were irrelevant intrusions into his realm. Moreover, Saheb argued, his people wanted him to live in luxury and would beg him to return if he no longer ruled. To Muehl, Saheb descended deeper and deeper into a mire of "pathetic self-deception of a debauching old sentimentalist." Muehl had little use for either Saheb's paternalistic nonsense or his ranting about the need to go to war against Pakistan.[20] Yet, the reactionary attitudes of the court, he was to learn, was to be matched equally by the conservative ways of the village, a troubling reality that haunted his journey across India.

Muehl's travels took him, among other places, to the village of Halvad in the state of Kathiawar where he settled in for a lengthy stay to experience village life and conditions. He characterized the place as a typically impoverished community in the outback of India's rural expanse.

> When you enter the village there are the usual disillusionments, the rubbish and the feces and the garbage underfoot. There are smells and the flies and the dirt in ugly contrast to the traditional beauties that command the scene from a distance. As you walk through the streets, the pye-dogs crawl past you, muzzles low to the ground and hind quarters dragging, a moment later to resume their fighting over garbage or to make frantic love, to the delight of the children. And the streets are disordered and dirty. They reach out into circular alleys and crazy cul-de-sacs, winding and twisting their nightmarish courses with the violent inanity of a chronic drunk . . . Halvad is like some madman's jigsaw puzzle, hammered together in pathetic and impossible ways.[21]

At first, Muehl's presence elicited a great deal of suspicion and curiosity. However, once ostracized by a surly local police patel with whom he sparred verbally, Muehl discovered that the villagers thereafter embraced him as one of their own, even if most of them could not speak Muehl's acquired Indian language, Hindustani. Unfortunately, the few who did speak Hindustani to Muehl were an obnoxious band of local banias (a reference to a specific Hindu mercantile caste) who sold drugs to locals, issued usurious loans and otherwise preyed upon villagers. They frequently taunted Muehl. They were particularly amused whenever he shaved, entering his hut to observe the daily ritual, mocking his movements and uttering sarcastic remarks. In addition to those aggravating incidents, Muehl was especially disgusted at the banias' habit (they were practicing Jains) of ceremoniously scattering sugar on the ground to feed migrating roaches and ants while at the same time ignoring the plight of several near-starving villagers in their midst. As further evidence of their indifference to their own species, Muehl complained that the "Jain banias can often be seen sowing bajri and jowar grains in the streets. And woe unto the hungry child of Halvad who robs the insects while the bania is watching!"[22]

Muehl's favorite villager was a nine-year old orphan named Baghwan. The boy had traveled extensively through India following his soldier-father's camps, learning Hindustani and seeing the world. Muehl took him on as a "servant-cum-interpreter," an invaluable guide to the ways of the village as well as an able assistant, delightful raconteur, and trusted companion. Muehl's fondest memories of Halvad were sitting about the hut drinking coffee while listening to Baghwan's many stories about peoples and escapades he had experienced on the road. Clearly, the boy was a Kim-like figure full of intrigue and bursting with a sense of adventure. According to Muehl, he could lie with the best of them but they were transparent ones, harmless and even useful in wiling away the long days and nights of village life. For the boy had accumulated a remarkable range of life experiences for a nine-year old. And he was fully aware of it, once remarking to Muehl that "We are men of experience; we understand each other." Meuhl fully agreed. He found Baghwan, even as a nine-year old, far more sophisticated and open to the world than the adult villagers about him.[23]

Muehl's journeys led to a turn of events where he accompanied an itinerant policeman as he made his rounds through villages in southern Gujurat. At first deeply hostile to the idea of traveling with a "baboo official," upon meeting and chatting with him Muehl found the man to be an extraordinary individual. Khan, the policeman, was a Muslim in a Hindu district but in spite of the religious difference Muehl could not detect that Khan held any prejudice against Hindus. Moreover, Khan was scrupulously honest, fair, and genuinely concerned about the people he served. Muehl had extensive opportunities to observe him. He noted Khan's lack of officiousness, his generous and warm nature towards local farmers, his patience at their resistance to revealing information. According to Muehl, the villagers were as astonished by Khan's behavior as he was. What made these tag-along travels particularly interesting was the fact that Khan was hunting for a killer named Zonia, a flamboyant character who bred horses, dressed in colorful Rajput fashions, and carried a pair of silver-handled pistols in grand swashbuckling style as he ran roughshod over the territory. Approximately a half-dozen policemen had been killed tracking him. Even Khan had nearly fallen victim to him one night, saved by a guard who fired at Zonia with a shotgun, wounding him seriously, and thereafter pledging revenge against his stalker. Muehl was fascinated with Khan's psychiatrist-like strategy of interrogating villagers, never asking questions about Zonia directly, but patiently and cleverly extracting innumerable tidbits of information that he stored and processed in his quest to catch the bandit. Through all of these experiences with Khan, Muehl observed that the policeman was a realist, fully aware of the victim status of villagers but seeing among them the same cycle of oppression, abuse, and manipulation that existed elsewhere in India. Khan remarked to Muehl: "The trouble is, you want to keep things just as they are, only changing the government, but it is impossible, for the villages are so corrupt themselves that they would contaminate a government of gods." According to Khan, the old order was horrific in many ways but a new one might bring something far worse—a sentiment echoed by many of the villagers he encountered in his day-to-day rituals. "You know," said Khan, "it takes a wise man to sympathize with the villages but it takes an even wiser one to be critical of them too!"[24]

Khan's reflections on village life made a profound impact on Muehl. The itinerant cop had taught him to forego easy judgments and generalizations without first peering more deeply into actual conditions, and to refrain from yielding to unwarranted preconceptions or the prejudices of one group against another. Muehl's wanderings through village India took its toll on him. By his own admission, the many months on the road were beginning to tell on his nerves, the strain of isolation, of continuous conversing in a foreign tongue to his debilitating trait of "becoming too emotionally involved in the villagers' problems." It wore him down. Muehl claimed, "You were spared nothing in Asia. That was the trouble. You lived knee deep in life's most horrid realities . . . it was blood and death and violence." These words were uncharacteristically melodramatic of him, yet it evidenced the effects of a journey through Indian village life that few Westerners had experienced. Muehl contemplated returning to the city for a time, but resisted the temptation. At the conclusion of his travel account he complained that he was "sick to death of those who prate of the glorious traditions of India." For Muehl, such glories only reside in the ornate ruins of the Maharajas' palaces—not in the horrible poverty, serfdom, and misery of village life. In short, constructing an idyllic image of the cheerful, contented Indian villager had little to do with reality. Yet, in the end, for all the misery and suffering he remembered most the ring of Halvad's raucous laughter, and for all the suffering, misery and death—in the final analysis—"India is life rather than death."[25]

Muehl's travel memoir amply illustrates the difficulties intrinsic to investing significant time in villages in order to gain a deeper understanding of India's *real* character. Solitary travelers like Muehl, even those armed with language skills, experienced a profound sense of isolation and even emotional upheaval when enduring prolonged absences from Western or urban influences. This tendency was and remains a common feature in travel writing. And the more remote and isolated the writer is in his or her experiences, the more likely it is that the travel narrative evidences traces of disorientation. In doing so another trait appears. The travel writer's prose takes on an increasingly personal tone, speaking more directly and intensely to the imagined reader, bonding as it were with an envisioned compatriot, far distant in miles but brought close in imaginary proximity to the writer's psychic presence in order to provide solace and stability in an alien land and culture. For the difficulty of travel through the countryside in search of the *real* India was about more than just a lack of creature comforts; even more compelling was the absence of emotional sustenance. Traveling to India's major centers, staying in hotels or in private residences, availing oneself of easily obtained guides, all tempered the difficult conditions of journeying through India. Those travel amenities frequently came with social comforts as well—people to talk to in one's native language—people of cosmopolitan airs and knowledge of the world seldom found in the outback of India's villages. It is no wonder that most Gandhian Age travel memoirs wrote little of Indian villages except for cursory observations and to propagate the usual cliché that therein could be found the *real* India. For the *real* India was no more in the villages than it was in the mosque, the Taj Mahal, Bombay's waterfront, or the ghats of Benares. Kaleidoscopic India was too complex and diverse to reduce to a single image or iconic concept. It was all of those things and more.

Octavio Paz, who served as Mexico's ambassador to the India in the 1960's, asked himself the question, "how does a Mexican writer view the immense reality of India?" In short, Paz, in his book of essays on India, *In Light of India*, modestly suggested that his observations were "merely glimpses of India; signs seen indistinctly, realities perceived between light and shadow." Paz noted Gandhi's deep attachment to village life, that civilizations appeared and departed, that the West and all of its innovations were part of that cycle and were dangerous to India's soul. Instead, Gandhi put his faith in the timeless solidarity of village farmers and artisans. Yet, as Frederick Muehl found, Paz believed for all his admiration of Gandhi that "history itself, in its blindest and most brutal form, has proven him wrong; the population explosion has smashed the dream of happy villages. Every village is a pit of misery and despair.[26] Such pronouncements represent the polar opposite of India's villages as idyllic domains where people of the soil, indifferent to hardship, toil on in blissful ignorance of their status. Thus, why disturb them? Why arouse discontent that can rarely if ever be remedied? Gandhi of course did so anyway for nationalistic purposes, even as he trumpeted village virtues, but expectations changed in the new, emerging India. India's villages were awakening from their seemingly timeless slumber while the British Raj and Princely States crumpled around them.

In today's India, millions are flocking from the countryside to the cities even as village life is changing, but not entirely as various sources would suggest. In William Dalrymple's *The Age of Kali*, a collection of contemporary India vignettes, he writes of a journey to a Rajasthani village where the occurrence of the ancient Hindu practice of *sati* surfaced in the 1990's. *Sati* is a ritual sacrifice where a widow casts herself on her husband's funeral pyre in order to facilitate the successful rebirth of her departed spouse. Even though it was banned by the British in the early nineteenth century and gradually died out through most of India, it continues to resonate in parts of village India, particularly in the state of Rajasthan. Dalrymple traveled to report on the case of a young widow named Roop Kanwar, who according to some accounts, was pressured by her in-laws and villagers to carry out the rite, even though the authorities and much of the general public were highly skeptical that a young, reasonably well-educated and not particularly religious woman would voluntarily succumb to the idea of burning herself alive. The case became a national sensation. Thirty-two men were prosecuted in a ten-year legal ordeal filled with conflicting accounts of what actually occurred. The defendants were eventually found innocent of murder charges. The case reveals a continuing divide in India between modernity and tradition. As Dalrymple observed, "while most urban Indians regard *sati* with horror, seeing it as a primeval custom unthinkable in contemporary India, in rural Rajasthan the villagers are quite unrepentant, and continue piously to revere past *satis*.[27]

The fairy tale world of Princely States, much like the Gandhian India in which they existed, has vanished into the mists of history. But the villages live on pulled into India's current political process by ambitious, often corrupt politicians preying upon their ignorance and historic dependence upon local elites. Villagers grapple with a changing India and millions seek to escape their lot for the promise of better jobs and a more promising way of life in the cities. For today's traveler, one can still find a slice of Gandhian India in rural outbacks. Unlike India's temples, mosques, its old palaces and ruins, the villages remain a living link to the past. But they may be just as impenetrable and troubling today as they were for Frederick Muehl decades ago. Thus, just as it would seem that one would have an opportunity to engage the *real* India, like everything else there, it blurs into a frustrating complexity.

## SOME FINAL THOUGHTS

Travel writers have often been accused of penning quick, glib treatments of the environments and peoples they encounter, seeking as it were, the *real* essence of places without sufficient time and experience to penetrate their core. Prolonged exposure to and engagement with such places, some have contended, ultimately discredit the art of travel writing as little more than a fleeting, shallow impression of travel sites and peoples. Yet, as argued previously in this study, the opposite is frequently true as well. Extended stays in foreign environments often dull the sensibilities to an environment's most salient and changing characteristics. Cultural calcification sets in, stock images dominate, and the freshness and openness that travelers bring to their descriptions are brushed aside as the ramblings of a novice. Memoirs written by "old India hands" readily reveal this tendency. Many of them, although informative, are even more deeply self-referential, personally and culturally, than those penned by travel writers on several-month itineraries through India. India, as subject, was sometimes re-colonized by old India hands through countless references to Britain's imperial venture. Even if understandable when interpreted in the context of an expatriate's life work in India (how could it not dominate, or at least figure prominently in their accounts?), nevertheless, the subcontinent is seldom seen on its own terms—only in context of the Raj's achievements and failings—usually the former. And, it should be added, like elsewhere, there was a pecking order (or mini-caste system) operating among those who traveled in India. Expatriates disparaged travelers and both demeaned tourists, even though such classifications can be highly suspect as demarcated realms. After all, at what point is an expatriate a "traveler" or perhaps nothing more than a "tourist" to indigenous eyes? Similarly, "travelers"—those who ostensibly journeyed through India for months—were arguably quite tourist-like to expatriates and Indian residents. Even those Indians who had emigrated to the West and who later returned to visit family or survey changes to their ancestral homeland could assume the persona of the fleeting tourist or traveler. Yet, they were all seeking, in some sense, the *real* India. What they found returns us to the mantra of the Gandhian Age travel writer—that India was a kaleidoscope—a wonder of ever-changing form and color. Perhaps to twenty-first century sensibilities the symbol of a kaleidoscope as perceptual lens for seeing India has a quaint if not dated quality. But as has been evident from travel writer memoirs, one could never fix on the *real* India. The place was terminally elusive. And as several travel writers noted, India could no more be condensed into a digestible geographic and cultural entity than could Europe from France to Russia. In fact, it could be argued that Europe was far more heterogeneous religiously, ethnically, and culturally than India. In the end, travel memoirs of India during the Gandhian Age were always infused with political and cultural baggage that filtered their perceptions. There is no escaping such representational quandaries. Nevertheless, travel writers such as the "armchair" practitioners featured in this work, brought a diverse and dynamic India to a Western public eager to learn of this Eastern wonderland, filled with glorious antiquities, great physical beauty, thoroughly engaging peoples, and a charismatic political leader and dramatic political movement that never ceased to fascinate. And they invited prospective readers to journey vicariously with them to experience the India they were discovering—a part of the world that few would have an opportunity to discover on their own. Such was and remains the utility and the charm of the travel memoir genre. For those of us ever curious about the rest of the world, travel writers will always be welcome compatriots to our lives.

## NOTES

1. Paul Bowles, *Their Heads are Green and Their Hands are Blue* (New York: Harper Perennial, 1957), 39. Bowles traveled about India in the early 1950's, the journey logging about 8,000 miles across the subcontinent. Bowles admitted that at the journey's end he knew little more about India than he did upon his arrival, having only a "somewhat more detailed and precise idea of my ignorance than I did in the beginning."

2. E.J. O'Meara, *I'd Live it Again* (Philadelphia: J.B. Lippincott, 1935), 110–113.

3. Maurice Dekobra, *The Perfumed Tigers: Adventures in the Land of the Maharajahs* (Oxford: Brewer & Warren, 1930), 150.

4. David Cannadine, *Ornamentalism: How the British Saw Their Empire* (Oxford: Oxford University Press, 2001), xv–xxi; 41–45. Cannadine interprets Britain's relationship to its imperial possessions as essentially determined by common cause between reciprocating elites, what Cannadine terms *Ornamentalism.* He articulates this view in part as a direct challenge to Edward Said's seminal work *Orientalism.* Said's study of European representations of the "Orient" (the Middle East or what is sometimes referred to today as West Asia) has spawned a burst of scholarship in recent decades deconstructing imperial sources more from the perspective of "gender and race, cultural and language" than that of "class." But according to Cannadine it was *class* not *race* that most prominently dictated relations between Britain and its Indian 'crown jewel' (among other colonial possessions). However, neither *Ornamentalism* nor *Orientalism* excludes the roles of the other's theoretical emphasis. Likewise, travel writers in this study usually found issues of race and class prominently displayed in their interactions with British and Indian contacts. And such issues were often blurred or melded within their own symbiotic perceptual structures, depending upon whom they talked to or the topic of the moment.

5. Michael Pym, *The Power of India* (New York: G.P. Putnam's Sons, 1930), 119–121, 269–271.

6. Cecil Beaton, *Far East* (London: B.T. Batsford, 1945), 41.

7. Henry Noel Brailsford, *Subject India* (New York: John Day Co., 1943), 128–131.

8. *Eye Witness Travel Guides: India* (London: DK Publishing, 2002), 398.

9. Lady Lother, *Land of the Gold Mohur* (London: Phillip Allan, 1932), 36–38.

10. Ibid, 45–46, 58.

11. Nilla Cram Cook, *My Road to India* (New York, L. Furman, Inc., 1939), 264–265.

12. Ibid, 270.

13. E.M. Forster, *The Hill of Devi* (New York: Harvest Books, 1953), 56. The remark originated from Malcolm Darling who served as guardian and tutor to the young prince beginning in 1907. The dual kingdom of Dewas was something of an anomaly, having two rulers who ruled over two palaces, two armies, and other were organized along other split arrangements.

14. Ibid, 55, 76, 114, 149, 150, 265.

15. Paul Scott, *Staying On* (London: Arrow Books, 1977), 167–169.

16. Santha Sama Rau, *Home to India* (London: Harper & Brothers, 1939), 147–151.

17. John Hay Beith, [Ian Hay, pseud.], *The Great Wall of India* (London: Hodder & Stoughton, 1933), 17.

18. Walter Roper Lawrence, *The India We Served.* (London: Cassell & Co., 1928), 43.

19. John Frederick Muehl, *Interview with India.* (New York: John Day Co., 1950), 4.

20. Ibid, 12–15.

21. Ibid, 46–47.

22. Ibid, 52–57.

23. Ibid, 52–55.

24. Ibid, 114–117, 127–128.

25. Ibid, 128, 243–245, 302–303.

26. Octavio Paz, *In Light of India* (New York: Harvest Books, 1995), 32–33, 194.

27. William Dalrymple, *The Age of Kali: Indian Travels & Encounters* (Oakland: Lonely Planet Journeys, 1998), 133–140.

# Bibliography

## PRIMARY SOURCES


Alter, Stephen. *Sacred Waters: A Pilgrimage up the Ganges River to the Source of Hindu Culture*. New York: Harcourt, 2001.

Bamford, Alfred J. *Turbans and Tails; or Sketches in the Unromantic East*. London: Sampson, Low, Marston, Searle, & Rivington,1888.

Beaton, Cecil. *Far East*. London: B.T. Batsford, Ltd., 1945.

_____. *Indian Album*. London: B.T. Batsford, 1945. [photo album].

Beith, John Hay [Ian Hay, pseud.]. *The Great Wall of India*. London: Hodder & Stoughton, 1933.

Bemis, Albert Farwell. *A Journey to India, 1921–1922*. Boston: Privately Printed, 1923.

Bernays, Robert. *"Naked Faquir."* New York: Henry Holt & Co., 1932.

Blackman, Robert J. *Incomparable India: Tradition, Superstition, Truth*. London: Sampson, Low, Marston & Co., n.d.

Boulnois, Helen Mary. *Mystic India*. London: Methuen & Co., 1935.

Bowles, Chester. *Ambassador's Report*. New York: Harper & Row, n.d.

Branson, Clive. *British Soldier in India: The Letters of Clive Branson*. London: Communist Party, 1944.

Brailsford, Henry Noel. *Subject India*. New York: John Day Co., 1943.

Brunton, Paul. *A Search in Secret India*. London: Arrow Books, 1934.

Burr, Agnes Rush. *India: The Land That Lures*. Boston: L.C. Page & Co., 1929.

Caine, W.S. *Picturesque India: A Handbook For European Travelers*. London: George Routledge & Sons, 1891.

Channing, Mark. *India Mosaic*. London: J.B. Lippincott Co., 1936.

Clouston, D. *From the Orcades to India*. London: Oliver & Boyd, 1936.

Cook, Nilla Cram. *My Road to India*. New York, L. Furman, Inc., 1939.

Darling, Malcolm Lyall. *At Freedom's Door*. Oxford: Oxford University Press, 1949.

Dekobra, Maurice. *The Perfumed Tigers: Adventures in the Land of the Maharajahs*. Oxford: Brewer & Warren, 1930.

Durant, Will. *The Case for India*. New York: Simon & Schuster, 1930.

Elliott, Richard Maurice. *The Sunny Side of Asia*. New York: Century Co., 1928.

Field, Harry H. *After Mother India*. New York: Harcourt, Brace and Co., 1929.

Forster, E.M. *A Passage to India*. New York: Harvest Books, 1924.

_____. *The Hill of Devi*. New York: Harvest Books, 1953.

Frater, Alexander. *Chasing the Monsoon: A Modern Pilgrimage Through India*. New York: Henry Holt & Co., 1990.

Fuller, J.C.F. *India in Revolt*. London: Eyre & Spottiswoode, 1931.

Gardner, Mona. *The Menacing Sun*. New York: Harcourt, Brace & Co., 1939.

Grant, T.J. *The Spirit of India*. London: B.T. Batsford, 1938.

Hagan, Louis. *Indian Route March*. New York: Pilot Press, 1946.

Hamilton, Norah Rowan. *Through Wonderful India and Beyond*. London: Holden & Hardingham, 1915.

Hardie, J. Keir, M.P. *India: Impressions and Suggestions*. New York: B.W. Huebsch, 1919.

Hadley, Leila. *A Journey with Elsa Cloud*. New York: Penguin Books, 1997.

Hamilton, Norah Rowan. *Through Wonderful India and Beyond*. London: Holden & Hardingham, 1915.

Hendley, Charles. *Trifles of Travel*. New York: Rider Press, 1924.

Hoyland, John S. *Indian Crisis: The Background*. New York: Macmillan Co., 1943.

Huxley. Aldous. *Jesting Pilate: The Diary of a Journey*. London: Chatto & Windus, 1948.

*India: A Reprint of the Special Number of 'The Times.'* London: London Times, 1930.

Iyer, C.S. Ranga. *Father India: A Reply to Mother India*. New York: Louis Carrier & Co., 1928.

James, Edward Bolton. *I Tell Everything: The Brown Man's Burden (A Book on India)*. Geneva: Imprimerie Kundig, 1931.

Johnston, George H. *Journey Through Tomorrow*. Melbourne: F. W. Cheshire Pty., 1947.

Kendall, Patricia. *Come With Me to India*. New York: Charles Scribner's Sons, 1935.

Lawrence, Sir Walter Roper. *The India We Served*. London: Cassell & Co., 1928.

Lother, Lady. *Land of the Gold Mohur*. London: Phillip Allan, 1932.

Loti, Pierre. *India*. New York: Frederick A. Stokes Co., 1929.

MacDonald, Sarah. *Holy Cow, An Indian Adventure*. Mission Point, Australia: Broadway Books, 2002.

Mathews, Basil. *India Reveals Herself*. London: Oxford University Press, 1937.

Matisse, Maarten. *Wanderer from Sea to Sea*. New York: Harcourt, Brace and Co., 1936.

Mayo, Katherine. *Mother India*. New York: Harcourt, Brace & Co., 1927.

_____. *Volume Two*. New York: Harcourt, Brace & Co., 1931.

Miller, Olive Thorne. *Little People of Asia*. New York: Dutton, 1888.

Mitchell, John W. *The Wheels of India*. London: Thornton Butterworth, 1934.

Mistry, Rohinton. *A Fine Balance*. New York: Vintage Books, 1995.

Muehl, John Frederick. *American Sahib*. New York: John Day Co., 1946.

_____. *Interview with India*. New York: John Day Co., 1950.

Mukerji, Dhan Gopal. *Disillusioned India*. N.p.: E.P Dutton & Co., 1930.

Murray's Indian Handbook. *A Handbook for Travelers in India, Burma and Ceylon.* 14th ed. London: John Murray, 1933.
Naipaul, V.S. *Area of Darkness: A Discovery of India.* New York: Vintage Books, 1964.
_____. *India: A Wounded Civilization.* New York: Vintage Books, 1976.
Newby, Eric. *Slowly Down the Ganges.* Oakland: Lonely Planet Journeys, 1966.
Nichols, Beverley. *Verdict on India.* London: Jonathan Cape, 1944.
O'Meara, E. J. *I'd Live It Again.* Philadelphia: J.B. Lippincott, 1935.
O'Reilly, James and Larry Habegger, eds. *Travelers' Tales Guides India: True Stories of Life on the Road.* San Francisco: Travelers' Tales, 1998.
Orwell, George. *Homage to Catalonia.* London: Harvest Books, 1952.
Paz, Octavio. *In Light of India.* New York: Harvest Books, 1995.
Pinney, Peter. *Dust on My Shoes.* New York: Bobbs-Merrill Co., 1951.
Powell, E. Alexander. *The Last Home of Mystery.* Garden City, NY: Garden City Publishing Co., 1924.
Pym, Michael. *The Power of India.* New York: G.P. Putnam's Sons, 1930.
Rau, Santha Rama. *Home to India.* New York: Harper & Brothers, 1939.
Roosevelt, Eleanor. *India and the Awakening of the East.* New York: Harper & Brothers, 1953.
Shahani, Ranjee G. *Indian Pilgrimage.* London: Michael Joseph, 1939.
Sharp, Sir Henry. *Good-Bye India.* London: Oxford University Press, 1946.
Sinclair, Gordon. *Foot-Loose in India.* New York: Farrar & Rinehart, 1933.
Sitwell, Constance. *Flowers and Elephants.* London: J. Cape, 1927.
Spender, J.A. *The Changing East.* London: Casell & Co., 1926.
Sucitto, Ajahn and Nick Scott. *Rude Awakenings: Two Englishmen on Foot in Buddhism's Holy Land.* Boston: Wisdom Publications, 2006.
Taleyarkhan, Homi J. H. *Roads to Beauty Around Bombay.* Bombay: Popular Book Depot, 1953.
Thomas, Lowell. *India: Land of the Black Pagoda.* New York: P.F. Collier & Sons, 1930.
Tibbits, Mrs. Walter. *Veiled Mysteries of India.* London: Eveleigh, Nash & Grayson, 1929.
Tracy, Jane A. *See India With Me.* Boston: Stratford Co., 1928.
Wheeler, Post. *India Against the Storm.* New York: E.P. Dutton & Co., 1944.
Williams, Gertrude Marvin. *Understanding India.* New York: Coward-McCann, 1928.
Wright, Eugene. *The Great Horn Spoon.* Indianapolis: Bobbs-Merrill Co., n.d.

## SECONDARY SOURCES

Adiga, Aravind. "My Lost World." *Time*, June 26, 2006, 44–45.
Allen, Charles Allen, ed. *Plain Tales from the Raj, Images of India in the Twentieth Century.* London: Futura Publications, 1975.
Anderson, Benedict. *Imagined Communities: Reflections on the Origin and Spread of Nationalism.* London: Verso, 1983.
Andrews, A.N. *After the Victorians, The Decline of Britain in the World.* New York: Picador, 2005.

Bowles, Paul. *Their Heads are Green and Their Hands are Blue*. New York: Harper Perennial, 1957.

Brantlinger, Patrick. *Rule of Darkness: British Literature and the Imperialism, 1830–1914*. Ithaca, NY: Cornell University Press, 1988.

Buruma, Ian. *The Missionary and the Libertine*. New York: Vintage Books, 1996.

Cannadine, David. *Ornamentalism: How the British Saw Their Empire*. Oxford: Oxford University Press, 2001.

Childress, David Hatcher. *Lost Cities of China, Central Asia & India.* Kempton, IL: Adventures Unlimited Press, 1985.

Crossette, Barbara. *The Great Hill Stations of Asia*. New York: Basic Books, 1999.

Dalrymple, William. *The Age of Kali: Indian Travels & Encounters.* Oakland: Lonely Planet Journeys, 1998.

_____. *City of Djinns: A Year in India.* New York: Penguin Books, 1993.

Das, Gurcharan. "The India Model." *Foreign Affairs*, July/August 2006, 2–16.

Eames, Andrew, ed. *Insight Guides: India.* 5th ed. Boston: Houghton Mifflin Co., 1995.

Elliott, Michael. "India, Inc." *Time*, June 26, 2006, 38–39.

*Eye Witness Travel Guides: India* (London: DK Publishing, 2002), 446.

Hansen, Thomas Blom. *The Saffron Wave: Democracy and Hindu Nationalism in Modern India*. Princeton: Princeton University Press, 1999.

Hopkirk, Peter. *Quest for Kim: In Search of Kipling's Great Game.* Oxford: Oxford University Press, 1996.

Hutchinson, John A. *Paths of Faith*. New York: McGraw Hill Publishing Co., 1981.

Hutnyk, John. *The Rumour of Calcutta: Tourism, Charity, and the Poverty of Representation.* London: Zed Books, 1996.

James, Lawrence. *Raj: The Making and Unmaking of British India*. New York: St. Martin's Griffin, 1997.

Keay, John. *India, A History.* New York: Grove Press, 2000.

Kleinfield, N. R. "Modern Ways Open India's Doors to Diabetes." *New York Times*, September 13, 2006, 1, 12–13.

Kraft, Scott. "Get Me to the Taj on Time." *Los Angeles Times*, Travel Section, April 29, 2007.

Lamont, Peter. *The Rise of the Indian Rope Trick: How a Spectacular Hoax Became History*. New York: Thunder's Mouth Press, 2005.

Luce, Edward. *In Spite of the Gods: The Strange Rise of Modern India*. New York: Doubleday, 2007.

McKay, John P., Bennett D. Hill and John Buckler, eds. *A History of World Societies*. Vol. B. 3rd ed. Boston: Houghton Mifflin Co., 1992.

Mehta, Suketu. *Maximum City: Bombay Found and Lost.* New York: Alfred A. Knopf, 2005.

Metcalf, Barbara D. and Metcalf, Thomas R. *A Concise History of Modern India.* 2nd ed. Cambridge: Cambridge University Press, 2006.

Mishra, Pankaj, ed. *India in Mind.* New York: Vintage Books, 2005.

Mohan, C. Raja. "India and the Balance of Power." *Foreign Affairs*, July/August 2006, 17–32.

Owen, Nicholas, ed. *Human Rights, Human Wrongs— Oxford Amnesty Lectures*. Oxford: Oxford University Press, 2003.

Pagden, Anthony. *Peoples and Empires.* New York: Modern Library Chronicles, 2001.

Paine, Jeffery. *Father India: How Encounters with an Ancient Culture Transformed the Modern West.* New York: HarperCollins Publishers, 1998.

Paz, Octavio. *In Light of India.* New York: Harvest Books, 1995.

Perry, Alex. "Bombay's Boom." *Time*, June 26, 2006, 40–44.

Roy, Arundhati, ed. *India: A Mosaic.* New York: New York Review Book, 2000.

Royle, Trevor. *The Last Days of the Raj.* London: John Murray, 1989.

Seal, Mark. "Meera Gazing." In *The Road Within, True Stories of Transformation and the Soul*

*Eye Witness Travel Guides: India*. Edited by Sean O'Reilly, James O'Reilly, and Tim O'Reilly. San Francisco: Travelers' Tales, 2002.

Silvers, Robert B. and Barbara Epstein, eds. *India: A Mosaic.* New York: New York Review of Books, 2000.

Spear, Percival. *A History of India*. Vol. 2. London: Penguin Books, 1978.

Spivak, Gayatri Chakravorty. "Righting Wrongs," in *Human Rights, Human Wrongs.* Edited by Nicholas Owen. Oxford: Oxford University Press, 2002.

Strobel, Margaret. *European Women and the Second British Empire.* Bloomington: Indian University Press, 1991.

Tarnas, Richard. *The Passion of the Western Mind.* New York: Ballantine Books, 1991.

Tharoor, Shashi. *India: From Midnight to the Millennium.* New York: Arcade Publishing, 1997.

Watson, Catherine. *Roads Less Traveled: Dispatches from the Ends of the Earth.* Minneapolis: Syren Book Co., 2005.

Wilson, A.N. *After the Victorians: The Decline of Britain in the World.* New York: Picador Press, 2005.

Winchester, Simon, ed. *Calcutta.* Oakland: Lonely Planet Publications, 2004.

# Index

www.ingramcontent.com/pod-product-compliance
Lightning Source LLC
Chambersburg PA
CBHW071522100726
47908CB00004B/1261

* 9 7 8 0 7 6 1 8 3 9 4 9 1 *